Essentials of Abnormal Psychology

Essentials of Behavioral Science Series

Founding Editors, Alan S. Kaufman and Nadeen L. Kaufman

Essentials

of Abnormal Psychology

Andrew R. Getzfeld

 John Wiley & Sons, Inc.

Published by John Wiley & Sons, Inc., Hoboken, New Jersey.
Published simultaneously in Canada.

For general information on our other products and services please contact our Customer Care Department within the United States at (800) 762-2974, outside the United States at (317) 572-3993 or fax (317) 572-4002.

Wiley also publishes its books in a variety of electronic formats. Some content that appears in print may not be available in electronic books. For more information about Wiley products, visit our website at www.wiley.com.

Library of Congress Cataloging-in-Publication Data:

Getzfeld, Andrew R.
    Essentials of abnormal psychology / by Andrew R. Getzfeld.
       p. ; cm. — (Essentials of behavioral science series)
    Includes bibliographical references and index.
    ISBN-13: 978-0-471-65623-4 (pbk. : alk. paper)
    ISBN-10: 0-471-65623-2 (pbk. : alk. paper)
      1. Psychology, Pathological. I. Title. II. Series.
    [DNLM: 1. Mental Disorders. WM 140 G394e 2006]
RC454.G455 2006
616.89—dc22

                                                                        2005020241

Printed in the United States of America.

10 9 8 7 6 5 4 3 2 1

I dedicate this book to the memory of my father, Robert B. Getzfeld,
whom I miss more each day; his endless love, compassion, and support
always pushed me to surpass my potential.

CONTENTS

SERIES PREFACE

I n the *Essentials of Behavioral Science* series, our goal is to provide readers with books that will deliver key practical information in an efficient, accessible style. The series features books on a variety of topics, such as statistics, psychological testing, and research design and methodology, to name just a few. For the experienced professional, books in the series offer a concise yet thorough review of a specific area of expertise, including numerous tips for best practices. Students can turn to series books for a clear and concise overview of the important topics with which they must become proficient to practice skillfully, efficiently, and ethically in their chosen fields.

Wherever feasible, visual cues highlighting key points are utilized alongside systematic, step-by-step guidelines. Chapters are focused and succinct. Topics are organized for an easy understanding of the essential material related to a particular topic. Theory and research are continually woven into the fabric of each book, but always to enhance the practical application of the material, rather than to sidetrack or overwhelm readers. With this series, we aim to challenge and assist readers in the behavioral sciences to aspire to the highest level of competency by arming them with the tools they need for knowledgeable, informed practice.

Essentials of Abnormal Psychology concentrates on the most common types of psychopathologies and examines the various subtypes within each *DSM-IV-TR* diagnostic category (the author presumes rudimentary understanding of the *DSM-IV-TR* classification system). In addition, etiologies and potential treatment modalities are explored, including psychopharmacological modalities that were current at the time of publication. This book will not be as extensive or as exhaustive as a traditional abnormal psychology text, and it was not written as such. Therefore, this book does not concentrate on child and adolescent psychopathologies, and could not concentrate on all of the *DSM-IV-TR* categories. The author found that in many abnormal psychology classes, all *DSM-IV-TR* categories were not covered, and those that are often eliminated have also been eliminated here. Please note that this is not due to their perceived lack of importance. This book can be used by upper-level undergraduate or graduate students as a stand-alone text, or as a supplement for those who have trouble understanding material in class or in their primary text. Professionals who wish to have a handy guide to review the most common psychopathologies and treatment methods will also find this book very useful. Researchers and those who are preparing for certification, licensure, or those who are preparing to take the GRE in psychology will also benefit from this book.

The book begins with a brief history of abnormal behavior and treatment modalities and then examines the *DSM-IV-TR*. Chapter 2 looks at the most common Anxiety Disorders, and Chapter 3 examines Mood Disorders, considered by some to be the most common mental illness. Chapter 4 examines Substance-Related Disorders, specifically the Alcohol Use Disorders, which continue to be a significant problem faced by psychologists. Chapter 5 examines the Eating Disorders Anorexia Nervosa and Bulimia Nervosa and focuses on Bulimia Nervosa, the most common eating disorder and one which is being treated rather successfully today. Chapter 6 looks at sexual and gender identity disorders, examining Sexual Dysfunctions and the Paraphilias, in particular Pedophilia. Chapter 7 extensively examines the Schizophrenic Disorders, the latest treatment modalities at the time of publication, and the current etiological perspectives (as well as some historical ones). The book concludes with a comprehensive discussion of the Personality Disorders, examining them based on their clusters as grouped in the *DSM-IV-TR*.

Alan S. Kaufman, PhD, and Nadeen L. Kaufman, EdD, Founding Editors
Yale University School of Medicine

ACKNOWLEDGMENTS

Many individuals have both helped and encouraged me as this project took shape. I wish to thank the patients described within this book for their generosity in allowing me to share their situations in an anonymous, disguised fashion.

I wish to express special thanks to Tracey Belmont at Wiley, whom I bothered to no end as the deadline approached and who always showed incredible confidence and optimism toward an increasingly pessimistic author (Good Luck to you!), and to Isabel Pratt, whom I met (finally) for the first time at APA 2005 in Washington, DC! An extra special thanks to Dr. Barry Cohen for initially suggesting that I write an *Essentials* book; on to the next project once I regain my sanity!

Of course this book would have been impossible without the continued and invaluable support of my family. I am indebted to my lovely wife, Gabriella, to our extremely precocious daughter, Anya Rose Getzfeld, and to my mother, Paula Getzfeld, easily the best family one could possibly have. Thanks for having the patience to put up with my endless frustrations with this project, my moods bordering on clinical depression at times, my never-ending late hours, and for having the patience to accept me as an author, university professor, husband, father, and a son. A special shout-out to my sister Lisa Gardner, her husband Ken, and their daughter Emily (you know why). I know I've not been a joy to be around as the manuscript neared completion, but I think it was worth it (Anya, you'll understand one day, and yes, Daddy can play with you now). I will be forever indebted to my late father, Robert B. Getzfeld, and to his father, Henry Getzfeld. They both always encouraged me to challenge myself and taught me to persevere no matter how overwhelming the odds might be. This book is for you, guys; we did it again!

Essentials of Abnormal Psychology

One

INTRODUCTION TO ABNORMAL PSYCHOLOGY AND THE *DSM-IV-TR*

bnormal Psychology. Psychopathology. These are terms that continue to fascinate psychologists and other helping professionals, especially those outside of the field. In this chapter we will give a brief overview of abnormal behavior and its treatment throughout history. Before we get to that, we need to examine the various ways in which *abnormal behavior* is defined.

If you were to take a poll of most people outside of the helping professions (e.g., psychologists, social workers, and psychiatrists), they would probably tell you that they know abnormal behavior when they see it. Let us look at an example:

You live in a large urban area. One day you hear out of your apartment window a man singing an aria. You look out the window and watch him walking down the street, singing in an operatic tenor, for everyone to hear. The man is well dressed in a work uniform, appears well kempt, and is not really interacting with other people. The aria fades as he continues down the street. You detect nothing unusual in his behavior except for the fact that he was singing, and doing so rather loudly. Some people were obviously annoyed; some even crossed the street to avoid him.

Is his behavior abnormal? Does his behavior present a danger to himself or, more importantly, to others? This is the goal of those in the helping professions: to ascertain whether an individual's behavior is indeed abnormal. Therefore, it is important to define abnormal behavior.

DEFINING ABNORMAL BEHAVIOR

Generally speaking, we define abnormal behavior by using three perspectives: the statistical frequency perspective, social norms perspective, and maladaptive behavior perspective. Statistical frequency labels behavior as abnormal if it occurs rarely or infrequently in relation to the behavior of the general population. Let us return to our aspiring opera soloist for the moment. Do people rarely or infrequently sing on the street, especially opera?

Social norms consider behavior to be abnormal if the behavior deviates greatly from accepted social standards, values, or norms. *Norms* are spoken and unspoken rules for proper conduct. These are established by a society over time and, of course, are subject to changes over time. Thus, is our friend a deviant, based on this perspective? Would it be easier to evaluate him if he were walking around half naked or if he had not showered for a week?

Finally, the maladaptive perspective views behavior as abnormal if it interferes with the individual's ability to function in life or in society. Is this man able to function in everyday life? By this we mean able to work, take care of himself, and have normal social interactions. See Rapid Reference 1.1 for a summary of the three perspectives used to define abnormal behavior.

As you can see, one key feature needed when defining abnormal (or normal!) behavior is the need for as much information as possible before making a diagnosis. It should also be quite clear that determining whether behavior is abnormal is a difficult process indeed. Before we learn a bit more about our operatic fellow, let us consider two other features that we use to define abnormal behavior. First, is the individual's behavior causing danger to him- or herself or to other people? In many instances, the exact opposite is true. The notion that many mentally ill individuals are slashers like the movie characters Freddy Kruger or Jason or deranged psychopaths like Jeffrey Dahmer or Charles Manson is simply not the case. If these individuals are dangerous, it is more likely that they pose a threat to themselves and not to other people.

Finally, is the individual's behavior causing him or her distress? Not all abnormal behavior causes stress to the individual. In many cases, the

Rapid Reference 1.1

Defining Abnormal Behavior

Statistical Frequency: The behavior is abnormal if it occurs rarely or infrequently in relation to the behavior of the general population.

Social Norms: The behavior is abnormal if the behavior deviates greatly from accepted social standards, values, or norms.

Maladaptive Perspective: The behavior is abnormal if the said behavior(s) interfere(s) with the individual's ability to function in life or in society.

individual's family or loved ones are more distressed than the individual himself! Does this qualify? How about our friend? Let us see if more information about him helps to clear up the picture.

This gentleman goes to work every day in a uniform. In fact, he is a building superintendent who has a side hobby of singing arias. In his opinion, he has a wonderful voice, and he desires to share it with others. He knows he will never sing at the Met, but for him music is about making people happy and spreading his goodwill. Thus, he sings as

> **CAUTION**
>
> The term *insanity* really has little to do with psychology, and you will not find it in the *DSM-IV-TR* (American Psychiatric Association [APA], 2000). *Insanity* means that an individual, while in the act of committing a crime, was unaware of the nature of the act or did not know the difference between right and wrong. This has also been called the *M'Naghten Test* (sometimes called the *M'Naghten Rule*). The courts determine whether an individual is insane. Psychologists often provide testimony and administer tests to help the court decide.

he walks to work in the morning and when coming back from lunch. He has held his job for 12 years, and, by his report, no one really complains about his singing. If they do, he just sings louder.

Does this help? Is this man's behavior abnormal based on the aforementioned perspectives? Perhaps he is what Weeks and James (1995) call an *eccentric*. Eccentrics have odd or unusual habits but are not mentally ill. As you can see, it is difficult to clearly define abnormal behavior. To help us in our diagnosis, we must also look at factors such as duration, age of onset, and the intensity of the behavior(s). We have now laid the groundwork, so let's examine the history of abnormal behavior and how it was treated before we consider some other issues.

A BRIEF HISTORY OF ABNORMAL BEHAVIOR AND TREATMENT

The history of abnormal psychology (or psychopathology; the terms are used interchangeably) dates back hundreds if not thousands of years. Stone Age civilizations (the dates vary, but most agree that this era occurred approximately 2 million years ago in Asia, Africa, and Europe; in the Americas, it began about 30,000 years ago!) evidently believed that serious mental illness or abnormal behavior was due to being possessed by evil spirits (an idea that some people still believe today). Archaeological finds have discovered skulls that have holes bored into them. This process was called *trepanning*. A small instrument was used to bore holes in the skull, the idea being that the holes would allow the evil spirits to leave the possessed person. In later societies exorcisms were performed, usually by a priest. This was a noninvasive way to drive out the evil spirits in the possessed individual. Exorcisms, although rare, are still performed today.

Views on abnormal behavior were significantly advanced by Hippocrates (460–377 B.C.), the father of modern medicine. He viewed abnormal behavior—and illnesses in general—as having internal causes, and thus having biological natures or etiologies. Hippocrates' prescriptions for the ill included rest, proper diet, sobriety, and exercise—many prescriptions that are still used today. Hippocrates also had a key belief that if you took care of your body, your mind would also stay well. See Rapid Reference 1.2 for a discussion of the *Hippocratic Oath*.

During the Middle Ages (approximately the fifth to the fifteenth century), the view that demons were causing mental illnesses in certain people once again became popular, and the ancient Greek and Roman views that saw physiological causes of such behaviors lost favor. Plagues were common during these times, and exorcisms reemerged as a form of treatment for mental illnesses. One key concept was the idea that evil supernatural forces were to blame; oddly enough, this took some of the responsibility off of the mentally ill.

During the Renaissance (around 1400–1700 A.D.), the treatment of the mentally ill improved significantly. The mentally ill were seen as having sick minds, and, therefore, their minds needed to be treated along with their bodies. During the early

≡Rapid Reference 1.2

The Hippocratic Oath

The Hippocratic Oath itself is not a part of typical psychological training or practice, but its tenets are expected to be followed. In sum, the oath states that physicians or healers will not deliberately harm an individual who seeks their help; they will treat anyone who comes seeking their aid; they will not give a deadly drug if the patient requests it; and they keep all information about doctor-patient professional relationships confidential. Like all vows and oaths, this one is open to interpretation. Many of those in the helping professions follow the oath's tenets.

part of the Renaissance, asylums were created. Even though the name connotes bad feelings and scenes of patient abuse today, this was not how they were run at their founding. Their sole purpose was to treat the mentally ill in a humane fashion. Unfortunately, they soon became overcrowded, and the treatment soon turned to punishment and torture. Reforms in mental health treatment really did not occur until the nineteenth and twentieth centuries. See Rapid Reference 1.3 for a discussion of Bedlam.

Two important figures arose during the nineteenth century. Philippe Pinel (1745–1826) is seen as one of the early reformers in the

≡ *Rapid Reference 1.3*

The Origin of Bedlam

Bethlehem Hospital in London was founded in 1247 as a typical hospital for the poor of London. In the early 1400s, it began to be used as a facility to house the mentally ill. Eventually, during the sixteenth century, Bethlehem Hospital was used solely to house the criminally insane. *Bedlam* was the shortened version of Bethlehem Hospital and was the term used by Londoners. Bedlam became associated with the chaotic conditions within its own walls and with mental illness as well as with a place or situation where mass confusion reigns (http://www.new advent.org/cathen/02387b.htm).

proper treatment of mentally ill individuals. Pinel, a Frenchman, advocated that the mentally ill be treated with sympathy, compassion, and empathy—not with beatings and torture. Dorothea Dix (1802–1887) helped to establish many state mental hospitals in the United States during her nationwide campaign to reform treatment of the mentally ill. She was directly responsible for laws that aimed to reform treatment of this population.

The Twentieth Century

Many changes occurred during the twentieth century. Emil Kraepelin (1856–1926) was indirectly responsible for the seeds that led to the creation of the *DSM* series. He also espoused the concept that physical factors were responsible for mental illnesses. (How ironic that it took over two millennia to revert back to Hippocrates's ideas!)

In 1897 the sexually transmitted disease syphilis was discovered by von Kraft-Ebing (1840–1902). This was important because syphilis sufferers demonstrated delusions of grandeur, which *can* be a sign of a mental illness. General paresis was a disease that was caused by syphilis and was not curable. This was a critical discovery because now there was medical evidence that physical illnesses could mimic symptoms of mental illnesses and, more importantly, that physiological factors were, at the least, somehow involved with some if not all of the mental disorders known at that time.

For many psychologists the most important figure of the twentieth century began his work in the 1890s in Vienna. Sigmund Freud (1856–1939) was initially a researcher who was studying the reproductive systems of eels. Josef Breuer (1842–1925), another Viennese physician, treated patients who suffered from hysteria, which literally means "wandering uterus." Hysteria during the 1890s meant something quite different than it does today: Breuer's patients told him that they had physical illnesses. However, after examination, he discovered that they had no physical symptoms. Breuer, following Anton Mesmer's work, discovered that in some cases their symptoms eased or disappeared once his patients discussed their past with him in a safe environment without censure and while under hypnosis. Breuer discussed these ideas with Freud, who expanded on them and created psychoanalytic theory, thus leading to an entire movement that is still popular today. Freud's basic tenet is that unconscious processes, motives, and urges are at the core of many of our behaviors and difficulties.

Freud had some very famous disciples, including Carl Jung, Alfred Adler, and his daughter, Anna Freud, whose views differed from his regarding personality, human nature, and treatment procedures. Many of these individuals continued the doctor-patient paradigm initiated by Freud. In these instances, the doctor (therapist) was viewed as being in a power position, and the patient was a sick individual who would take the doctor's words as unassailable fact.

CAUTION

Freud and his followers only treated patients who today would be considered to have mild to moderate mental illnesses, such as Anxiety Disorders and mild Mood Disorders. Freud did not work with the chronically mentally ill, psychotic individuals, or those that required hospitalization. Some people in the helping professions do not see psychoanalysis, even short-term analysis, as being helpful to seriously ill individuals.

As is typical within a field, changes and differing viewpoints on human nature, personality, and mental illness and treatment exploded once Freud's ideas were publicized and published. B. F. Skinner (1904–1990) was considered by many to be the father of behaviorism. Interestingly, he did not do much research with human subjects! Skinner believed that any behavior that was reinforced or rewarded would be more likely to increase or recur; any behavior that was either not reinforced or was punished would be more likely to decrease or be extinguished. The simplicity of Skinner's basic tenets is remarkable. One positive feature of Skinner's concepts is that they are testable through controlled experiments.

Albert Bandura (1925–) created Social Learning Theory, also known as Modeling. Bandura postulated that we could learn based upon what we observed in a model (in real life, on television, in the movies) and then copying, or modeling, those behaviors. Modeling is especially effective when the model's behavior is reinforced. Modeling itself is a very powerful form of learning. How did you learn to read, ride a bicycle, or drive a car (especially a stick shift)? How did you learn to use a computer or beat the latest PlayStation 2 game? Perhaps through modeling!

Behaviorists tend to act like teachers in therapy sessions, often giving homework assignments and taking a very active role in sessions. Behavioral methods are quite effective when used in short-term therapy sessions and for individuals with behavioral problems (such as acting out in class or in public), and are welcomed in today's managed care environments.

Albert Ellis (1913–) takes a somewhat different approach. He believes that we get depressed and develop other mental illnesses because of our faulty thinking. He created Rational Emotive Behavior Therapy (REBT) with this concept in mind. For example, Ellis says that some people set themselves up to fail because of "musterbation." This means that you create a series of mental "musts"

DON'T FORGET

Many of Freud's ideas are archaic and seem sexist today. However, in Victorian Europe, a woman's status was not as high as it is today in many countries. Do not forget that Freud did not have access to the scientific devices and, more importantly, the technology and computing power that we now have. Nevertheless, Freud's theories still have reverberations in the psychological community today.

CAUTION

Bandura's theory was controversial because he demonstrated that learning could occur without *direct* reinforcement, something that many radical Skinnerians would say is impossible.

that are virtually impossible to satisfy. For example, "Everyone must love me. I must always get any job I apply for. I must always be happy." These are unrealistic goals, and when some of them are not met, the individual gets depressed. Rational Emotive Behavior Therapy works well with Anxiety Disorders and some Mood Disorders; it does not work well with lower-functioning individuals or with those who are not very verbal (or verbally astute).

Carl Rogers's (1902–1987) client- or person-centered therapy changed the therapeutic paradigm yet again. Here the psychologist is seen as someone who is a skilled listener, not judgmental, and certainly not powerful or omniscient. Rogers was a humanist: someone who believes in the innate goodness of all people and in the ability of all people to grow and to lead constructive lives. Rogers theorized that dysfunction begins in infancy. Children who have unconditional positive regard from their parents early in life will grow up to become constructive and productive adults, even though they will have flaws. They realize that they and their contributions are valued even with these flaws. In Rogerian therapy, clients attempt to look at themselves as being valuable, worthwhile human beings. Empathy, feeling for someone, is a critical component. According to Prochaska and Norcross (2003), about 5 percent of clinicians (this includes clinical and counseling psychologists and social workers) use client- or person-centered therapy techniques in their practice. See Rapid Reference 1.4 for definitions of key terms.

≋ Rapid Reference 1.4

Key Terms to Know

Reinforcement: This is any response that leads to an increase in the demonstrated behavior; any response that strengthens a behavior.

Punishment: This is any response that leads to a decrease, or extinction, of a behavior. Punishment must always decrease a behavior.

Modeling: This is the "do-as-I-do" concept; learning by observing what a model does in an identical or similar situation.

Rational Emotive Behavior Therapy (REBT): This is Albert Ellis's theory that we get into trouble because we develop and continue to feed into our irrational beliefs.

Empathy: This is feeling for someone; figuratively, it means jumping into that person's body and seeing the world through his or her eyes.

CAUTION

It is easy to place too much emphasis on dysfunctional upbringing as being the major contributor toward manifesting mental illness. It is indeed a critical factor; however, mental illness is much more complicated than any one etiological factor. Many psychologists take an eclectic viewpoint, seeing the etiologies of mental illnesses as emanating from a variety of different areas.

CAUTION

Many people confuse negative reinforcement with punishment. Negative reinforcement strengthens a behavior by removing a noxious stimulus (for example, the seatbelt buzzing in a car will only cease if you buckle up; once you do, the sound stops). You are therefore more likely to repeat this behavior next time (regardless of the fact that if you are caught while not buckled up, you could pay a hefty fine!). Punishment, by definition, always decreases the likelihood of a behavior recurring. The term *negative* is what confuses many people.

The field of abnormal psychology reached a major milestone in the early 1950s. During this decade Henry Laborit (1914–1955) introduced Thorazine (generically known as chlorpromazine[1]) for the treatment of Schizophrenic Disorders. Initially this medication was used to tranquilize surgical patients, but Laborit noticed that chlorpromazine managed to calm patients *without* putting them to sleep. This led to its widespread use for the treatment of Schizophrenic Disorders. Thus, the field of psychopharmacology was unofficially born, and the nature of mental illness treatment changed forever.

DON'T FORGET

Medications are not panaceas. They work well (for some) in alleviating the symptoms of some mental illnesses, but they do not eliminate all of the concerns that bring someone in for treatment. They also have side effects, some of which are quite significant, and some classes of medications have addictive potential. Medications should be seen as a treatment adjunct, not as a sole treatment modality.

[1]Generic names of all medications will be provided in this book in parentheses next to the medication's trade name. All generic names begin with a lowercase letter; all trade names begin with a capital letter.

Today many mental illnesses are treated with a combination of talk therapy and medications. Some of the more commonly used medications will be examined in the ensuing chapters.

THE DIAGNOSTIC AND STATISTICAL MANUALS

A second landmark in the helping professions was the publication of the *Diagnostic and Statistical Manual of Mental Disorders* (*DSM*) in 1952. It contained about 60 different disorders and was based on theories of abnormal psychology or psychopathology. However, the *DSM* and *DSM-II* (1968) were considered to have many limitations. Arguably, the major limitation was that the concepts had not been scientifically tested; in addition, all of the disorders listed were considered to be reactions to events occurring within the individual's environment, and there was really no distinction between abnormal and normal behavior. In effect, everyone was considered to be abnormal to a certain degree, depending on the severity of their behavior.

The first two *DSM*s also described the differences between neurosis and psychosis. The term *neurosis* is now considered archaic, while *psychosis* is still used. If an individual is demonstrating psychosis, that person experiences a break from reality, including hallucinations, delusions, and disorganized or illogical thinking patterns. Schizophrenia is an example of a psychosis. A person with a neurosis will be distorting reality without actually breaking (or splitting off) from it. Neuroses are considered milder disorders than psychoses and tend to respond better to treatment. Most of Freud's patients suffered from neuroses. Today we call neuroses Anxiety Disorders; they can also include some of the milder Mood Disorders.

The diagnostic field changed significantly in 1980 with the publication of the *DSM-III*. The psychoanalytic basis for the *DSM*s was abandoned, and the diagnostic criteria were now based on the medical model and on clinical symptoms, not on theories. The five-part multiaxial system was also introduced. The *DSM* was revised twice more, until the current *DSM-IV-TR* was published in 2000. This volume is heavily research based and includes much information about the etiologies of all of the disorders. The next revision (*DSM-V*) is scheduled to come out in 2011 at the earliest. See Rapid Reference 1.5 for a brief outline of the multiaxial system.

≡Rapid Reference 1.5

The *DSM-IV-TR* Multiaxial System

Axis I: Clinical Disorders and Other Conditions that May Be a Focus of Attention

Axis II: Personality Disorders and Mental Retardation

Axis III: General Medical Conditions

Axis IV: Psychosocial and Environmental Problems

Axis V: Global Assessment of Functioning

(From APA, 2000)

The Medical Model

The medical model is simple to understand. All mental illnesses described in the *DSM-IV-TR* are seen as having similar symptoms in common within each diagnostic category and subcategory. For example, all individuals suffering from Schizophrenia, Disorganized Type will demonstrate hallucinations, delusions, and illogical thoughts and confused speech patterns. In effect, the mental illnesses are seen as being similar to physical diseases, that is, all influenzas have the same general symptoms. This is critical because it allows the helping professions to have a common language in which to communicate.

DON'T FORGET

Many students, when they first encounter the *DSM-IV-TR*, have the following reaction: "Where is all the information on how to treat this disorder?" The *DSM-IV-TR* does not include treatment information; it is only, as its title states, a diagnostic manual that describes the disorders within. The authors presume that the years of expensive higher education have taught the user how to properly treat the disorders within the text.

Problems with the DSM System and Some Ethical Concerns

With the advent of the *DSM,* it seemed that the helping professions would have a common language and theoretical orientation. However, no field is problem free, and psychology especially tends to be a somewhat unscientific science at times. Widespread use of the *DSM* system has led to problems, some of which are preventable.

The first problem, and perhaps the most significant, is that once an individual is labeled or diagnosed, it becomes very difficult for that person to come out from under that label or diagnosis. For example, will people be able to see Monica Lewinsky as a woman, or will they only be able to associate her with joke punch lines? If someone in your family suffers from Alcohol Dependence, will you ever be able to disassociate that diagnosis from that individual? We need to be extremely careful before assigning a diagnosis (or diagnoses) to someone, as this may well alter that person's life forever.

What do helping professionals do if they do not believe in the medical model but instead regard mental illness as problems in living or as fictitious categories created by the powers that be in society (Szasz, 1984)? R. D. Laing thought that the people who are mentally ill are sane people who cannot handle the everyday stress and craziness of life. Thus, they go off into the peace of their own worlds, leaving normal people to suffer in everyday life. If nothing else, these viewpoints are worth considering and debating. Therefore, some in the helping professions are anti-*DSM* and do not see mental disorders as being real illnesses with potential biological and environmental etiologies, regardless of what the latest research presents.

A serious issue is that of *comorbidity*, which refers to the appearance of two or more disorders at the same time in the same person. Certainly patients can (and often do) have multiple diagnoses, sometimes on Axes I–III. For example, when many bulimic women come into treatment, they also present signs and symptoms of depression. Is the depression causing the bulimic symptoms, or is it the other way around? Suppose this young woman also had Alcohol Dependence, a digestive disorder, and liked to hurt herself—but had no intention of killing herself? What do we do then with all of these possibilities?

A concomitant issue is the fact that the *DSM* will not be updated again until 2011 at the earliest. The world changes more rapidly every year, and undoubtedly new disorders, or new wrinkles on present disorders, will present themselves. For example, you have no doubt heard of *road rage*. How would you diagnose this condition? Should we be creating a separate subcategory for those who survived the September 11, 2001, terrorist attacks in New York and Washington, DC and those people in New Orleans who survived Hurricane Katrina?

An issue that is often debated is how to handle disorders that do not have a known cause or a known viable treatment modality—or both. Autistic Disorder (autism) is one such example. How can we accurately diagnose autism if we are unsure of its cause(s)? Is observation enough? Are there not degrees of impairment across individuals with autism? See Rapid Reference 1.6 for the definition of *ethics*.

Rapid Reference 1.6

What Does *Ethics* Mean?

Ethics means doing what is right and correct for yourself, for others, or both. They are moral principles adopted by an individual or a group to provide rules for proper conduct in certain situations and, perhaps, in life. What is ethical behavior for one person may be unethical for the next (for example, accepting gifts from patients). This is why ethical dilemmas are so difficult to resolve; there are no set answers for them.

PURPOSE OF THIS BOOK

Abnormal psychology encompasses hundreds of disorders, and to cover them all would require a larger-sized book. We have selected what we consider to be the most commonly seen mental illnesses by helping professionals—those that are the most debilitating—or those mental illnesses that are often misunderstood. Because of this, certain categories could not be included in this book. In addition, in the interest of space, every specifier for each disorder's subtype could not be included.

The focus of this book will be on describing the features and diagnostic criteria for each of the disorders, examining their etiologies when known or hypothesized, and describing various treatment modalities. Current psychotropic medications (at the time of publication) will also be examined in each chapter, even if they are not in common usage or if they are not terribly efficacious. This format is designed for the intended audience of this book: students, educators, and professionals who may need an easy-to-use reference for abnormal psychology and may need assistance in making *DSM-IV-TR* diagnoses. This book is not designed to replace the *DSM-IV-TR* nor anyone's clinical judgment and experience.

 **TEST YOURSELF**

1. **Statistical frequency sees behavior as abnormal if**
   (a) the said behavior interferes with the individual's ability to function in life or in society.
   (b) the behavior deviates greatly from accepted social standards, values, or norms.
   (c) the behavior occurs rarely or infrequently in relation to the general population.
   (d) it can be classified with a *DSM-IV-TR* diagnosis.

2. **An *eccentric***
   (a) is a diagnostic category.
   (b) is someone who is mentally ill.
   (c) is what a lunatic used to be called.
   (d) is someone who has odd or unusual habits but is in fact not mentally ill.

3. **_Hysteria_**
   (a) literally means "wandering uterus."
   (b) was one of the concepts that led Freud to develop his theory of psychoanalysis.
   (c) refers to individuals who presented physical symptoms but had no physical illnesses.
   (d) All of the above are correct.

4. **By definition, reinforcement will always lead to an increase in the desired behavior.** True or False?

5. **_Empathy_ means**
   (a) feeling sorry for someone.
   (b) feeling for someone.
   (c) directly parroting back to the patient what he or she has just told you.
   (d) demonstrating patient or therapy bias.

6. In the medical model of abnormal psychology

(a) all psychological disorders are seen as diseases where the symptoms across the patient subpopulation are similar.

(b) psychotropic medications are the primary treatment modality.

(c) the therapist-patient relationship gives all of the power to the therapist.

(d) treatment efficacy is rapidly realized.

7. The *DSM-IV-TR* includes all of the following *except*

(a) specific codes for each disorder.

(b) the proper and most effective treatment modalities and how to apply them.

(c) gender breakdowns of each disorder.

(d) etiologies of each disorder.

8. Hippocrates viewed mental illnesses as being caused by evil spirits. True or False?

Answers: 1. c; 2. d; 3. d; 4. True; 5. b; 6. a; 7. b; 8. False

Two

ESSENTIALS OF ANXIETY DISORDERS

Anxiety Disorders are very common in the United States. A recent report from the National Institute of Mental Health (NIMH; 1999) stated that Anxiety Disorders affect about 14 percent of the United States population. This is an extremely large percentage, which makes Anxiety Disorders one of the most prevalent mental illnesses in the United States. *Anxiety* is best defined as an uneasy feeling of fear or apprehension, usually accompanied by increased physiological arousal symptoms such as increased heart rate, increased blood pressure, sweating, pupils dilating, and so forth. Anxiety, which is an emotional reaction, can be seen as an exaggerated fear response to environmental threats. *Fear* is a response that occurs when faced with real danger. Unlike fear, which is directed at the present threat, anxiety occurs because of the anticipation of future bad occurrences. Let us look at an example to illustrate this difference before we continue.

Let us assume that you are going about your daily routine, which includes walking through a plaza to get to your car at the end of your workday. You have made this walk many times before, and rarely has anything unusual occurred. One day you have had a wonderful day at work, and you are going home to your partner, who has prepared a great meal. As you head across the plaza, you see, out of the corner of your eye, people fleeing with terrified looks in their faces. You turn completely around and suddenly you see a huge lion charging straight for you! You are momentarily paralyzed. You feel your heart pounding, you break out in a cold sweat, and you get ready to run for your life!

We have just described a fear response, where you are reacting to a true life-threatening situation. The intensity builds quickly and prepares you to either fight or flee (in this case you obviously made the wise choice). The next day, you are shaky as work ends. You have to get to your car, but as you approach the plaza, your heart races, you feel like you are about to vomit, and you get

16

dizzy. You thus avoid crossing the plaza and find an alternate route to your car. As this occurs, your heart slows down, and the waves of nausea cease. You soon realize that you need to avoid crossing the plaza at all costs, and you therefore always find another route to your car. You have thus created a phobia, in that crossing the plaza brings about unrealistic fear responses in you. You *expect* the worst to happen, even though it is extremely unlikely that it will recur. In fact, many phobias, as we will see, are strengthened through these types of avoidance behaviors.

The *DSM-IV-TR* (APA, 2000) recognizes many subcategories of Anxiety Disorders. The subtypes are based upon descriptive features,

CAUTION

Not all anxiety is bad for you! Low levels of anxiety signal to us that we need to get ready for an upcoming event that produces some tension, such as final exams, a wedding, a major presentation, or an audition. Some people call this *positive anxiety,* as it gives you an added energy boost. Anxiety becomes detrimental and crippling when it is too high, thus harming concentration and performance.

DON'T FORGET

Worry is defined as an uncontrollable series of negative and emotional thoughts and images that may be concerned with possible future threats or dangers.

not on etiologies. We will focus on four of these subtypes: Panic Disorder with Agoraphobia, Social Phobia, Obsessive-Compulsive Disorder (OCD), and Posttraumatic Stress Disorder (PTSD). We are not examining Generalized Anxiety Disorder (GAD) as the diagnostic reliability of GAD tends to be lower than the other Anxiety Disorders (Chorpita, Brown, & Barlow, 1998). GAD also tends to overlap highly with the other Anxiety Disorders, making its validity as a separate diagnostic category questionable. Kessler, Keller, and Wittchen (2001), however, note that GAD appears to be an independent subtype of an anxiety disorder. The research, and the debate, continues.

HISTORY OF ANXIETY DISORDERS

Anxiety Disorders have been documented at least since Freud's time, if not earlier. There are those who believe (the author is not one of them) that the girls who identified the witches during the Salem witch trials suffered from

> **DON'T FORGET**
>
> Early versions of the *DSM* series grouped Anxiety Disorders under the category of neurosis. The critical facet: The individual was aware of his or her neurosis. By definition, this would be a higher functioning individual, one ideal for Freudian analysis.

Anxiety Disorders, perhaps even Panic Disorder. Anxiety Disorders were previously called neuroses; that term is archaic, even though many people still use it.

Freud became famous (and remains so) for the work he did with Anxiety Disorders. Freud worked with individuals who had phobias, OCD, and GAD. The specific symptoms of the disorder were not as critical to Freud as were the underlying causes in one's unconscious.

Freud and his disciples would see anxiety as a warning signal that dangerous or threatening id impulses (either sexual or aggressive) were about to enter the conscious mind. Although life would be rather interesting if we allowed this to occur (and rather dangerous as well), the ego prevents this from occurring, to the best of its ability. Ego defense mechanisms either distort or deny reality, thus preserving the individual's psyche and enabling him or her to get through the day. Freud thus focused on mental conflicts in the psyche (i.e., the id's impulses conflicting with the ego's defense mechanisms and the superego's impossible-to-meet standards of purity) and the sexual and aggressive impulses of the individual.

Repression, an ego defense mechanism, typically works on anxiety. The ego realizes that the individual is about to act on a sexual or an aggressive impulse that is considered inappropriate (such as lashing out at a parent or making a sexual advance toward the opposite-sex parent). When repression works, the anxiety is reduced because these forbidden impulses are blocked from reaching the conscious mind. Thus, the individual's behavior adapts properly to the situation and to proper social norms.

Unfortunately, according to Freud, this system can, and often does, fail. Extreme trauma can lead to an excessive amount of anxiety, which Freud would call free-floating anxiety. Thus, the ego will use additional defenses to combat this increased anxiety; Freud would state that this would lead to phobias and compulsions. As we will note throughout this book, the psychodynamic perspective is difficult to research and measure accurately. Many people in psychology do not give his theories much credence today.

≋ Rapid Reference 2.1

Key Terms to Know

Fear: Fear is a response that occurs when faced with real danger; directed at present threats.

Anxiety: Anxiety is a more general emotional reaction than fear; this is seen as an exaggerated fear response to environmental threats; occurs because of the anticipation of bad occurrences.

Worry: Worry is an uncontrollable series of negative and emotional thoughts and images that may be concerned with possible future threats or dangers.

Ego Defense Mechanisms: These are from Freud; these alleviate anxiety in the short term but are not designed for long-term use. They tend to become less effective the longer they are used on a regular basis.

Repression: This is from Freud; this is an ego defense mechanism where forbidden id impulses are blocked from reaching the conscious mind.

We do need to note the importance of Freud's concepts as he stressed biological impulses beyond our control, learning experiences that we had as a child, and the conflicts that can arise when past experiences clash with current experiences. If nothing else, Freud taught us that it is critical to examine an individual's past in order to gain clues to the etiologies of his or her current problems. Therefore, we will stress that it is extremely important to obtain an individual's history, to the best of your ability. See Rapid Reference 2.1 for definitions of terms related to Anxiety Disorders.

Symptoms of Anxiety Disorders

All Anxiety Disorders have one key feature in common: The affected individual experiences an emotional reaction—typically fear—that is well out of proportion to environmental threats. This anxiety causes a general problem with the person's ability to have a normal

CAUTION

Defense mechanisms are *not* bad for an individual when they perform properly. They are designed to alleviate anxiety in the short term, and, according to Freudians, they are quite effective in doing so. They are not designed for long-term use, and they tend to become less effective the longer they are used on a regular basis.

DON'T FORGET

Lacking information about a situation often creates more anxiety than having knowledge, even if that knowledge is negative (a blood test that finds cancer, for example). The anticipation is often worse than the actual situation. This is similar to situations when the anticipation of a positive event (a cool trip) is often better than the trip itself ("That's it? I expected more.").

everyday routine and a normal life. Typically, all of these disorders lead to a pessimistic outlook on life and a feeling of loss of control over an upcoming bad situation. This feeling of lack of control, and the fear of the unknown future, is typically found within most of the Anxiety Disorders.

We will begin by examining Panic Disorder with Agoraphobia, an especially fascinating disorder.

PANIC DISORDER WITH AGORAPHOBIA

Panic Disorder can either be diagnosed with or without Agoraphobia. Agoraphobia is an exaggerated fear of open spaces. (The *agora* was an open marketplace in ancient Greece, usually at the center of town. People would meet, catch up on the news, and do their daily shopping.) The *DSM-IV-TR* (APA, 2000) defines Agoraphobia as follows: The affected individual has extreme anxiety about being in situations where escape is very difficult or embarrassing. The Agoraphobia is presumed to have originated because the individual had a panic attack in a public place and was embarrassed by it or had no easy way to exit the public place. Thus, the individual will end up avoiding open places or places that offer no easy egress, or he or she will experience extreme stress and anxiety when he or she has to be in such places. Therefore, the individual will avoid these situations, will experience them but have

CAUTION

One can be diagnosed as having Agoraphobia alone if one does not have a history of panic attacks. One can also have Panic Disorder without Agoraphobia if Agoraphobia is not present.

extreme anxiety about doing so, or will have to be in the company of another individual (friend or loved one) who will ideally provide comfort, safety, and a sense of security (APA, 2000).

For an individual to be diagnosed with Panic Disorder, the individual must first have experienced recurrent, unexpected panic attacks. Simply put, a panic attack mimics a heart attack. Some symptoms include chest pain, nausea, chills, fear of dying, a feeling of choking, and profuse sweating (APA, 2000). A heart attack can be caused by severe panic attacks. However, the heart itself is not damaged specifically because of a stroke caused by severe panic attacks, or because of a disruption of the heart's blood and oxygen supply caused by severe panic attacks. The individual also experiences intense fear and discomfort during this episode, which occurs without warning and peaks after about 10 minutes (APA, 2000).

In addition, at least one of the panic attacks must have been followed by at least 1 month of having persistent concern about having additional attacks, being worried about the implications of the attack, or having a significant change in behavior related to the panic attacks. In other words, because of the initial panic attack, the individual now is extremely anxious, wondering when the next unannounced panic attack will occur. An individual may spend more time worrying about when the next attack will occur than about carrying on his or her daily activities. You can already see how avoidance behaviors of certain situations may help to reduce an individual's anxiety, while at the same time reinforcing avoidance of the situation. In other words, avoiding open spaces will reduce anxiety and thus be reinforced, making the pattern even harder to treat.

Next, the panic attacks must have certain potential causes ruled out before a definitive diagnosis can be made. In this instance, the clinician must establish that the panic attacks are not due to the direct physiological effects of a substance such as a drug of abuse, like cocaine or marijuana, or due to the individual taking a specific medication. Certain medications can produce symptoms similar to a panic attack. For example, reserpine is an antihypertensive. Some side effects may include dizziness, faintness, anxiety, and heart palpitations—all Panic Disorder symptoms. Some individ-

DON'T FORGET

Rule out means to examine the individual for the presence of other mental or physiological illnesses that might be mistakenly diagnosed as a mental illness or might lead to a *DSM-IV-TR* misdiagnosis. For example, if an individual is addicted to amphetamine (speed), they will demonstrate some symptoms of Panic Disorder without actually having Panic Disorder.

uals have even developed phobic reactions while taking reserpine. General medical conditions can also produce panic attack-like symptoms, such as hyperthyroidism; these general medical conditions also need to be ruled out.

Finally, we need to rule out the possibility that the panic attacks are not better accounted for by another mental disorder, for example, Social Phobia. Social Phobia can cause panic attacks or panic attack-like symptoms when the individual is exposed to feared social situations, such as public speaking. We also need to rule out Specific Phobia. The *DSM-IV-TR* defines Specific Phobia as a phobia (an exaggerated fear response) that is set off by the presence or anticipation of a specific object or situation, such as flying, blood, heights, dirt, black cats, and so on. Separation Anxiety Disorder also needs to be ruled out as a differential diagnosis. A panic attack (or symptoms) can occur if the individual is responding to being away from home or away from close relatives. This generally occurs in children and is typically a response to starting full-day school or being away from their mother or father (or both). Finally, PTSD needs to be ruled out; we will examine this next.

POSTTRAUMATIC STRESS DISORDER (PTSD)

Posttraumatic Stress Disorder (PTSD) has been around for decades but has only somewhat recently entered public awareness. This had been called *shell shock* in the past and was applied to combat veterans who had returned home and who would demonstrate stress reactions and might even reexperience combat through flashbacks. Initially, many laypeople attributed this to drugs or noted that the individual was having a nervous breakdown (which is not a clinical term) and was, in fact, crazy. Neither was correct. In fact, the individual was producing a delayed reaction caused by traumatic events. After the terrorist attacks on September 11, 2001, many expected that PTSD incidences would increase, and they were correct. Of course, whether this increase was mainly attributed to the attacks or to something else is debatable. Keep the September 11 attacks in mind as we examine the diagnostic criteria. Regardless, PTSD is often misunderstood, perhaps because it has so many symptoms. In the interest of space, we will examine the categories but not all of the subcategories. For a more detailed description, please see the *DSM-IV-TR* (APA, 2000).

In order to be diagnosed with PTSD, the individual must have been exposed to a traumatic event, and he or she must reexperience this traumatic event persistently. The exposure to the traumatic event must have involved actual or threatened death, serious injury, or a threat to oneself or to others. Second, the individual's response to this event must have involved intense fear, helplessness, or horror. Children might instead express this by demonstrating either disorganized or agitated behavior. Thus, we are already beginning to see how mental illness symptoms are defined differently for children. You can see how experiencing wartime combat can lead to PTSD. Keep in mind that crime victims (not necessarily violent crimes) can also have PTSD. An important facet to realize is that PTSD is not unusual for rape victims, along with other concerns.

Next, the traumatic event must be persistently reexperienced. The individual will have recurring *daymares* (a term we use to denote daytime nightmares while awake) or will have nightmares reflecting the traumatic event. Again, we need to note that symptoms will appear different in children. Instead of the daymares, the child will demonstrate repetitive play, where the themes (or certain aspects) of the trauma might be expressed. This is critical as young children are not, as a rule, capable of expressing themselves as are adults. Thus, helping professionals should examine how they play, and they should also examine drawings where unexpressed feelings and trauma may appear (that is, if you believe in the utility of drawings as one type of diagnostic indicator). Children will also have nightmares, but if you ask them to tell you the content of those nightmares, it may be unrecognizable.

Third, the individual must somehow feel as though the traumatic event is recurring. This will include reliving the experience, having hallucinations, and seeing illusions that make the individual feel as though the event is recurring. What is most often associated with PTSD (to the lay public at least) is that the individual may have dissociative flashback episodes. *Dissociation* can be defined where a set of activities, thoughts, or emotions become separated from the rest of the individual's personality and function independently of him or her. The individual may feel detached, unreal, have a sense of déjà vu, or may feel numb in relation to specific events, in this case extreme trauma. These flashbacks can also occur once the individual wakes up or while he or she is intoxicated. With children (especially young children), trauma-specific reenactment may occur instead of flashbacks. Finally, the individual will experience extreme psychological and physiological distress if they are exposed

CAUTION

For many people, flashbacks are associated with "bad acid trips." The LSD user will have a recurrence of the bad trip weeks or months after the effects have dissipated. Flashbacks for the PTSD individual differ, but they are equally as frightening.

to situations that internally or externally cue an aspect of the traumatic events. This may, of course, lead to flashbacks.

Fourth, the individual will persistently avoid stimuli associated with the trauma. For example, the individual may avoid thoughts, feelings, or conversations that are associated with the attacks. They may remove themselves from social situations because of the *fear* that conversations might involve this topic. They will also have their overall responsiveness to situations numbed out; in fact, they may appear to be depressed (which is, of course, possible and likely). For example, they may have decreased interest in activities that might somehow be associated with the trauma, and they may limit their participation in such activities. A rape victim might leave the dating scene for a long period of time because going out with a male might lead the woman to reexperience the trauma associated with her rape.

The individual also might be unable to recall an important aspect of the trauma. This aspect is critical and creates problems when helping professionals and law enforcement work with PTSD individuals. We may ask them to recall the rapist's facial features, but she may be unable to do so. The following is an interesting example of this: Many individuals swear that they saw the first airplane hit the World Trade Center live on television, but this did not actually occur! It was the *second* plane crash that was televised live. The individual might also feel a sense of detachment or estrangement from others, which is a type of emotional numbness. He or she may demonstrate limited affect and may feel that his or her future is limited. For example, an individual may feel that his or her life is almost over and is also hopeless, as he or she believes they will not get married, have children, or have a normal life span.

Next, the individual will experience increased arousal and anxiety. Both of these emotions were not as extreme before the trauma. The individual may, for example, have difficulty falling or staying asleep or concentrating; he or she may be prone to angry outbursts or may have an exaggerated *startle response* (a startle response is an involuntary reflexive reaction to an unanticipated loud or sudden noise). This is the reaction you have when you hear a loud backfire of a car engine, a loud crash, or a sudden explosion. You will have muscle tightening, you may jump and recoil, and you may have a shocked look on your face. In PTSD victims this response is exaggerated; they may scream hysterically at the slightest unanticipated loud noise (like a horn blast or a siren).

So far it sounds like we are describing examples of anxiety, and we are. After reading this, you might be saying, "Well, I know I have PTSD, since I was a basket case after September eleventh." Many of my students asked the same question 5 days after the attacks: Do I have PTSD? The answer was easy: Not *yet*. The reason for this is simple: The disturbance (i.e., the PTSD symptoms that we listed) must have been occurring for at least 1 month. Thus, if you are reacting to a traumatic event 3 weeks after its occurrence, you are not experiencing PTSD—and may very well be experiencing a normal reaction.

Posttraumatic Stress Disorder also has two specifiers. If the symptoms have been occurring for less than 3 months, it is called PTSD, Acute; if the symptoms have lasted for 3 months or more, the diagnosis is PTSD, Chronic. The *DSM-IV-TR* also notes that PTSD can be classified as occurring with Delayed Onset. This refers to the symptoms not appearing until at least 6 months after the traumatic event has occurred; for a definition of key terms, see Rapid Reference 2.2.

≡ *Rapid Reference 2.2*

Key Terms to Know

Agoraphobia: This is an exaggerated fear of open spaces; it occurs when escape is very difficult or embarrassing; it may originate because the individual had a panic attack in a public place and was embarrassed by it or had no easy way to exit the public place.

Panic Attack: It mimics a heart attack; some symptoms include chest pain, nausea, chills, fear of dying, a feeling of choking, and profuse sweating.

Posttraumatic Stress Disorder (PTSD): This occurs when the individual has been exposed to a traumatic event; the individual must reexperience this traumatic event persistently.

SOCIAL PHOBIA

Social Phobia (sometimes called shyness) might be considered as a special type of Specific Phobia, so we will examine the diagnostic criteria for this first. The individual must first demonstrate a "marked and persistent fear that is excessive or unreasonable, cued by the presence or anticipation of a specific object or situation (e.g., flying, heights, animals, receiving an injection, seeing blood; APA, 2000, p. 449). In other words, the individual demonstrates an exaggerated fear response that is out of proportion to the real danger presented. Many situations can produce phobic responses; the *DSM-IV-TR* only lists some examples. The fear of heights (Acrophobia), of open places (Agoraphobia), and closed-in places (Claustrophobia) are some of the most well known.

The response cannot be considered phobic until two subsequent reactions occur. First, the individual, upon exposure to the phobia-producing stimulus, will almost always produce an immediate and extreme anxiety reaction, that is, an exaggerated fear response. This immediate response may produce a panic attack. If the phobic individual is a child, she or he may instead be crying, having tantrums, or be clinging to the mother/father/caretaker. The individual must also realize that his or her response is excessive and unreasonable and must then avoid the phobic situation. As we previously mentioned, avoidance is very common in Anxiety Disorders. However, even though avoidance provides temporary relief from the anxiety, it also becomes reinforcing and is thus strengthened as a response. Children may not realize how unreasonable or excessive their fears are. If avoidance is not possible, the individual will experience the situation, but with significant dread and anxiety. Of course, this will make them extremely uncomfortable.

Finally, the avoidance or the anxious anticipation will interfere with the person's daily routine and with

DON'T FORGET

Charlie Brown (of *Peanuts* fame) surely has many phobias; it was rumored that his creator, Charles Schulz, also had them. He may have social phobia, in that he never really gets up the courage to even speak to his secret love, the Little Red-Haired Girl (who is never visible in the comic strip). When he attempts to even approach her, he gets very nervous, and if he finally does approach her, he has no idea what to say!

his or her normal activities, with work or school functioning, or with social functioning. Thus, his or her daily life is seriously compromised and is focused on avoidance behaviors or fear and dread.

So what makes Social Phobia different from Specific Phobia? The critical additional factor is performance. These individuals will avoid social situations because they produce fear, sometimes crippling

DON'T FORGET

Some of the most famous celebrities have (or had) Social Phobia. Barbra Streisand and the late Johnny Carson are two of the most famous. Julie Kavner, an accomplished actor who is also the voice of Marge Simpson, is notorious for not giving interviews. Does this make her socially phobic, or is she just shy or private?

fear. These can be classified as performance anxiety, which means doing something in front of other people (or in front of a single person who may be judging that person's performance), or as interpersonal interactions, where the individual is at parties, in dating situations (as seen with Charlie Brown), or in sexual encounters. Theorists believe that this anxiety originates because of a fear of being humiliated or embarrassed in public. If the fear is related to a specific situation, such as giving a speech, performing sexually, or playing a musical instrument, the fear dissipates (and the task is readily completed) if the task can be performed privately. If the fear is more generalized to any social situation and thus creates avoidance, that person is generally viewed as being shy.

OBSESSIVE-COMPULSIVE DISORDER (OCD)

Contrary to popular belief, Obsessive-Compulsive Disorder (OCD) does *not* have to present with both obsessions and compulsions. Instead, according to the *DSM-IV-TR,* either obsessions or compulsions need to be present. However, most people who have OCD demonstrate both. Before we examine OCD's symptoms, we first need to define *obsessions* and *compulsions.* Many people confuse the two terms, as do the media.

Obsessions are intrusive or recurring thoughts, impulses, or images that the person tries to eliminate or resist but either cannot or has extreme difficulty doing so. It seems impossible for the person to control the obsessions; this leads to increased anxiety and to the method generally used to try to control the obsessions: compulsions. *Compulsions* are thoughts or actions that provide relief; they are used to suppress the obsessions. Compulsions can be seen as behaviors whose main purpose is to either suppress or eliminate the person's obsessions. The compulsions are not connected realistically with the obsessions, or they are obviously excessive in their nature. Typically, compulsions are of two types: checking behaviors and cleaning rituals. For the most part, checking behaviors can be annoying, while cleaning rituals may lead to self-injurious behaviors.

The *DSM-IV-TR* has some additional diagnostic criteria for obsessions. First, the thoughts, impulses, or images cannot be excessive worries about real-life everyday problems, such as mounting credit card debt, the requirement to buy a new car because yours is about to die, or worries surrounding work or school. Next, the individual must recognize that the obsessions (as well as the compulsions) are excessive and unreasonable. Therefore, the individual needs to demonstrate some insight into his or her behavior, and she or he has to also realize that these behaviors are not normal.

Next, the person must make attempts to ignore or suppress the obsessions. They may also attempt to neutralize these obsessions with other thoughts or actions, typically compulsions. Finally, the person must recognize that the obsessions are a product of his or her own mind. In other words, she or he must realize that these obsessions are not due to thought insertion or otherwise imposed on him or her from outside the body. This criterion is used to rule out paranoid thoughts.

A point of debate concerns how professionals should distinguish between normal behavior and compulsions. The *DSM-IV-TR* states that the obsessions or compulsions must cause marked distress and be time consuming, defined as taking more than 1 hour a day, each day. Therefore, is it obsessive to check the door locks each time you go out, presuming you go out many times each day? What is considered to be compulsive handwashing? Did Lady Macbeth, for example, suffer

CAUTION

The *DSM-IV-TR* allows for the individual to have poor insight into their obsessions or compulsions; this is the specifier "With Poor Insight." This is included as a specifier if, for most of the duration of the current OCD episode, the individual does not recognize that the obsessions and compulsions are excessive or unreasonable (APA, 2000).

from OCD (she is often mentioned as a literary example)? Do you compulsively wash your hands during cold or flu season?

Finally, the obsessions or compulsions must significantly interfere with the individual's daily life or everyday routines, whether that be in one's occupation, in school, or in social situations. We again see that the condition needs to somehow interfere with the person's everyday routine before it can be defined as a mental illness. Therefore, we can safely say that many of the mental illnesses we will discuss do indeed interfere (or cause problems with) the individual's normal everyday life. Finally, as we previously noted with other conditions, OCD cannot be due to the physiological effects of a substance, such as drugs of abuse, alcohol, or medications, nor can it be due to a general medical condition. For definitions of relevant terms, see Rapid Reference 2.3.

Rapid Reference 2.3

Key Terms to Know

Obsessions: These are intrusive or recurring thoughts, impulses, or images that the person tries to eliminate or resist but either cannot or has extreme difficulty doing so.

Compulsions: These are thoughts or actions that provide relief; their main purpose is to either suppress or eliminate the person's obsessions.

ETIOLOGIES OF ANXIETY DISORDERS

Many etiologies have been posited for Anxiety Disorders. We will briefly examine each perspective, beginning with the learning perspective (we previously covered the psychodynamic perspective). We will examine PTSD's etiologies in a separate subsection.

The learning (or behavioral) perspective is brilliant in its simplicity. This perspective views the individual's fears and anxieties as learned behaviors, which are acquired through either classical or operant (sometimes called instrumental or Skinnerian) conditioning. One perspective looks at a previously neutral stimulus, such as a peach, which, after it is paired with a strong unconditioned emotional response (called an unconditioned response), now takes on a negative value and subsequently becomes a conditioned stimulus (CS). For example, let us assume that a little boy is given a peach, and he is not told that there is a rock-hard stone (pit) in its center. He bites down hard in the center and he breaks a tooth, requiring a lengthy dental visit for the first time. The dentist gives him novocaine and uses loud drills. After this experience, the boy never goes near a peach again, and he also avoids the dentist at all costs. The peach and the dentist now have acquired a negative value through their association with negative events and consequences, and if either is presented to the boy, he would probably get extremely tense and nervous. Other examples of unconditioned stimuli might be sudden loud noises and sudden, unexpected, intense pain. The conditioned stimulus would be any neutral stimulus that was present when the fear reaction occurred. The CS now produces a response called the conditioned response (CR), which can occur only if the CS is presented to the individual. This model helps to explain how phobias are acquired and is supported by much research (for example, Merckelbach, Muris, & Schouten, 1996). A phobia may occur because an individual experiences an irrational fear after experiencing trauma.

Operant conditioning can also be involved with acquiring phobias. Anxiety relief *negatively reinforces* the avoidance behavior (negative reinforcement occurs when a behavior is strengthened due to the removal of a reinforcer). If the person is petrified of the dentist, avoiding him or her will alleviate the anxiety, and thus the avoidance behavior will become negatively reinforced. A Darwinist would point out that humans are predisposed to fear certain species that can harm us, such as spiders and snakes. This is called *prepared conditioning*. Finally, panic attacks are seen as occurring due to subtle environmental cues. Learning theories cannot and do not explain all Anxiety Disorders and their etiologies.

Operant conditioning can also be used to explain phobic behaviors. The key here is the avoidance behavior. The anxiety relief experienced by the individual due to his or her avoiding the threatening or traumatic situation is strengthened (or negatively reinforced) by the avoidance. For example, if the individual is petrified of going to a doctor for a routine physical (as many people are), avoiding the doctor will alleviate the anxiety, thus negatively reinforcing the avoidance behavior.

An interesting perspective is called the *preparedness model* (Ohman & Mineka, 2001). This model posits that we humans are biologically prepared to make certain types of associations in our lives. This model states that humans have a special module in the brain that has been changed and molded through evolution. Some of these modules are prepared to work automatically and unconsciously (shades of Freud!). These modules are also very selective in that they do not switch on to all stimuli; instead, they are very discriminative. These modules allowed humans to adapt and to survive. Note that the theorists state that these fears are not innate but, instead, are easily learned and maintained.

Research supports this model (Mineka & Ohman, 2002). Conditioned responses to truly threatening stimuli, such as snakes, spiders, and vermin, are much harder to extinguish than are fear responses to neutral or positive stimuli, such as roses and perfumes.

How would Bandura use modeling to explain Anxiety Disorders? Some phobias can develop by the individual witnessing a traumatic event happening to someone else or watching someone else behave with intense anxiety in a situation. Bandura's views differ and, to some, defy logic because the individual never has to directly experience an event in order for the event to produce a learning response. Watching an individual experiencing a trauma might be enough for the viewer to become traumatized and to acquire a phobia. The viewer needs to be interested enough to watch the trauma (or watch someone experiencing it) in order for learning to occur.

Cognitive theories posit that dysfunctional patterns of thinking may lead to Anxiety Disorders. Research has supported the hypothesis that cognitive factors play a key role in the etiology and maintenance of Anxiety Disorders. First, Albert Ellis states that individuals might develop phobias or an anxiety disorder because of his or her irrational beliefs and irrational thoughts. For example, an individual may have a fear of rejection in relationships because his or her perfect marriage ended in divorce. The divorce was bad, and it left a significant psychological wound. Therefore, he or she sees him- or herself as a failure and as being unable to handle any further encounters or relationships because he or she has to be perfect, and the marriage (or relationship) needs to be perfect. Anything less than perfection is considered a failure. Ellis notes that there is no way for this individual to be happy or to succeed because nothing (except the proverbial death and taxes) is 100 percent certain in life.

Oversensitivity to threat is a key symptom of Anxiety Disorders. Clark (1996) hypothesized that individuals with Anxiety Disorders may be overly sensitive to dangerous situations and thus may overreact and see danger where none exists, or they may seriously misinterpret bodily sensations or perceived threat. That is, these individuals may interpret normal physiological reactions in an alarmist way, going on the presumption that these sensations are signaling an impending catastrophe. Thus, they will experience a panic attack, and this will recur once the feared situation is reexperienced. A classic example is when an individual (let's presume that he has elevated cholesterol) also fears that there is something wrong with his heart. He wears a watch that is able to check his pulse and his heart rate. He notices one quiet morning that his heart rate is slightly elevated, as is his blood pressure. He believes that these are signs that a heart attack is imminent, and he continues to say this to himself and says that he will die because of this. This becomes a vicious cycle, and eventually the anxiety builds up to excruciating levels. The end result may be a panic attack and, subsequently, Panic Disorder. This theory, while fascinating, has not received overwhelming research support. For example, individuals can have panic attacks while asleep (Craske & Rowe, 1997). This should not occur based on this theory, as the individual needs to be awake to consciously misinterpret physical sensations. Thus, this theory, while interesting, needs more support and should be viewed cautiously.

Much research has examined the role of worrying, specifically looking at the cognitions that are involved. For some reason, people who are excessive worriers seem to be extremely sensitive to danger cues that signal the existence of perceived future threats. Attention is a critical component (Mathews & MacKintosh, 2000). What occurs is that the individual will attend to any signs of danger, no matter how minimal they are or how brief their appearance. He or she will attend to these cues, especially when they are under stress. What then occurs is another vicious cycle. The recognition of danger triggers this cognitive processes cycle, which can quickly lead to excessive anxiety. A presumption is that the threats are encoded in our long-term memory (LTM) as schemas that can be (and are) easily reactivated.

Thus, the anxious individual is worried that they will fail when encountering a future event, especially an event where the outcome is uncertain. These individuals use

DON'T FORGET

A *schema* is a general cognitive mental plan that serves as an action guide or as a structure for interpreting information.

many "what-if" statements. For example, "What will I do if she says 'no' to my marriage proposal?" Once this worrying cycle begins, the individual uses avoidance of the anticipated threatening events because they rehearse the anticipated (negative) consequences. The "what-if" questions are then activated by the threat schemas, and the individual's worrying and anxiety increase (Vasey & Borkovec, 1992). Thus, these individuals will continue to worry because this worrying is reinforced by a reduction in the uncomfortable physiological sensations. Note that this reduction is immediate and is temporary.

One cognitive theory involving OCD examines thought suppression (sometimes called thought stopping). Steketee and Barlow (2002), among others, posit that OCD may be related to maladaptive consequences of the individual attempting to suppress unwanted or threatening thoughts that he or she may view as being dangerous or forbidden. Let us presume that an individual has thoughts about sex that keep on entering his or her conscious mind (awareness). He or she tries to resist thinking about sex because he or she has been raised to believe that sex is dirty and that thinking about it is immoral. The individual therefore tries to block these thoughts through suppression or through distraction. Eventually these thought-stopping or thought-suppression methods become compulsions. The OCD individual, as was mentioned, becomes aware of these exaggerated reactions (the compulsions) and finds them unpleasant or embarrassing. He or she then tries to suppress or resist the emotions in order to control their overreactions to these forbidden or dangerous thoughts.

We once again see a vicious cycle occurring when the thoughts that are associated with the emotions that are present may become an obsession. Thus, OCD is seen as cyclical, where relapse can be cued by an intense emotional experience. What is ironic is that these compulsions will not serve their purpose and will fail because they actually increase the frequency of these bad thoughts. Avoidance behaviors only seem to make anxiety and, in this case, obsessions worse.

Research has also begun to support the hypothesis that biology plays an important role in the etiology and maintenance of Anxiety Disorders, especially in Panic Disorder. Genetics seem to play a role in Anxiety Disorders, specifically in GAD and in Panic Disorder (Barlow, 2002). Panic Disorder and GAD appear to have a familial component; there appears to be an increased prevalence of Panic Disorder or GAD among biological relatives of individuals who have Panic Disorder or GAD. We thus seem to inherit a tendency to panic. Twin studies also indicate that genetics are involved with the etiologies of several Anxiety Disorders, especially Panic Disorder.

Research has also indicated that the amygdala has a key role in the etiology of Anxiety Disorders (LeDoux, 2000). The amygdala (part of the brain's limbic system) is responsible for detecting and organizing a response to a threat or a certain danger. The amygdala itself is responsible for producing a fear response in humans.

The gamma aminobutyric acid (GABA) system also seems to be involved in the etiology and maintenance of Anxiety Disorders. Gamma aminobutyric acid, a neurotransmitter, reduces anxiety specifically by inhibiting neurons from exciting neighboring neurons. The concept here is that depleted GABA levels lead to increased anxiety caused by neurons firing too often. Support for this hypothesis actually comes from a treatment modality we will examine later in this chapter. Anxiolytics (also called antianxiety medications) are often used to treat Anxiety Disorders. The goal is to get the patient functional while in psychotherapy and then take them off of the anxiolytic. The benzodiazepine Valium (generically called diazepam) excites the GABA system, thus making it more likely that anxiety levels will decrease.

There are some problems with the GABA hypothesis, specifically the role of serotonin, another neurotransmitter. Serotonin is involved with appetite, mood, libido (sex drive and sex appetite), and perhaps sleep. Panic Disorder specifically seems to be linked to depleted serotonin levels. This hypothesis receives support because the antidepressant medication class known as selective serotonin reuptake inhibitors (SSRIs) seems to be rather efficacious in treating Panic Disorder. Examples of these medications include Paxil (paroxetine) and Zoloft (sertraline). In addition, the Food and Drug Administration (FDA) seems to agree: Paxil and Zoloft have FDA approval for the treatment of Panic Disorder with or without Agoraphobia (Bezchlibnyk-Butler & Jeffries, 2005). Other neurotransmitters that have been implicated include dopamine and norepinephrine. Some research has concluded that these neurotransmitters all have some implication in Anxiety Disorders' etiologies.

Klein (1994) has an interesting biologically based theory that refers specifically to Panic Disorder. He states that individuals who have Panic Disorder see their anxiety levels increase when they are faced with biologically dangerous situations, such as increased carbon dioxide levels in the blood, suffocation, asthma, or hyperventilation. Klein believes that a brain defect leads individuals who are more likely to panic to misinterpret cues related to suffocation (for example), such as increased carbon dioxide levels. Klein states that this will then lead to respiratory alarm, which leads to onset of a panic attack and the beginning of panic attack symptoms such as hyperventilation, rapid heartbeat, nausea, and hot or cold flashes. This perspective is still being investigated and has support both for and against its views.

Posttraumatic Stress Disorder (PTSD)

The definition of Posttraumatic Stress Disorder (PTSD) states that it is caused specifically because the individual experiences a traumatic event or receives traumatic stressors. However, not every person who experiences trauma develops PTSD. For example, not everyone, even some of those who were in the World Trade Center, developed PTSD. Researchers want to know why some people who experience (or are exposed to) traumatic stressors develop PTSD and why some people do not.

First, social and cultural factors have some influence. Researchers have discovered that two critical factors are the nature of the traumatic event and the individual's level of exposure to it, and whether the individual has a good social support system (i.e., family and friends). Individuals who experience trauma are more likely to develop PTSD if the trauma is more intense, life threatening, or if they have been exposed to the trauma for a greater length of time than someone else who has experienced the trauma. That is, if an individual witnessed the Twin Towers collapsing in person, while someone else observed both planes crashing into the towers and the subsequent horrific events that followed, the second individual would be more likely to develop PTSD (Foy, Resnick, Sipprelle, & Carroll, 1987). Interestingly enough, if the second individual has a strong social support system, this would *decrease* his or her chances of developing PTSD (Galea et al., 2002; Kilpatrick et al., 1989). Some research has also demonstrated that attempting to face the situation (and not using avoidance techniques) instead of becoming angry or blaming others also helps to decrease the chances of developing PTSD.

Foy and colleagues conducted some interesting research (Foy et al., 1987). They discovered that some people appear to be more vulnerable to developing PTSD than do other people, especially if that individual has a family history of Anxiety Disorders. Foy et al. (1987) also discovered that some individuals may place themselves in situations where experiencing trauma is more likely. Individuals who grow up in an unstable family situation seem to be at greater risk to develop PTSD if they experience traumatic stressors.

One final theory involves the hippocampus and the stress-related hormone cortisol and how these are related to memory disruption and memory loss. One research team discovered that some PTSD victims have short-term memory disruptions and are thus unable to recall certain events well, if at all (Vasterling, Brailey, Constans, & Sotker, 1998). The researchers hypothesized that PTSD victims suffer from chronic brain arousal due to the presence of cortisol; because of this, damage to the hippocampus can occur (the hippocampus is involved with memory functions and learning). This is one possible explanation why PTSD victims sometimes have problems recalling their traumatic events.

Before we begin to examine treatment modalities, we need to review the work of Davidson (2000) and Öhman and Mineka (2001). They hypothesize that an area of the brain—called the worry circuit—exists that signals danger to the individual. The worry circuit includes parts of the limbic system, and they hypothesize that this area of the brain is *constantly* sending alarm signals, which tell the individual to attend to the alarm immediately. This can lead to OCD. It is also hypothesized that the brain is dysfunctional in reducing repetitive behaviors. The *motor strip* has also been hypothesized to be dysfunctional; the motor strip controls movement. This may help to explain the handwashing and checking behaviors because the motor strip may be unable to stop these behaviors or may be inducing them through its dysfunction.

Thus, the best way to view the etiology of Anxiety Disorders is from an interactionist perspective or, perhaps, an eclectic approach. This includes biological and psychological perspectives as well as cognitive and learning theories. The research into Anxiety Disorders is continuing (for definitions of key terms, see Rapid Reference 2.4).

≡ *Rapid Reference 2.4*

Key Terms to Know

Negative Reinforcement: This occurs when a behavior is strengthened due to the removal of a reinforcer; it is often confused with punishment.

Thought Suppression (Thought Stopping): This is when an individual attempts to block undesired thoughts or wishes, either through suppression or through distraction.

Amygdala: This is a brain structure in the limbic system, it is responsible for producing a fear response in humans.

Gamma Aminobutyric Acid (GABA): This is a neurotransmitter that reduces anxiety specifically by inhibiting neurons from exciting neighboring neurons.

Anxiolytics: This is the technical name for antianxiety medications.

TREATMENT MODALITIES

One feature of most of the Anxiety Disorders is that they respond rather well to treatment and to interventions. In many instances, the combination of psychotherapy and pharmacotherapy (medications) are used. Historically, Anxiety Disorders have had documented treatment efficacy since Freud's time; thus, we will start with a brief examination of psychoanalysis.

Freud and his followers would emphasize the individual gaining insight into his or her unconscious motives, wishes, and fears that create and are seen as the primary cause of the individual's symptoms. One goal would be to bring these unconscious motives and desires to the surface so that they can be recognized and worked on during the psychoanalysis. Even though there are historical precedents with Freud's concepts, it does not hold up well in research and is not used by many therapists today.

Systematic desensitization techniques, a behavioral treatment method, were initially developed to treat specific phobias as well as Anxiety Disorders in general. The individual is first taught progressive muscle relaxation techniques. These are muscle relaxation techniques that can be readily learned with some at-home practice. Mental relaxation techniques, which use guided imagery, are more difficult to learn and are more difficult to put into effective practice. Then the therapist will make a list of the fear-producing stimuli, starting with those that produce minor fear, up to those that produce the most fear and might produce a phobic avoidance response or a panic attack. Finally, while the individual is relaxed (in the therapist's office), she or he is told to imagine the images, beginning with the least frightening one. This first image (let us assume it is thinking about a baby spider) is continuously presented until the individual no longer experiences anxiety when thinking about the baby spider. As the process continues the therapist moves up the ladder to stimuli that produce greater and greater fear responses.

Systematic desensitization has proven to be quite effective in treating phobias, with the key factor being systematic and maintained exposure to the fear-producing stimuli (Mineka & Thomas, 1999). An alternative form of systematic desensitization is called *flooding*, which has also proven to be quite effective. In flooding, the most frightening stimuli are presented to the individual first, instead of working up to those stimuli. Barlow and his colleagues (Barlow, Raffa, & Cohen, 2002) noted that these various exposure methods are quite efficacious; more importantly, the results are maintained at least several months after treatment has concluded.

Panic Disorder with Agoraphobia has been treated with a slightly different approach. In order to treat Agoraphobia (specifically the phobic avoidance behaviors that accompany it), situational exposure has been used. In this modality the individual repeatedly confronts the situation that he or she previously avoided. This will include open spaces such as malls, theaters, and large gathering places, such as train stations. This method is also used when methods of transportation, such as buses, trains, or airplanes have been avoided due to their producing a phobic response.

Panic attacks have been treated with an exposure method known as *interoceptive exposure*. Here the individual is taught to recognize the internal physical sensations that are often associated with the potential onset of a panic attack, such as increased heartrate, sweating, increased breathing, dizziness, and increased respiration. The idea here is to reduce the individual's fear of

DON'T FORGET

Relaxation training has been proven to be quite effective in treating GAD (Borkovec, Newman, Pincus, & Lytle, 2002). Many relaxation techniques, in order to continue to succeed, need to be practiced on a regular basis and can also be used to control anxiety, worry, and tension.

experiencing these sensations. What the therapist will do is involve the individual in exercises that produce these responses, such as hyperventilating, running in place or on a treadmill, or perhaps breathing through a coffee stirrer (a very narrow straw or tube). Craske (1999), among others, supports this technique and notes that this technique is very effective and is an important component in the treatment of Panic Disorder.

According to Franklin and Foa (2002), the most effective treatment modality for OCD is exposure with response prevention. First, the individual is deliberately exposed to a situation that would set off obsessive thoughts. This might be leaving the house or touching someone or something that he or she considers to be unclean. The next component, response prevention, refers to the individual attempting to physically prevent the compulsion (response) from occurring. Neither component on its own is successful; both must be used in order for treatment success to occur. Individuals with OCD use their compulsive behaviors to reduce the anxiety that usually occurs when an obsession appears, typically suddenly. As we have mentioned, the compulsion leads to avoidance, which strengthens the compulsion. More importantly, if the compulsive behavior occurs, exposure to the stimulus that produced the obsession is cut short, making it less likely that the individual will be able to face down the obsession. Eventually the individual would be able to handle the anxiety brought about by the obsession while at the same time not acting on the compulsion triggered by that same anxiety. While these techniques are not effective for all OCD patients, they remain one of the most effective techniques to effectively treat OCD (Abramowitz, 1998).

Breathing retraining is one effective way of treating Panic Disorder (Ley, 1999). This technique provides practice in learning how to breathe slowly and how to avoid hyperventilation (very rapid breathing, which can lead to lightheadedness and often occurs during a panic attack). In this technique, the individual learns to control his or her breathing by breathing from the diaphragm, not from the chest. The goal is to take short deep breaths, not short rapid breaths. Researchers report that while the technique is effective, the reasons for its effectiveness remain somewhat unclear.

Cognitive techniques are widely used to treat Anxiety Disorders; the most commonly used techniques were created by Albert Ellis and Albert Bandura. The approach is simple and is, as you will see in Chapter 3, similar to the approach used to treat unipolar depression. First the therapist

DON'T FORGET

Some common cognitive errors are all-or-none thinking (one mistake or rejection means total failure and that the individual is a total flop) and overgeneralizing ("That D in Psychology is the pits. Now I'll never be Freud's successor."). Jumping to conclusions before considering all of the evidence is an additional type of cognitive error or faulty logic. How often do you make these kinds of errors?

will work with the patient to help him or her identify the cognitions (thoughts) that are relevant to his or her anxiety, in this case his or her presenting problem. Then the therapist works with the patient to identify and recognize how these cognitions are related to the maladaptive emotional responses that are produced. In this situation these responses are the anxiety responses. Then the therapist will look at all of the present evidence that is either supporting or contradicting these beliefs, and, finally, the therapist will work with the patient to teach him or her more useful and adaptive ways of interpreting and viewing events that affect him or her in the patient's life or environment.

David Barlow examines the cognitive errors of his patients when they present with Panic Disorder. In addition, Barlow also uses an interesting technique called *decatastrophisizing*. Here Barlow asks the patient to imagine what would happen if his or her worst-case scenario actually came to pass. Once the patient has done this ("If she says 'no' to me, I will die and slit my wrists."), the therapist then helps him or her examine the faulty logic and cognitive errors she or he is making. Ideally, the patient will end up realizing that these gross exaggerations are nothing more than cognitive errors based on faulty logic. In order to reinforce the patient's seeing these assertions for what they truly are, homework assignments and practice sessions are assigned at the end of each therapy session, with the results to be reviewed during the next session. The patient is also encouraged to write down predictions (which are probably exaggerations based on faulty logic) that he or she makes about specific situations that will be encountered. The patient is then expected to make records of the actual outcomes of these situations.

Cognitive interventions are effective in treating Panic Disorder with or without Agoraphobia, GAD, Social Phobia, and OCD (see, for example, Ladouceur et al., 2000).

Medications

Anxiolytics

Medications are often used to treat Anxiety Disorders—specifically to treat OCD and Panic Disorder—although they are often prescribed to treat other Anxiety Disorders as well. Ideally, medications are used in conjunction with psychotherapy, although researchers remain somewhat unclear whether psychotherapy combined with medications are more efficacious than either psychotherapy alone or medications alone. Two classifications of medications are used to treat Anxiety Disorders.

We will first examine anxiolytics, also known as antianxiety medications. Some professionals and texts refer to these medications as *minor tranquilizers*. This term is confusing and is archaic.

The most common anxiolytics are the benzodiazepines; this class includes Valium (diazepam), Halcion (tricozolam) and Xanax (alprazolam). These medications reduce anxiety symptoms, help to relax the muscles, and will help to calm a nervous stomach. They will also reduce heart palpitations and perspiration. These drugs also reduce hypervigilance but are not as effective at reducing the individual's tendency to worry about future events. These medications work on the GABA system, which was previously mentioned; anxiolytics inhibit the activity of GABA neurons. Some anxiolytics have a long half-life, such as Valium. Xanax has an intermediate half-life, while Halcion's half-life is short-acting and thus has the shortest half-life of these three medications.

Benzodiazepines are quite effective in treating GAD and Social Phobia, but they are not effective for treating specific phobias and OCD. Positive effects are usually seen early on in treatment, and the effects may wane after 6 months of usage. The FDA recently approved Xanax for the treatment of Panic Disorder with or without Agoraphobia (Bezchlibnyk-Butler & Jef-

DON'T FORGET

Major tranquilizers are known today as antipsychotic medications. The former term is archaic, but it was used because the purpose of these medications, it was believed, was to sedate violently psychotic individuals. Minor tranquilizers were used to calm down an anxious individual who was not violent.

fries, 2005), and this remains the drug of choice for treating Panic Disorder. A critical concern is that many patients who have Panic Disorder with or without Agoraphobia have a tendency to relapse if they go off of their medications. As you will see throughout this book, this statement will be made quite often. A reasonable alternative would be to use exposure therapy with individuals who have Panic Disorder with Agoraphobia.

The side effects of benzodiazepines are somewhat problematic. Individuals may experience drowsiness and mild psychomotor and cognitive impairments. In the elderly these drugs can interfere with attention and memory, which is ironic because concentration and memory are often negatively affected by Anxiety Disorders! Patients on these medications should avoid operating a motor vehicle or heavy machinery because they interfere with judgment, motor, and cognitive behavior, and they can make the individual drowsy. There is one other side effect of benzodiazepines that makes their prescription very risky.

Benzodiazepines become physiologically addictive in a relatively short period of time (Bezchlibnyk-Butler & Jeffries, 2005). In addition to this, these medications do not mix well with alcohol. If the individual drinks alcohol while on these medications, the effects of the benzodiazepine are increased significantly. This is known as a drug interaction, where the combined effects of two substances are far greater than if either substance were used alone. One study showed that about 40 percent of the individuals who were taking benzodiazepines for at least 6 months demonstrated withdrawal symptoms if the benzodiazepines were removed (Michelini, Cassano, Frare, & Perugi, 1996). Withdrawal symptoms include sleep problems, difficulty concentrating, somatic concerns, and the return of anxiety. As you might expect, the withdrawal symptoms are most significant with individuals who quit taking benzodiazepines quickly, especially if the medications are those that have short half-lives, such as Xanax. As a rule, the risk for dependence increases if the individual also has a history of Substance Abuse or Substance Dependence, especially with alcohol, another central nervous system depressant and muscle relaxant. Because of these concerns with benzodiazepines, we recommend that their usage be short term and used only as needed.

One alternative is to use BuSpar (buspirone), which acts on serotonin, not on GABA. BuSpar is effective in treating GAD; its efficacy in treating the other Anxiety Disorders is unclear (Apter & Allen, 1999). Buspar does not cause drowsiness and does not have a drug interaction with alcohol; therefore, its tendency to be addictive is lower that the benzodiazepines. The main disadvantage is that therapeutic onset of BuSpar is longer for patients who have severe anxiety compared with benzodiazepines.

Antidepressants

When one thinks of antidepressants, one immediately thinks of medications that are used solely to treat unipolar depression or perhaps to treat Bulimia Nervosa (we will examine this usage in Chapter 5). What is not widely known is that antidepressants, specifically the SSRIs, are now the preferred form of medication to treat many of the Anxiety Disorders (Bezchlibnyk-Butler & Jeffries, 2005). The SSRIs include medications that are very prominent in psychology and psychiatry: Zoloft (sertraline), Paxil (paroxetine), Prozac (fluoxetine), and Luvox (fluvoxamine). Research supports their usage and also supports the hypothesis that they are at least as equally effective as tricyclic and other antidepressants in reducing anxiety and, therefore, in effectively treating many types of Anxiety Disorders (e.g., Roy-Byrne & Cowley, 2002).

There are other significant advantages to using SSRIs. They tend to have fewer side effects than other antidepressants and anxiolytics; some of the most common side effects are nausea, jitteriness, constipation, a change in libido (sex drive), and dry mouth (Bezchlibnyk-Butler & Jeffries, 2005). The SSRIs are safe to use and have a low overdose potential, unlike the tricyclics and anxiolytics, and their addiction potential is minimal. Finally, withdrawal symptoms are not as significant when their usage is decreased. One reason for this is that it takes a while for the medication to completely wash out of the bloodstream. Thus, the SSRIs are now considered the front-line medication (i.e., the first choice of the psychiatrist) when treating Panic Disorder, Social Phobia (social anxiety disorder), and OCD (Bezchlibnyk-Butler & Jeffries, 2005). It should also be noted that Paxil (paroxetine) has recently been approved by the FDA for the treatment of Social Phobia.

One of the older antidepressants is the tricyclic Tofranil (imipramine). Tofranil has been used for over 40 years to treat Panic Disorder, and research has supported its efficacy (Bezchlibnyk-Butler & Jeffries, 2005). One major advantage of Tofranil over anxiolytics is that Tofranil is less likely to cause physiological dependence and thus has little chance of being abused.

However, prescribing Tofranil leads to some concerns. First, the length of time before it reaches clinical efficacy is longer than that of the SSRIs. The therapeutic effect for Tofranil is seen after 7 to 28 days. Of greater concern are the side effects produced by Tofranil. Some of the side effects of Tofranil and some other tricyclic antidepressants include sedation and drowsiness, decreased libido, and anticholinergic side effects. Anticholinergic side effects include constipation, blurred vision, confusion, poor memory, and hypotension (Maxmen & Ward, 1995; Bezchlibnyk-Butler & Jeffries, 2005). Some label these side effects antihistamine effects, as they are similar to those produced by over-the-counter allergy pills such as Benadryl and Chlortrimetron. An additional problem is that these side effects might also cause the patient to discontinue their medication treatment prematurely, leading to the anxiety symptoms returning.

Anafranil (clomipramine), a tricyclic antidepressant, has been used effectively to treat OCD for a number of years. Even though Anafranil has about a 60 percent efficacy rate with OCD, like all of the tricyclic antidepressants, it has significant and unpleasant side effects (Bezchlibnyk-Butler & Jeffries, 2005). When Anafranil is removed, patients tend to have a high relapse rate (Maxmen & Ward, 1995; Bezchlibnyk-Butler & Jeffries, 2005).

Psychiatrists and psychologists generally agree that antidepressants are the medication of choice when treating PTSD. The FDA approved Zoloft for PTSD treatment in 1999, and in 2002 they approved Paxil for PTSD treatment. These medications seem to alleviate the anxiety and panic attacks that can occur with PTSD. Paxil is somewhat unique in that it also has significant anxiolytic effects. These medications may be effective because researchers have established a relationship, and comorbidity, between PTSD and unipolar depression (Bezchlibnyk-Butler & Jeffries, 2005). Once again, as with the previous medications, many patients will relapse once the medications are withdrawn.

We can thus conclude that Anxiety Disorders are often treated best with a combination of medications and psychotherapy. Medications alone may alleviate the symptoms, but more needs to be addressed before the patient can safely be on the road to recovery; see Rapid Reference 2.5 for definitions of key terms.

CAUTION

Research has demonstrated that benzodiazepines and other typical antianxiety medications do *not* have therapeutic efficacy in treating PTSD.

≡ *Rapid Reference 2.5*

Key Terms to Know

Benzodiazepines: This is a class of anxiolytics that includes Valium (diazepam) and Xanax (alprazolam); they reduce anxiety symptoms, help to relax the muscles, and will help to calm a nervous stomach.

Selective Serotonin Reuptake Inhibitors (SSRIs): This is one class of antidepressant medications.

Tricyclics (TCAs): This is one class of antidepressant medications.

Putting It Into Practice

The Case of Tillie Cornered

Tillie is a 24-year-old Caucasian female who is a receptionist for a business firm. She has worked for them for about 2 years, and she loves her job. She came in to see us because she has been getting very nervous lately, especially "when I'm in an elevator, in an office, or sometimes when I'm taking the train home. I get so shaky and nervous that I've gotten sick on occasion. I also get bad shakes in these situations." Tillie was concerned because these reactions were making it very difficult for her to encounter these situations. "I need to get home, and, if I pull a major freak-out while on the train or getting near it, that's no good. I can't always bum rides from people, and sometimes I get woozy and shaky when I'm in a car as well. Sometimes I even get a choking feeling like I can't breathe. That really happens when I'm in an office, not a cubicle." Tillie's reactions have been occurring since she started this job and have gotten progressively worse. Her coworkers and friends noticed her shaking in these situations, and "a coworker mentioned that I should see a doctor about this. I did, and he said I should see a psychologist for an examination. I know I've got some kind of psychological illness. I just need whatever it is fixed."

Thus, it appears at first glance that Tillie has an anxiety disorder, perhaps either a Specific Phobia or Panic Disorder. We gathered more information before we made a diagnosis. We asked Tillie about the history of this condition. "As I said, it's been getting a lot worse the past two years since I started work. It's gotten to the point where these silly behaviors are sabotaging my work and social lives. I'm not sure what happened, but I've never been like this before. At times I feel totally crippled, and I know the reasons

(continued)

are idiotic. I can tell you that I feel better when I don't go into an elevator, or on the train, or when I'm shut inside of a small office."

It appears that Tillie has a Specific Phobia, which most likely is Claustro-phobia (fear of enclosed places). We needed more information to clarify and support this impression. Most phobias need a precipitating event, so we asked Tillie to try and recall what might have occurred in her past. She replied quickly, "Shoot, that's simple. The earthquake and the closet. When I was little we lived in California and a big quake hit, really suddenly and re-ally big. The whole house shook and beams came down. We knew how to act, but I was scared out of my nut. I was downstairs, and I ran into a closet. Once things ended my Mom had problems finding me. I was so scared that I must have lost my voice, and the closet door jammed so I couldn't get out. My Mom found me eventually, but it was dark in there, and I was scared that the house would begin to shake again. I threw up shortly afterwards, and I couldn't sleep for days. No one was hurt, and the house sustained some damage, but the main damage was done to me. I've been terrified of closed places since then, and I also am afraid of the dark. Needless to say, my social life—men—is problematic because of these insane fears and my equally crazy reactions to offices and trains. I deal with it, but I'm sure I'll get an ulcer because of how stressful this is for me."

Tillie thus demonstrates a fear that is excessive and unreasonable and is set off (or cued) by either the presence or the anticipation of having to ride the train, go into an office, or go into an elevator. When she encounters these situations, her reactions are immediate anxiety responses, which at first glance may appear to be panic attacks. Tillie prefers to avoid these situa-tions, but if they have to be endured, she does so with extreme dread and fear. The anxiety, avoidance, and anticipation have caused significant impair-ment in her work, home, and interpersonal lives, and her phobia has lasted for at least 6 months. Finally, she recognizes that these fears are unreason-able and excessive. Thus, she meets all of the *DSM-IV-TR* diagnostic criteria for a Specific Phobia:

Axis I: Specific Phobia, Situational Type   300.29
Axis II: No Diagnosis   V71.09
Axis III: None
Axis IV: Occupational Problems
Axis V: GAF = 70 (Current)

The Situational Type refers to a phobia that is cued (or set off) by a specific situation. In Tillie's case, her phobia is cued by entering, being near, or antici-pating entering enclosed places. The age of onset for situational phobias is bimodal, with the first peak in childhood (which matches Tillie's history), and the second peak in the mid-20s (APA, 2000).

We know that Tillie does not have Panic Disorder because she is not having panic attacks outside of the specific phobic situations. That is, she has not seen these anxiety attacks occurring when she is in the park jogging, in a restaurant, making presentations, and so on. If she were having these panic attacks outside in an open place, in a restaurant, or while making a presentation (outside of the specific phobic situation), then she would be diagnosed with Panic Disorder.

Treatment Plan

Tillie was admitted to the clinic and was involved with individual therapy. We used systematic desensitization techniques, specifically structured and supervised exposure exercises. We supervised this because if left alone Tillie might try to do too much too soon. We gradually exposed Tillie to the phobia-producing stimuli, in this instance enclosed places and spaces. We openly asked Tillie to discuss her fears with us, and we began by showing her photographs of elevators, very small offices, and studio apartments, all the while asking her to tell us what was occurring. Tillie told us that the photos made her "nervous, and I could feel my throat closing up." She shied away from the photos when we held them close to her. We also taught Tillie progressive muscle relaxation techniques. Our goal was to get Tillie to use these techniques whenever she felt anxious about a claustrophobic situation. We gradually built up Tillie's resistance to the phobic-inducing situations by asking her to imagine herself in a claustrophobic setting (although not the worst one) while using the relaxation techniques. Once she was able to accomplish this, we continued on, eventually exposing her to the elevator in our building. We asked Tillie to bring in her best female friend to help out, and her friend was happy to assist.

Eventually Tillie exposed herself to more and more threatening situations, until she felt comfortable in enclosed places. Tillie also learned through the exposure exercises and through therapy that offices and trains are rarely threats. At discharge, Tillie was able to face her fears and the feared situations directly and was able to handle any adverse anxiety reactions. She was discharged after 4 months of weekly individual sessions with a prognosis of Good.

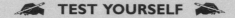

TEST YOURSELF

1. *Fear* **is best defined as**

    (a) a response that occurs when faced with real danger.

    (b) an exaggerated response to environmental threats, usually occurring because of the anticipation of bad occurrences.

    (c) a purely innate response.

    (d) None of the above.

2. *Anxiety* **is best defined as**

    (a) an uncontrollable series of negative and emotional thoughts and images that may be concerned with possible future threats or dangers.

    (b) an exaggerated fear response to environmental threats, usually because of the anticipation of future bad occurrences.

    (c) anger turned inward, according to Freud.

    (d) a response that occurs when faced with real danger.

3. **Repression is**

    (a) an ego defense mechanism that unconsciously blocks out forbidden id impulses.

    (b) an ego defense mechanism that consciously blocks out forbidden id impulses.

    (c) a reaction to a phobic situation.

    (d) a neurochemical reaction.

4. **A panic attack**

    (a) has symptoms similar to a flashback.

    (b) often occurs with Agoraphobia.

    (c) mimics a heart attack.

    (d) does both b and c.

5. **Posttraumatic Stress Disorder is definitely caused by**

    (a) an exaggerated fear response.

    (b) being exposed to a traumatic event.

    (c) a neurotransmitter imbalance.

    (d) experiencing bad consequences after being exposed to a neutral, everyday situation.

6. Obsessions are

(a) thoughts or actions that provide relief in OCD.

(b) most commonly checking and cleaning behaviors.

(c) intrusive or recurring thoughts, impulses, or images that the person tries to eliminate or resist but either cannot or has extreme difficulty doing so.

(d) similar to a panic attack.

7. Compulsions are

(a) behaviors whose main purpose is to either suppress or eliminate the person's obsessions.

(b) intrusive or recurring thoughts, impulses, or images that the person tries to eliminate or resist but either cannot or has extreme difficulty doing so.

(c) most commonly checking and cleaning behaviors.

(d) both a and c.

8. Anxiolytics include medications such as Anafranil (clomipramine) and Tofranil (imipramine). True or False?

Answers: 1. a; 2. b; 3. a; 4. d; 5. b; 6. c; 7. d; 8. False

Three

ESSENTIALS OF MOOD DISORDERS

Mood disorders, which include the Depressive Disorders and Bipolar Disorders, affect anywhere from 15 to at least 30 million adults in the United States. When most people think of mood disorders (called Affective Disorders in the past), they think of depression, sometimes called unipolar depression. Some very famous individuals suffer (or have suffered) from depression as of this writing. Mike Wallace; Colin Powell's wife, Alma; and the late Charles Schulz (the *Peanuts* creator) have all been afflicted. Lorraine Bracco, who plays Dr. Melfi the psychologist on *The Sopranos,* has also recently admitted to suffering from depression and has made advertisements stating this. Jane Pauley has stated that she suffers from Bipolar Disorder.

Mood is defined as one's general emotional feeling over a period of time. This feeling may vary over this time period, although mood fluctuations are normal for everyone. The term *affect* refers to the physical (in this case, facial) display of the present mood. The easiest way to understand affect is to look at the individual's facial expressions and reactions and to define them behaviorally. For example, people who suffer from depression typically will have a flat (unemotional) affect. Note that affective changes can change or influence an individual's overall mood if the affective patterns are consistent over time.

Thus, a mood disorder can be diagnosed when the individual's moods shift more dramatically, more frequently, or last longer. The *DSM-IV-TR* (APA, 2000) has two classifications of Mood Disorders. The first subcategory is *Depressive Disorders,* in which the individual has persistent sadness and finds little or no enjoyment in life and in things that led to enjoyment in the past (this last aspect is known as *anhedonia*). These individuals will also lack energy, in some cases so severe that they find it difficult to leave the house or to even get out of bed. Depressive Disorders are also known as *unipolar depressions,* meaning that these types of disorders have no evidence of mania or manic states and only have periods of depression. The opposite of depression is *mania,* which is characterized by extreme energy, elevated mood, euphoria, irritability, little need for sleep, and flight of ideas.

The *Bipolar Disorders* are the second subtype. These disorders are characterized by mood swings, or shifts, between mania and depression. Bipolar Disorder is commonly known as *manic depressive illness* or *manic depressive psychosis,* but these

> # CAUTION
>
> As we will soon discuss, Bipolar Disorders are often misdiagnosed by helping professionals. Part of the reason for this might be the fact that this group of disorders is relatively rare, so when it does appear, clinicians may mistake the mood swings as being caused by something else, such as drug usage. When an individual uses speed (methamphetamine), she or he will appear to be in a manic state.

terms are not clinically correct. The latter term may be considered pejorative.

Before we begin to examine the two subtypes of Mood Disorders, we need to look at another individual. Miss Q. is a 33-year-old single female who comes to you one day and tells you that she is having sleep difficulties; these have been occurring for at least 2 years. Specifically, she often wakes up in the middle of the night and cannot fall back to sleep. Her appetite has also decreased, she does not have a lot of energy, and her sex drive (libido) has become almost nonexistent. She gets weepy at times but cannot have a good cry. However, she manages to hold down a high pressure job that pays almost $300 thousand per year and manages to take care of her 3-year-old son every night after she gets him from daycare. In fact, she is in line for a promotion this year at work. She will have a glass or two of wine on occasion to "help her ease down and to sleep."

Does this sound like someone to you who is suffering from a mood disorder? After all, she is holding down a high paying job and raising a child on her own and seems no worse off. Her main concern is her sleep difficulties. Some professionals would send her to a medical doctor in the hope that she might be prescribed barbiturates or sleeping pills. How would you handle Miss Q.?

SYMPTOMS OF MOOD DISORDERS

We will examine the two types of Mood Disorders recognized by the *DSM-IV-TR.* Depressive Disorders include Major Depressive Disorder and Dys-

DON'T FORGET

Bipolar Disorder can also lead to suicidal behavior. In fact, it is rather common among these individuals who are not receiving treatment or for whom treatment is not effective. The risk is exacerbated here because of the volatility and the extremes of the mood swings. They can last for months and prove to be quite tiring for the individual. She or he may get sick of the varying moods and see suicide as a reasonable alternative.

thymic Disorder. Bipolar Disorders include Bipolar I Disorder, Bipolar II Disorder, and Cyclothymic Disorder.

Before proceeding, we should examine an important myth that surrounds Depressive Disorders: all individuals with a mood disorder, especially a depressive disorder, attempt to commit suicide. While suicidal ideation and suicidal behaviors are common among these individuals, Mood Disorders are not the sole disorder in which an individual will feel suicidal or perhaps act on these feelings. For example, Substance-Related Disorders (especially Alcohol Dependence) oftentimes lead to suicidal ideation. Schizophrenic individuals may be suicidal because of delusions or because no treatment works for them (Roy, 1992). Individuals who suffer from Panic Disorder with Agoraphobia (PDA) may be suicidal (Friedman, Jones, Chernen, & Barlow, 1992). Thus, suicidal ideation and suicidal behavior is not limited to Mood Disorders (Beck, Steer, Kovacs, & Garrison, 1985).

Symptoms of Depressive Disorders

Dysthymic Disorder

When we identify and define Depressive Disorders, we generally are considering either Major Depressive Disorder or Dysthymic Disorder. We will first examine Dysthymic Disorder, which some helping professionals consider to be not as debilitating and not as dangerous as Major Depressive Disorder.

Typically, when someone suffers from Dysthymic Disorder, they will tell you that they have been depressed for many years or as long as they can remember, which ultimately is a lifetime for them. An immediate concern is that these depressed feelings become a trait and are often considered to be normal for them. In fact, the *DSM-IV-TR* (APA, 2000) states that this depressed mood must have been present for at least 2 years for adults or for at least 1 year for children and adolescents. Additionally, there can only be a 2-month absence of the depressed mood during the 2-year period. Thus, the individual must have been depressed for at least 22 months during the past 2 years.

Before we continue, consider the preceding statement. For many people (Dysthymic Disorder affects about 6 percent of the population; Sadock & Sadock, 2003), this is hard to imagine. It is normal and natural for everyone to be depressed at some point during the year, if not multiple times. No doubt you have been in that kind of situation. However, try to imagine being depressed for months on end, every day appearing gray or perhaps black. If you have never suffered from a mood disorder, specifically a unipolar depression, you probably cannot imagine how it feels to be going through this recurrent mood. The interesting feature is that these individuals manage to cope and maintain relatively normal lives, holding down jobs; having families, friends, and relationships; and managing to function somewhat normally if not normally (again, Charles Schulz is a good example of this as are Mike Wallace and Tipper Gore).

The additional problem occurs when treatment becomes necessary. Because these individuals have become used to their depressed moods, they oftentimes do not see anything that needs to be discussed in psychotherapy. Thus, if they participate, they often will drop out before the treatment has concluded.

We will examine some other diagnostic criteria for Dysthymic Disorder, and you will soon see why this can be difficult to treat. First, while the individual is depressed, she or he must have had at least two of the following symptoms: either poor appetite or overeating, insomnia or sleeping too much, low energy, low self-esteem, poor concentration or difficulty in making decisions, and feelings of hopelessness. As we mentioned, these symptoms must have been present for at least 22 of the past 24 months (APA, 2000). Do not forget that all of us have experienced some or all of these symptoms at some point in our lives. The difference here is the length of time that the symptoms are present.

DON'T FORGET

The helping professions have a specific term for those who drop out of treatment early, against their better interests: *against medical advice* (AMA).

DON'T FORGET

We cannot stress often enough how important it is to ask new patients or clients if they have had a complete physical before we engage them in psychotherapy or before therapy has progressed for a lengthy period of time. In some instances, medical conditions can mimic psychiatric disorders and as many of us are not medical doctors, we are not properly qualified to perform a physical examination and to run diagnostic tests (such as a blood workup). Finally, alcohol or drug abuse or dependence must be ruled out in some situations, as their use can mask, contribute, or mimic psychiatric disorders.

Next, a manic or hypomanic episode must never have been present, and the criteria for Cyclothymic Disorder (we will examine this later) have not been met. Next, during the first 2 years of this disturbance in mood, a Major Depressive Episode must not have occurred. However, if this has occurred in the past, complete remission must have occurred.

The mood disturbance in Dysthymic Disorder must not have been part of a chronic psychotic disorder (such as a Schizophrenic Disorder) or the result of drug or alcohol abuse or dependence or caused by a medication or a general medical condition. This criterion is critically important, as it tells us that other conditions may contribute or mimic psychiatric disorders.

Finally, the symptoms must cause clinically significant impairment or distress in the individual's important areas of functioning. This last criterion is somewhat subjective. Does this mean that the individual cannot function on a daily basis? Perhaps this means that the individual can function decently but is unable to remain stable at times during the day. Or does this mean something else? Again, in our experience, many of the individuals who suffer from Dysthymic Disorder do manage to function and may compensate by overemphasizing other areas of their lives, so much so that we professionals may miss key diagnostic indicators.

Major Depressive Disorder

We will next examine Major Depressive Disorder. The *DSM-IV-TR* (APA, 2000) states that the individual must have experienced at least one Major Depressive Episode in the absence of any history of manic episodes. The *DSM-IV-TR* lists nine criteria for a Major Depressive Episode; the individual must have evidenced at least five of them during the same 2-week period.

A change in previous functioning must also have occurred. Finally, at least one of the symptoms must either be depressed mood or a loss of interest or pleasure. Take note that many of the criteria are physiological symptoms.

First, the individual must have had a depressed mood most of the day, nearly every day. This must be

> **CAUTION**
>
> While some individuals do indeed experience only one Major Depressive Episode in their lives and then make a complete recovery, this is rather rare. Most individuals suffering from unipolar depression have repeated major depressive episodes occurring intermittently.

indicated by either a subjective report (they tell you that they feel hopeless, sad, empty, and so on) or based on an observation(s) made by other people (someone else tells you that the individual is teary a lot). This might appear to be an irritable mood in children and adolescents.

Next, the individual will demonstrate anhedonia, which means a significantly decreased interest or pleasure in all, or almost all, activities most of the day, almost every day. This is how most media portray depression and is of course a classic (and stereotypical) criterion.

Third, the individual will demonstrate a significant weight loss when not dieting, a significant weight gain (a change of at least 5 percent in a month), or demonstrate a decrease or increase in appetite nearly every day. In children, we would look for a failure to make expected weight gains. Let us examine this criterion for a moment. Many people think that depressed individuals only lose weight; gaining weight, they might say, makes no sense, as they have no energy to eat. Consider this scenario: You have had an especially bad day. You were pilloried at work because you messed up a huge project, then you get home to get an e-mail from your partner that he or she "needs some space." You think, "This is the thanks I get after committing two years!" You then head to the freezer, pull out a pint of Häagen Daz (chocolate, please), and proceed to devour the entire pint in 15 minutes. Oddly enough, you feel better afterward.

Depressed individuals sometimes do similar things. They will eat a lot of comfort or junk foods because it might make them feel better. Additionally, these foods are extremely easy to eat and are addictive. Thus, while psychologists will typically see depressed individuals who are not eating much, we will come across those who are, in fact, eating too much.

CAUTION

We need to be careful so as not to confuse unipolar depression with an eating disorder like Anorexia Nervosa or Bulimia Nervosa. In these disorders, eating (and to a degree appetite) is disrupted. The individual might eat little, if anything, or they might eat a tremendous amount in one sitting. It might appear as though their appetite has either significantly decreased or increased; thus, they might be depressed. This is, of course, not the case. As we will discuss in Chapter 5, there *does* appear to be a link between unipolar depression and Bulimia Nervosa.

Fourth, the individual will have sleep difficulties, specifically insomnia (difficulty falling asleep) or hypersomnia (sleeping too much) nearly every day. An odd phenomenon can also occur: The individual will wake up in the middle of the night (say, 3 or 4 A.M., which is unusually late for *them*), and he or she finds that he or she is unable to fall back to sleep. This nighttime wakefulness often happens in depression and can get overlooked by helping professionals because we typically will expect depressed individuals to be sleeping at least 10 hours a day.

Fifth, the individual will evidence psychomotor agitation (he or she will appear to be hyper or manic) or psychomotor retardation nearly every day; either of these must be observable by others. Sixth, the individual will feel fatigue or loss of energy nearly every day. Seventh, the individual will have feelings of worthlessness or excessive or inappropriate guilt nearly every day; this does not include guilt about being sick. We need to exercise some caution here because, as a rule, many of our patients will have low self-esteem and may be feeling worthless quite often when they come to us seeking help. Also, how can we operationally define *inappropriate guilt?*

Eighth, the individual must demonstrate a diminished ability to concentrate or think, or demonstrate indecisiveness, nearly every day. Again, we need to exercise some caution as an inability to concentrate, think, or remember is a criterion for some Anxiety Disorders. However, what we can say is that many mental illnesses do in fact interfere with the individual's ability to concentrate and think clearly.

Finally, the individual will have recurrent thoughts of death (not just a fear of dying), recurrent suicidal ideation without a specific plan, or a suicide attempt or a specific plan for committing suicide (APA, 2000). Of course these are classic

≡ *Rapid Reference 3.1*

Key Terms to Know

Mood: This is one's general emotional feeling over a period of time.

Affect: This is the physical (in this case, facial) display of the individual's present mood.

Depressive Disorders: This is one subtype of Mood Disorders; the individual has persistent sadness and finds little or no enjoyment in life and in things that led to enjoyment in the past.

Bipolar Disorders: This is the second subtype of Mood Disorders and is characterized by mood swings, or shifts, between mania and depression; it is incorrectly known as manic depressive illness or manic depressive psychosis.

CAUTION

You might be saying to yourself, "I've had many of these symptoms in my life; I must be depressed!" While it is common for many, if not everyone, to have experienced many, if not all, of the above nine criteria, it does not mean that everyone who has done so is depressed. In the helping professions we look at the duration of the symptoms among other factors and considerations. "Medical student syndrome" means that medical students, when learning about each new disease, think that they in fact have every new disease they learn about.

criteria for depression, so much so that the media and laypeople think that anyone who commits suicide *must* have been depressed. Of course, nothing could be further from the truth. In fact, some psychologists believe that those who suffer from Bipolar I Disorder are in fact more likely to attempt and to commit suicide. Suicidal behavior is also seen in the Schizophrenic Disorders, in some of the Substance-Related Disorders, in PTSD, and sometimes in Eating Disorders and in Personality Disorders. For key terms, see Rapid Reference 3.1.

DON'T FORGET

Some professionals consider Dysthymic Disorder and Major Depressive Disorder to be two aspects of the same disorder. These professionals will often describe the combination of these two disorders as double depression.

Symptoms of Bipolar Disorders

The *DSM-IV-TR* (APA, 2000) lists three types of Bipolar Disorders. All of these types include either a Manic Episode or a Hypomanic Episode. A Hypomanic Episode is characterized as a period of increased energy that is not sufficient or severe enough to qualify as a Manic Episode. In order to be diagnosed as having Bipolar I Disorder, the individual must have experienced at least one Manic or Mixed Episode. In a Mixed Episode, criteria for both a Manic Episode and a Major Depressive Episode are met nearly every day during at least a one week period (APA, 2000). Typically, these individuals will also have experienced major depression.

Those individuals who are diagnosed as having Bipolar II Disorder will have experienced at least one Major Depressive Episode, at least one Hypomanic Episode, and *no* manic episodes. The symptoms for a Hypomanic Episode are the same as those for a Manic Episode; however, the key differences involve the duration and the severity. Before we consider the slight difference between the two, we need to examine the *DSM-IV-TR* criteria for a Manic Episode.

First, the individual must have experienced a period of abnormally and persistently elevated, expansive, or irritable mood that lasts at least 1 week (or has occurred at all if hospitalization is required). You might think that it would be great to be energized and be this happy for such a long period of time. Consider how tiring this would be, and consider what might be waiting at the end of the mania—depression.

Next, during this period of mood disturbance, the individual must have demonstrated at least three or more of the following symptoms (four if the mood is only irritable). The symptoms must also have been present to a significant degree:

First, the individual must have inflated self-esteem or grandiosity. Thus, one criterion includes a feature of narcissism. Second, the individual will have decreased sleep needs, that is, he or she will feel rested after having slept only 3 hours. Again, do not take this criterion out of context. Medical school residents and interns, students cramming for finals, new (and not so new) parents of a young child, and everyday individuals either might not be getting enough sleep or might not need a lot of sleep.

Third, the individual will be more talkative than usual, or he or she will feel pressure to keep on talking. In other words, the individual is a motor mouth, and he or she will also often talk rapidly. It is almost as though the individual is an auctioneer who continues to talk rapidly—and nonstop—for hours on end. Fourth, the individual will demonstrate flight of ideas or have the subjective impression that his or her thoughts are racing.

Fifth, the individual will be distractible, that is, his or her attention will be easily diverted to things that are unimportant or irrelevant. You could be conversing with the individual and he or she will constantly notice imperfections in your office, on your clothes, on the windows, and so on. Sixth, the individual will have an increase in their activity levels at work, at home, at school, or in sexual situations. For example, an individual might go clubbing, then come home early in the morning and paint the house. If the individual is an artist, he or she might produce two paintings in 2 weeks.

Finally, the individual will have excessive involvement in pleasurable activities that will most likely lead to undesirable consequences. Classic examples of this would be hitting the spending limits on one's credit cards, having multiple sex partners (or affairs if the individual is married), getting involved with foolish investments, or engaging in similar types of episodes.

For someone to be diagnosed as having a Hypomanic Episode, the symptoms need to have been present for minimally 4 days, unlike 1 week for a Manic Episode. Additionally, the mood change that occurs in a Hypomanic Episode must be noticeable to other people, but this mood disturbance cannot be severe enough to impair the individual's social or occupational functioning or require hospitalization. Thus, hypomania is a shorter, less severe type of mania.

We will end this section with a brief discussion of Cyclothymic Disorder. This is a chronic but less severe case of Bipolar Disorder. The individual must experience numerous hypomanic episodes and numerous periods of depression over the course of 2 years. There may be periods of normal moods lasting as long as 2 months. During the first 2 years, there cannot be any evidence

=== *Rapid Reference 3.2*

Key Terms to Know

Mania: This is a period of abnormally and persistently elevated, expansive, or irritable mood that lasts at least 1 week (or has occurred at all if hospitalization is required).

Flight of Ideas: This is a symptom of mania where the individual's conversation shifts rapidly from topic to topic, only occasionally making sense or being coherent.

Hypomania: This is a shorter, less severe type of mania. The elevated, expansive, or irritable symptoms need to have been present for minimally 4 days, unlike 1 week for a Manic Episode; the mood change that occurs in a Hypomanic Episode must also be noticeable to other people.

of a Manic Episode or any history of major depressive episodes. Some see this as the equivalent of Dysthymic Disorder; thus, it might be a Bipolar Disorder "lite," if you will. For key terms, see Rapid Reference 3.2.

ETIOLOGIES OF MOOD DISORDERS

Unipolar Depression

Overall, Mood Disorders affect anywhere from 15 to 30 million people in the United States. The higher figure becomes more pronounced when you realize that Mood Disorders may affect about 1 in 10 people in the United States! Unipolar depressions are much more common than Bipolar Disorders, outnumbering Bipolar Disorders by a ratio of at least 5:1. Research into Mood Disorders continues, of course, yet the public still seems to frequently misunderstand what they are.

One fact that is well established is that women are at least 2 to 3 times as likely as men to develop unipolar depression (see, for example, Kessler, 2000). What is more interesting to us is that this difference vanishes when examining the gender difference between men and women for Bipolar Disorders. One study reports the lifetime prevalence rate for men as 0.7 percent and for women 0.9 percent, a difference that is not significant.

There have been many posited explanations for this gender difference. Many people note that women are more likely to be diagnosed with depression than men or are more likely to seek treatment than men, especially because of the stigma surrounding mental health treatment. Some also posit that men, in the United States culture at least, are raised not to admit feelings of hopelessness, helplessness, or a loss of libido. Indeed, if a male admits to a loss of libido, he is usually described as being crazy, a male homosexual who has not admitted it, a wimp, and so on. These explanations have not been supported by research. Thus, the differences are probably real and are not due to bias, poor experimental technique, or extraneous variables.

Stress appears to play a key role in the development of unipolar depression. Stressful events might include unemployment, relationship problems, physical illness, economic troubles, problems with children, and school-related issues. People might also develop depression when they believe that they are responsible for bad things occurring in life; in other words, that they have the *reverse Midas touch,* where everything with which they are involved goes bad. Because they end up believing that they have this kiss of death, they end up acting in a way that things in their lives will be more likely to go wrong, like a self-fulfilling prophecy.

One way to make it less likely that a person develops a mental illness is to make sure that person has a strong social support system (Karel, 1997). Certain people can resist stress better than other people, and helping professionals believe that the lack of a good social support system makes it harder for someone to succeed in treatment and also may make them more likely to suffer from unipolar depression. For example, one often-cited study found that divorced or separated people are twice as likely to commit suicide as married people (Weissman, Bruce, Leaf, Florio, & Holzer, 1990). This study, when cited by the media, was used to support the institution of marriage, but we must presume that married people are happy in their marriages.

Age also needs to be considered. Many helping professionals (and the media as well) believed or currently believe that unipolar depression is much more common among senior citizens than among any other age group. Usually this is based on life-altering events that many seniors encounter. These include a loss of health (or their health being compromised), lack of services and overall support in the United States, retirement or relocation (either to another state or to a retirement community), and the loss of significant others. Bereavement, grief, and overall sadness do not always equal unipolar depression, however.

Data from a major study dispute this and demonstrate that, in fact, unipolar depression was significantly lower for those over 65 (Robins & Regier, 1991). Robins and Regier interviewed about 20,000 people in five communities. Their study was called the *Epidemiologic Catchment Area* (ECA) study. They discovered that unipolar depression was most frequent among young and middle-aged individuals, especially among 30- to 44-year-olds. Bipolar Disorders were also quite low in the 65 and older group. Explanations for these differences are not supported empirically, but they still need to be examined. One possibility is that those who are severely (and chronically) depressed often commit suicide and thus do not survive into old age. One other possibility is that seniors may have memory impairments or memory lapses and thus may be unable to recall episodes of depression while in a research study, such as ECA, or in a clinical setting. While these theories make sense, research conducted after the ECA study again found that Mood Disorders were indeed less common among the elderly compared with younger adults (see Hammen & Garber, 2001, for example).

Freud and his followers believed that depression is simply anger turned inward toward oneself instead of outward and toward individuals and significant others. The anger arises from a threatened or real loss of a significant other, such as a family member or a close friend. Freud also believed that those who become depressed are extremely dependent on others for the maintenance of their self-esteem. This occurs due to an oral fixation, where the infant is totally dependent on others for need gratification.

According to Freud, when an individual loses a significant other, pathological mourning will occur in an individual, especially if this individual has ambivalent feelings toward the loss of that significant other. The individual then has ambivalent feelings toward the significant other. They love and feel anger toward them at the same time. The anger gets to the point where it is uncontrollable. The superego then comes into play, making sure that the individual feels guilt for these emotions. The anger stays inside and becomes self-hatred, self-blame, and self-abuse, which then becomes depression. There is little support for this concept, as you might expect. However, we need to realize that some of his ideas remain usable. Paykel (1982) found that the loss of significant others can lead to depression. Of course this is common sense and should not surprise you. Some research has also discovered that depressed people are quite dependent and have a greater tendency to becoming depressed following rejection (Nietzel & Harris, 1990).

Aaron Beck's cognitive perspective (Beck, 1976; Beck, Rush, Shaw, & Emery, 1979) is one of the most important theories examining causal factors of unipolar depression today, and its influence is justifiably widespread. Depression develops in childhood and adolescence because of what Beck calls *negative schemes,* or the tendency to see the world pessimistically or negatively. These schemes are acquired by the individual because of the death of a parent, social rejection of peers, one tragedy after another, and so on; they are activated whenever the individual experiences a new situation that is similar to the conditions in which the negative schemes were learned. These individuals are also prone to misinterpreting reality. Thus, they think irrationally and may believe that they are responsible for all of their family's ills, that they are totally worthless, and so on. They may end up seeing themselves as unable to succeed and as incompetent and may see their chances of future success as limited or nonexistent.

These negative schemata and the accompanying cognitive distortions support the *negative triad.* Beck outlined this as follows: The person maintains a negative view of him or herself ("I'm no good, I rot, I'm a total and complete hopeless failure, and I am Satan."). The person also maintains a negative view of the environment ("This job is a dead end; school is the pits; my major is a waste; no human could live in *this* town with *these* people."), and, finally, the person has a negative view of the future and sees things as hopeless ("No matter what I do, things will always turn out bad for me, so it is really hopeless to even try."). Individuals who follow this triad set themselves up for failure and most likely depression by adopting these schemata. If they experience stress or disappointment, the likelihood of becoming depressed increases.

Learning theories look at the environment, specifically the lack or loss of positive reinforcement, to explain the onset of depression. These theories see depression as occurring because an individual's behavior does not get enough positive or negative reinforcement from the environment (Lewinsohn, 1974). Let us briefly look at an example. You have a friend who has worked especially hard during the past year. She was passed over for a promotion the first time, but this past year she always stayed late, kissed up to the boss, was always the first one there every morning, and often volunteered to work holidays. Once promotions were handed out again, she was once again passed over. Therefore, this lack of reinforcement or punishment will lead to depression and anger.

Family members can also contribute to the individual's depression by trying to help the individual, by trying to cheer him or her up, and so on. What occurs here is that the family member(s) take(s) away the individual's responsibilities, which makes him or her even more lethargic and thus exacerbates the depression. Other lifestyle changes, such as chronic or sudden illness, can also disrupt the flow of positive reinforcement. This concept has research support, but it remains unclear which comes first: depression or the reinforcement disruptions.

Martin Seligman's (1975) theory of learned helplessness is especially fascinating. Many times in psychology, the simplest concepts or theories are, in fact, the most brilliant. Seligman sees individuals developing depression because they see themselves as helpless in controlling the reinforcers in their environment and, therefore, the environment itself. They are therefore helpless in making positive changes in their lives. Thus, people see themselves as helpless to change their lives; they are prisoners of their environment and of their situation. They will eventually give up the fight and just basically take the situation that is given to them. If an individual is constantly experiencing bad incidents (he or she might tell you that they are having an especially bad month), Seligman would say that, eventually, the individual would resign him- or herself to fate and just take it or "bite the bullet," so to speak. Avoidance and escape behaviors then disappear and the individual sees him- or herself as helpless to escape. Seligman's theory does not account for the reasons why depressed individuals have low self-esteem, and it does not explain why some individuals' depressions are more resistant to treatment.

Seligman and his colleagues later revised this theory and renamed it the *reformulated helplessness theory*. Seligman explains that people who develop unipolar depression do so because they associate the causes of negative events to three types of attributions. First, *internal factors* are beliefs that failures reflect personal inadequacies. Second, *global factors* reflect flaws in the individual's personality. Finally, *stable factors* are beliefs that failures reflect fixed personality factors.

We will conclude this subsection by briefly examining some biological perspectives. Mood Disorders seem to have a familial component and may run

≡ *Rapid Reference 3.3*

The Egeland Study

In 1997, Egeland and her colleagues examined the Old Order Amish, an extremely religious sect in Pennsylvania known for their insularity and extended families and for the presence of Mood Disorders, specifically Bipolar Disorders. She discovered a dominant gene on the short arm of chromosome 11, which supported the heritability of Bipolar Disorders. Unfortunately, the study couldn't be replicated, and later researchers concluded that chromosome 11 was most likely not involved (Kelsoe, 1997). The moral of this story is that no matter how interesting or important research results might be, they have little value if the study that produced them cannot be replicated.

in families. What is most interesting is that genes play a more prominent role in determining the risk factors for developing Bipolar Disorders. Concordance rates have been reported being as high as 67 percent for identical twins and 20 percent for fraternal twins (Bertelsen, Harvald, & Hauge, 1997). The research strongly supports the idea that Bipolar Disorder may very well be inherited.

Genetic factors are not as influential when examining unipolar depression. If anything, the genetic influence is slight, if not somewhat strong. Genetics may be more influential in women than in men (e.g., Silberg et al., 1999). Dysthymic Disorder seems to be influenced less so by genetic etiological factors than major depression or Bipolar Disorder. See Rapid Reference 3.3 for a discussion of the Egeland Study.

Bipolar Disorder

As we just mentioned, Bipolar Disorder is considered to be biologically and genetically based. It remains somewhat unclear if Bipolar Disorder itself is inherited or the diathesis (meaning the vulnerability) is inherited. Stress appears to be able to lead to the manifestation of Bipolar Disorder. Stress can also lead to new bipolar episodes if Bipolar Disorder has already developed. Some research has hypothesized that families who were at high risk for developing Bipolar Disorder were also a high risk for developing unipolar depression, Substance Use Disorders, and Anxiety Disorders (for example, Crad-dock & Jones, 1999).

One intriguing viewpoint sees manic episodes serving a defensive or pro-tective function for the bipolar individual. What is actually being defended is unclear. Even more interesting is the fact that for most bipolar individu-als, they are relatively calm and well-adjusted between manic episodes. One study discovered that individuals with mania, even when they are between episodes, have low self-esteem (Winters & Neale, 1985). Later research sup-ported this conclusion (Lyon, Startup, & Bentall, 1999). While this may be somewhat surprising, it should not be, in our opinion. Low self-esteem seems to be a requirement for individuals who are suffering from a mental illness. What *is* surprising is that individuals with mania, who by definition are acting grandiose during the manic episodes, *still* suffer from low self-esteem even then! We can conclude that low self-esteem impacts many individuals with mental illnesses, even those who are manic.

NEUROCHEMISTRY OF MOOD DISORDERS

We saved this section for last because the research is still arriving as we write. Much of the research has arrived at two conclusions involving two neuro-transmitters: low levels of serotonin lead to depression and low levels of nor-epinephrine (also called *noradrenaline*) lead to depression and, more critically, to a high level of mania. These two theories arose because of the efficacy of the medications used to treat unipolar depression and Bipolar Disorder.

Tricyclic antidepressants act by preventing some reuptake of norepineph-rine and serotonin, basically leaving more of each neurotransmitter avail-able when the synapse fires again. One example of a tricyclic antidepressant is Elavil (amitriptyline). Monoamine oxidase inhibitors (MAOIs), another class of antidepressant medications, also work by increasing the amount of norepinephrine and serotonin in the synapse. Later research examined Pro-zac (fluoxetine) and other SSRIs, a class of medications that is especially effective in treating unipolar depressions. The efficacy of the SSRIs, along with the fact that they act specifically to compensate for low serotonin lev-els in depressed people, supports the serotonin hypothesis. Current research focuses more on the postsynaptic effects of the antidepressants, specifically whether the sensitivity of serotonin and norepinephrine postsynaptic receptors are altered (see, for example, McKim, 2003).

Research on Bipolar Disorder has begun to examine the reasons why Lithium is effective in reducing the manic and depressed episodes of Bipolar Disorder. This suggests that Lithium may act on a neurotransmitter that either increases *or* decreases brain activity. High levels of G proteins have been found in individuals who have mania, and low levels of G proteins have been found in individuals who are depressed. According to one line of research, it has been hypothesized that Lithium may act by regulating G proteins (Manji et al., 1995).

Rapid Reference 3.4

Key Terms to Know

Serotonin: This is a neurotransmitter; low levels have been implicated in the etiology of depression.
Norepinephrine (noradrenalin): This is a neurotransmitter; low levels have been implicated in the etiology of depression and of mania.

We can conclude that much remains unknown about the etiologies of Mood Disorders, specifically Bipolar Disorders. We are also uncertain as to the exact reasons why some of the medications work, or why they work as well as they do. For key terms, see Rapid Reference 3.4.

TREATMENT MODALITIES

Fortunately, several treatment modalities, used alone or in combination, have proved to be successful in treating the Mood Disorders. We will first examine treatment modalities for unipolar depressions, and we will then examine Bipolar Disorders.

Unipolar Depressions

One aspect of unipolar depressions, or depressions that occur with Bipolar Disorder, is that most depressions will lift and spontaneously remit in a few months without any form of treatment. While this is a positive aspect, helping professionals still need to treat episodes of depression as soon as they can, if for no other reason than the individual is no doubt experiencing considerable suffering. In addition, we see unipolar depression, as we do most mental illnesses, as family illnesses. That is, the affected patient's significant others are also affected by his or her mental illness. Therefore, those mental illnesses that seem to lift or disappear after several months still require treatment as soon as we are able to intervene.

As we stated, Freudians view depression as anger that is unconsciously turned inward. It also arises from a repressed sense of loss. The most critical aspect is that the conflict and emotions involved with depression are kept in the unconscious mind. The goal of Freudian analysis is to help the patient gain insight into the repressed conflict(s) and to enable and encourage a *catharsis:* the release of this repressed anger. By releasing this anger in a safe environment, the patient will eventually feel better. The overriding goal is to uncover these repressed feelings and motivations that contribute to, or manifest themselves, as unipolar depression.

Another way to treat depression is to work with the patient to try to examine childhood memories that may either be repressed or have been forgotten. The notion here is that feelings of loss and inadequacy occurred in childhood due to trauma or due to a parental incident. The patient perhaps feels guilt because, in the patient's eyes, she or he may blame him- or herself for the lack of affection displayed by the patient's parents (this assumes an intact biological family). However, she or he cannot express these feelings because to do so would, initially, alienate the patient's parents. In addition, by expressing or experiencing these feelings, the patient will therefore experience anger and pain. Of course, ego defense mech-

CAUTION

One additional reason why mental health professionals should treat unipolar depression as soon as they can is because if left untreated, it is possible that the individual will become suicidal (or have suicidal ideations) if they are not already at that point. More critically, the individual may make an actual lethal attempt if their depression is untreated.

CAUTION

Catharsis (the release of pent-up or repressed emotions) is a technique that some psychologists successfully use today. However, the results, if the psychologist is not well trained, can be detrimental to the patient. Repressed emotions that are expressed in an unsafe environment, those emotions that are expressed before the patient is ready to accept them, or those emotions that, when expressed, take the psychologist by surprise can all cause more harm than good in therapy sessions.

anisms then go to work, protecting the patient and eventually causing these feelings to manifest themselves as unipolar depression.

A more modern psychodynamic approach is called *interpersonal psychotherapy* (IPT; Klerman, Weissman, Rounsaville, & Chevron, 1984). This is a briefer form of psychodynamic therapy that focuses on the relationship between the patient and his or her social relationships (significant others and so on). Unipolar depression occurs within these social relationships; thus, relationships need to be focused upon in treatment. The treatment typically will last from 9 to 12 months. The most important aspect is that the focus in IPT is on *current* interpersonal relationships, not on early childhood experiences or on past experiences. The patient's social relationships are not pleasurable, and it is presumed that something about the patient's behavior(s) is/are contributing to this. Typically, IPT will focus on social skills and on better communication. Interpersonal psychotherapy appears to maintain the positive results attained in psychotherapy, not something that should be underestimated.

Behavioral or learning theories presume that depressive behaviors are learned and are being reinforced by environmental reinforcers. Therefore, if the individual were to see a behaviorist, the therapist would work with the individual to unlearn the negative or aberrant behaviors. Because the depressed behaviors have been learned, they should be able to be unlearned. As you know, behaviorists focus on present-day observable behaviors and attempt to modify or extinguish them. Radical behaviorists would, in fact, not emphasize past behaviors, unconscious thoughts, wishes, and so on, and they would not try to plan for the future. One of the best aspects of using behavioral therapy for treating unipolar depression is that results can often be seen in a somewhat short time frame. Of course, insurance companies like and expect this.

Cognitive theorists (such as Beck) would work with the patient on changing his or her distorted and dysfunctional thought processes and negative schemata. Beck would use a variety of techniques, but we want to briefly mention two of them. First, he would attempt to get the patient to change his or her

DON'T FORGET

We have discovered that many problems that bring patients into the therapist's office oftentimes are exacerbated by poor communication or a lack of proper communication skills. We will examine this concept further in Chapter 6 when we examine Sexual Disorders.

view of him- or herself by altering these dysfunctional and self-destructive thought processes. For example, I worked with a patient who would always mention how terrible she was and, more importantly, how horrible her life was. Not a day would go by when something "awful or crappy" would not occur, thus derailing her for the rest of her waking moments. We then pointed out to her the positives that occurred during her day and, in line with Beck's précis, she was in fact either not noticing these positive instances or was discounting them, considering them meaningless or worthless. From this perspective, it is virtually impossible to be a total loser; even Charlie Brown has *some* good days! Beck would also presume that the patient spends more time focusing on how bad she or he feels instead of focusing on the thoughts that are involved with these feelings.

Secondly, Beck's theory is similar to Albert Ellis' REBT. Beck and Ellis would focus on the patient's irrational thoughts, which lead to the individual acting depressed and thus becoming depressed, self-destructive, and so on. For example, this same patient of mine thought that she "was a total cow, a hag" if any man she fancied was not interested in hooking up with her. Thus, she needed to be perfect and needed to be liked by everyone. This belief is of course irrational, and it is easy for an outsider to see this. However, the patient is blinded and sees these beliefs as being normal and appropriate. Beck and Ellis would point out the irrationality of these beliefs and also work with her to help her realize that no one is liked (or loved) by every single person. Even if this were possible, it would make for a rather uninteresting life!

Ellis and Beck would also take a leading, almost professorial role, during treatment. This, of course, differs from traditional analysis where the analyst says little during the sessions. Ellis especially would be confrontational (in a pleasant way) with the individual, believing that this is the best way to break

DON'T FORGET

Ellis' irrational needs seem to be modifications of Horney's neurotic needs. Horney stated that everyone has these needs (the need for approval, the need for power), but *neurotics* (an archaic term) react to these needs in an extreme fashion, thus causing problems and leading them into a psychologist's office if their situation became too debilitating. We have often hypothesized that many of the theories subsequent to Freud's have borrowed concepts and have modified and modernized them. What do you think?

through irrational beliefs. Much research exists supporting the efficacy of Beck's cognitive methods in treating unipolar depression and in preventing relapses (e.g., Hollon, DeRubeis, & Seligman, 1992).

Before we conclude this section, we need to briefly examine Mindfulness-Based Cognitive Therapy (MBCT; Segal, Williams, & Teasdale, 2001). This modality focuses on relapse prevention after successful treatment for unipolar depression. The theory behind this modality is that the previously depressed individuals have maintained the negative thinking patterns, and, in fact, they can be reactivated by sad moods or discouraging events. In other words, these individuals will have thoughts similar to those when they were depressed if they encounter negative situations in their lives. Therefore, the reemerging thought patterns maintain the mildly depressed (perhaps melancholic?) state, which allows this state to intensify and more than likely become a Major Depressive Episode.

The concept here implies that unipolar depression is not really cured but is in remission, which means that there is always the possibility that the depression can recur. Overall, this is not a bad way to view many mental illnesses, as it will make the individual somewhat cautious when he or she encounters significant life stressors, which, of course, eventually will occur. The goal of MBCT is to get patients to detach themselves from these negative thoughts and feelings that exacerbate and recall past negative thinking patterns, thus hopefully derailing the potential path to the remanifestation of unipolar depression. Research is presently scarce on MBCT, but its potential should not be overlooked.

Finally, we will spend some time examining pharmacotherapy, or drug therapy, for the treatment of unipolar depression. Antidepressant medications have helped millions of individuals to either control or eradicate their depressive symptoms. If the medications are effective, some improvement will be seen within 2 months, even though the patient is expected to continue taking the medications for at least 1 year after the depressive symptoms have either been alleviated or eradicated (DePaulo & Horvitz, 2002). Antidepressants have been in existence since the 1950s, and even though four general drug classes presently exist, one group is prescribed more often than the other three combined!

Tricyclic antidepressants (TCAs) are some of the earliest antidepressant medications and are some of the oldest medications used in psychology and

DON'T FORGET

Side effects typically drop out after a 1- to 2-week time period. The patient needs to be made aware of this. However (and this is critical), if the side effects do not disappear during an appropriate time frame, the patient should inform the psychiatrist (or psychologist) as soon as possible. This indicates that the patient should be switched to another medication.

psychiatry. This class of medications includes Elavil (amitriptyline), Norpramin (desipramine), and Tofranil (impiramine). The TCAs work by blocking the reuptake of norepinephrine and, to a lesser degree, serotonin. Since the advent of SSRIs, the TCAs have declined in usage. This is not surprising once one examines the TCAs more closely. Many of the TCAs (such as Elavil) have significant side effects that are bothersome and rather significant. Typical side effects include dry mouth, constipation, drowsiness, spaciness, sedation, and blurred vision. These are called *anticholinergic side effects* or sometimes *antihistamine side effects,* similar to the effects produced by Benadryl and Contac. Most of the TCAs have similar efficacies and similar side effects. Elavil has some of the most bothersome anticholinergic side effects.

The second class of antidepressants, MAOIs, were discovered at approximately the same time as the TCAs. The MAOIs include medications such as Nardil (phenelzine). The MAOIs block the enzyme monoamine oxidase that breaks down neurotransmitters, such as serotonin and norepinephrine. The effects are similar to the TCAS. The MAOIs tend to have fewer anticholinergic side effects than the TCAs, and thus the patient will be less uncomfortable while taking them and may also be more compliant as well. Additionally, the MAOIs tend to have a faster therapeutic onset than the TCAs. These medications have not been as widely prescribed as the TCAs for two reasons.

First, the patient needs to be on a tyramine-free diet. This means foods containing tyramine need to be avoided: This includes foods such as cheese, chocolate, sauerkraut, beer, and red wine, to name a few. If the individual consumes any or all of these foods, they may experience high blood pressure and perhaps death. It is difficult enough to get many depressed individuals to eat, much less to eat properly. Placing this extra restriction on them while they are in treatment could easily cause them to drop out. Finally, many other drugs can interact with MAOIs, including cold remedies, over-the-counter stimulants, sleep aids such as Sominex, appetite suppressants, and antiasthma drugs such as Primatene (Bezchlibnyk-Butler & Jeffries, 2005).

As we mentioned in Chapter 2, MAOIs have been used rather successfully in treating Agoraphobia and panic attacks.

The SSRIs have been around since the 1980s and are the most frequently prescribed class of antidepressant medication. They include Prozac (fluoxetine) and Zoloft (sertraline). One major difference between the SSRIs and the TCAs is that the SSRIs were developed specifically because of the hypothesized role of serotonin in the etiology and maintenance of Mood Disorders, specifically unipolar depressions. The SSRIs specifically block the reuptake of serotonin in the individual's brain; some of the SSRIs also block norepinerphrine and dopamine.

The SSRIs have some significant advantages over the TCAs and the MAOIs. First, their period of therapeutic onset is generally shorter than the TCAs: approximately 2 weeks contrasted with approximately 3 to 4 weeks for the TCAs. The SSRIs have a long half-life, which means that missing a dose is not a critical concern. Perhaps most important, they have fewer side effects, which increases the likelihood of medication compliance. In general, the SSRIs do not produce anticholinergic side effects. However, the SSRIs can produce sexual dysfunction (Prozac is well known for this), lowered sexual desire (occurring in at least 50 percent of the men and women who take an SSRI), insomnia, nausea, and headaches. The SSRIs also produce weight gain, an average of about 20 pounds while on the medication. There is another big advantage of the SSRIs: It is very difficult to overdose on them, especially on Prozac. Finally, addiction or abuse of any of the antidepressant medications is highly unlikely. According to current research, the TCAs, MAOIs and SSRIs all have similar efficacy rates (Bezchlibnyk-Butler & Jeffries, 2005). See Rapid Reference 3.5 for definitions of key terms.

≡ *Rapid Reference 3.5*

Key Terms to Know

Catharsis: This is the release of pent-up or repressed emotions; it is a psychoanalytic term.

Interpersonal Psychotherapy (IPT): This is a briefer form of psychodynamic therapy that focuses on the relationship between the patient and his or her social relationships.

Mindfulness-Based Cognitive Therapy (MBCT): This modality focuses on relapse prevention after successful treatment for unipolar depression.

Monoamine Oxidase Inhibitors (MAOIs): This is a subclass of antidepressant medications.

DON'T FORGET

Prozac and Zoloft are two medications approved by the FDA for the treatment of Bulimia Nervosa. This implies that the FDA (or at least the drug company lobbyists who influence the FDA) sees a connection between Bulimia Nervosa and unipolar depression.

CAUTION

Suicidal behavior is connected to the Mood Disorders. It is not too difficult to overdose on the TCAs and the MAOIs, especially if they are combined with alcohol. Alcohol's effects are significantly increased if one takes TCAs or MAOIs at the same time. Therefore, it becomes rather risky giving any of these medications to someone who may have suicidal ideations.

Bipolar Disorder

We can now turn toward medication options for Bipolar Disorder. These medications are called mood stabilizers for obvious reasons. Sometimes antidepressant medications are used when treating Bipolar Disorder, but there is a risk involved. Antidepressants have been known to switch the individual from experiencing depression to experiencing a Manic Episode or a Hypomanic Episode. Research remains inconclusive regarding long-term usage of antidepressant medications with bipolar individuals.

Many individuals with Bipolar Disorder are helped, in some cases significantly, by taking Lithium (Lithium carbonate or Lithium citrate; one trade name for Lithium carbonate is Eskalith). Lithium, which is a naturally occurring element in the environment, is taken in the form of a salt. It will reduce manic episodes and in some cases will reduce depressive episodes for the bipolar individual, but Lithium is not very effective for patients that have unipolar depression. Prien and Potter (1993) report that Lithium provides some benefit for up to 80 percent of the bipolar individuals who take this medication.

Because its therapeutic effects occur gradually and not suddenly, Lithium is often taken with an antipsychotic medication initially. The antipsychotics, taken at a small dosage, are useful antianxiety medications. In this scenario, they would be used to help calm the bipolar individual until the Lithium reaches maximum efficacy in the patient's bloodstream. An antipsychotic that has a very long half-life such as Haldol (haloperidol) or Prolixin (fluphenazine) is typically used.

The biggest risk in using Lithium is that it is extremely toxic, and so the patient's blood levels need to be monitored closely. The difference between effectiveness and lethality is quite small (the term for therapeutically effective levels of Lithium is known as the *therapeutic window*). Lithium toxicity will present symptoms ranging from nausea, tremor, vertigo, and confusion to more serious symptoms such as seizures, coma, and death. Some conditions, like diabetes and weight-loss diets, may elevate the levels of Lithium in the blood, also increasing the risk of toxicity. Perhaps the most interesting aspect of Lithium is this: We still are not exactly certain why and how it works.

There are two additional risks of using Lithium. First, if a patient ceases its use, the risk for a recurrence of the mood swings may actually increase (see, for example, Suppes, Baldessarini, Faedda, & Tohen, 1991). Therefore, many helping professionals (including the author) recommend that the bipolar patient be on Lithium for the rest of his or her lifetime (see also Bezchlibnyk-Butler & Jeffries, 2005; Bowden et al., 2000) or minimally at least 1 year. If the bipolar patient has evidenced several episodes of mania or hypomania or has had recurring episodes of depression, he or she should remain on Lithium indefinitely.

There is one additional risk: The patient may actually do his or her best to remove themselves from Lithium for the simple reason that they miss the manic or hypomanic episodes, that is, the highs. This is quite logical, for if you know that you will be depressed (which, unless you are a masochist, is not pleasant), you may as well have something to look forward to during the course of your mental illness. In other words, the highs (perhaps they are natural highs) are often missed by bipolar patients.

Lithium has an additional problem if it is used to treat bipolar individuals who have *rapid cycling*. This is defined as having four or more episodes of mood swings within the past 12 months. For this particular subclassification of bipolar

CAUTION

Although this may seem pessimistic, some therapists make a point of anticipating that the bipolar patient will eventually make an attempt, perhaps surreptitiously, to go off of his or her Lithium. It is ethically responsible for the therapist to do his or her best to inform the patient of the ramifications of this action. It is better to be prepared than to be surprised and have to handle the consequences of this action.

individuals, Lithium, when used without any other medication, may take up to 1 year to reach therapeutic effectiveness. The most commonly used medications today to treat rapid cyclers are the anticonvulsant medications, which control seizures.

Three major anticonvulsants are Tegretol (carbamazepine), Klonopin (clonazepam), and Depakene (valproic acid). Tegretol and Depakene are the two anticonvulsants most often used to treat rapid cycling Bipolar Disorder individuals. Additionally, anticonvulsants are prescribed when the individual cannot tolerate Lithium or if its side effects do not drop out. Some research has demonstrated that Depakene is more effective in treating rapid cycling bipolar patients. Research results are mixed regarding how effective the anticonvulsants are in reducing the likelihood of preventing future bipolar episodes. One study concluded that Depakote (divalproex sodium) is as effective as a placebo in preventing future bipolar episodes (Bowden et al., 2000). However, Depakote was superior to placebo in terms of lower rates of discontinuation for either a recurrent mood episode or depressive episode. Some of the side effects of the anticonvulsants include nausea, vomiting, diarrhea, and sedation. Like Lithium, these medications need to be taken throughout the patient's lifetime.

We cannot conclude this section without briefly mentioning psychotherapy for bipolar patients. At the least, psychotherapy can address any concerns the patient may have about taking a mood stabilizer for an extended period of time. Therapy can also work with the patient's coping strategies and skills and teach him or her how to cope with life's everyday stresses. Psychotherapy can also encourage the patient to remain on his or her medications, as it is presumed that there will often

CAUTION

Some research has pointed out that attempting to treat Bipolar Disorder with antidepressants may actually *exacerbate* the bipolar symptoms and the eventual course of Bipolar Disorder with *some* individuals. Helping professionals need to be aware of this possibility.

DON'T FORGET

For rapid cycling bipolar patients, it is recommended to prescribe Lithium along with Depakene. For some reason, Lithium seems to increase the antidepressive and antimanic effects of Depakene (Bezchlibnyk-Butler & Jeffries, 2005). Thus, do not be surprised if you see this combination with a rapid cycling bipolar patient.

be temptation to remove the medications. One interesting perspective views recurring episodes of either mania or depression as being precipitated by some type of life stressor or a disruption in social rhythms; these refer to working a swing shift, for example, and therefore not having regular bedtimes or work hours. Frank, Swartz, and Kupfer (2000) emphasize examining the relationship between these social rhythm dysfunctions and the onset of manic or hypomanic episodes. The goals in therapy are to help the patient put his or her sleeping-waking cycles in order and to help him or her to effectively resolve any interpersonal

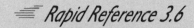

Rapid Reference 3.6

Key Terms to Know

Lithium: This is a mood stabilizer, prescribed for Bipolar Disorder. It will reduce manic episodes and in some cases will reduce depressive episodes.

Rapid Cycling: This is having four or more episodes of mood swings within the past 12 months in a bipolar individual.

Anticonvulsant Medications: The front-line indication is to control seizures. Three major anticonvulsants are Tegretol (carbamazepine), Klonopin (clonazepam), and Depakene (valproic acid).

conflicts he or she may have. Thus, prevention is a key goal of their therapy, called *interpersonal and social rhythm therapy* (Frank et al., 2000).

In sum, much more research is needed on which types of treatment modalities besides medications are effective in treating Bipolar Disorder. Most of the success stories are anecdotal and are subject to self-report bias. For key terms, see Rapid Reference 3.6.

A Treatment Alternative: Electroconvulsive Therapy (ECT)

Most likely you have seen the movie *One Flew Over the Cuckoo's Nest* with Jack Nicholson, where ECT was used to control violent patients, of which R. P. McMurphy was one. Electroconvulsive therapy is still used today but is seen as a last resort when treating individuals with severe unipolar depression who do not respond to medications. Electroconvulsive therapy still receives much negative press and has stigma attached to it as well.

The negative publicity is only part of the problem. The goal of ECT is to induce a seizure that includes convulsions by passing an electrical current between the brain that ranges between 70 and 130 volts (seizures where the individual first loses consciousness and then convulses are called *Tonic-Clonic seizures*). In the past, electrodes were placed on both sides of the forehead; this allowed the current to pass through both brain hemispheres. Today, the more common method is to pass the current through the non-dominant hemisphere only. The former method is known as bilateral ECT; the latter is known as unilateral ECT. In the past, as was the case in *One Flew Over the Cuckoo's Nest,* the patient was awake while the seizure was occurring. As you probably know, this is frightening to see and is painful for the patient.

The seizure itself is not painful, but if the patient remains conscious, she or he can suffer muscle strains and perhaps even fractures. Today the patient is giving a short-term anesthetic and is also given a powerful muscle relaxant before the seizure is induced. Once the seizure is occurring, the muscle spasms are almost imperceptible. The patient will either be aroused or will wake up a few minutes later having recalled nothing about the entire procedure. What the doctors seek are the after-effects of the seizure. The patient will probably have wet themselves and may have defecated. More critically, they will report that they feel calm and relaxed and would just like to go to sleep.

The question remains as to the reasons why any one person or family member (if the person is unable to make a rational decision for him- or herself) would opt for this treatment method. My students think that the individual must be insane or psychotic to willingly undergo a procedure that may lead to memory loss and confusion and creates a situation that, at the very least, is uncomfortable and could potentially result in death. Electroconvulsive therapy is often used at the last resort to treat individuals with unipolar depression for whom all other treatment methods have been unsuccessful. Recent research (Gagne, Furman, Carpenter, & Price, 2000) has demonstrated that this remains an extremely effective treatment method for these individuals. Fink (2001) also found that ECT appears to be effective in treating rapid cycling bipolar individuals and unipolar individuals who have psychotic features.

In sum, many individuals may view ECT as the lesser of two evils.

DON'T FORGET

Even though ECT has been around since approximately 1938 (an Italian physician named Ugo Cerletti [1877–1963] used it on a schizophrenic individual), we still do not know its mechanism of action. It is hypothesized that it may somehow reduce depressive brain activity as the convulsions may reduce blood flow to the brain.

CAUTION

Convulsive seizures in a controlled environment (such as a hospital setting) are considered relatively safe (no seizure, in our professional view, is totally safe, just as no medication is totally safe). Convulsive seizures (i.e., mostly Tonic-Clonic seizures) can in some cases lead to death, either due to the seizure itself or, more often, due to the consequences of having a convulsive seizure. For example, the individual could be on a high ladder or a platform and then lose consciousness or could suffer a concussion by hitting the concrete while losing consciousness. The seriousness of a convulsive seizure (or any type for that matter) should never be underestimated.

Imagine yourself in that situation. Your loved one has had unipolar depression for years and has been unresponsive to medications and to psychotherapy. He or she has been in and out of psychiatric hospitals, having made numerous suicide attempts. You noticed lately that he or she has become delusional, seeing herself as the devil and being evil. You hear about ECT and discuss it with a psychiatrist, who tells you that this is the last resort. Thus, you try it and handle whatever consequences may occur, or you leave your loved one untreated, most likely leading to a successful suicide attempt. This is obviously a question that requires much informed thought, and it is our responsibility to point out both sides of the ECT issue. Let us hope that you are not put in the position where you must be involved in such a decision.

Putting It Into Practice

The Case of Fannie Bluenote

Fannie is a 59-year-old African American female who was urged to come into the clinic by her husband and by her general practitioner, Dr. Jack. "Dr. Jack was concerned about me because I complained to him during my last visit that my mood has been really low the past year or so. Initially I didn't think much of it, figured I was going through some womanly things like very late postmenopausal stuff, but he was concerned about me. My moods have been weird lately. I'm sleeping a lot more than usual, sometimes twelve hours a day. I thought this was due to some kind of illness or getting older, but my health checked out fine." (We confirmed this with Dr. Jack; Fannie

(continued)

also brought in a copy of his evaluation.) "I usually wake up in the middle of the night, and I can't get back to sleep, and my appetite has fluctuated, but now it's minimal except for ice cream, sandwiches, and other junk food. I've lost quite a bit of weight, probably at least twenty pounds." (Fannie's normal weight is 130 pounds at her height of 5'5.5".) "I can't gain it back since I have no appetite. My sex life . . . nonexistent, but due to no fault of Rudy, my husband. He wants some very often, and I can't provide it. I just have no desire for sex, and I used to be quite frisky, actually a bit wild in bed. Now, I'm dead. I told Dr. Jack that I also feel empty and hopeless, like life is not worth the constant hassle and effort at times."

We see that Fannie is in touch with her feelings and is aware that something is not right with her mental health. She has followed the appropriate path in checking things out medically first just to be sure. We would have sent her to her general practitioner or to her ob-gyn if she had not already visited them. When we spoke with Dr. Jack, he told us that based on what Fannie said to him, he was quite sure that she suffered from some type of unipolar depression. He was most concerned because her moods seemed to be going deeper and deeper into depression.

Because Rudy came in with Fannie, we asked him what he saw. "Well, she's really been in the dumpster lately, or more than lately. She sleeps so much that nothing gets done at home. She stays at home now, but she used to work before she started missing too many days of work because she was always sleepy or sleeping too much. Her energy level really sucks. We have little life together, even at home. She's often in bed and doesn't want to talk."

Does this sound like typical behavior for a 59-year-old? In fact, many older individuals and senior citizens suffer from depression. Because this is often misinterpreted by medical doctors, seniors may be mistakenly prescribed anxiolytics or sedative or hypnotics and take them when their use is not warranted. This can lead them to fall down and break bones or a hip, which might hospitalize them and perhaps end up killing them if they get an infection or pneumonia.

Because we suspected that Fannie suffered from unipolar depression, we administered the Beck Depression Inventory-II (BDI-II), a paper and pencil self-report measure developed by Dr. Aaron Beck and his colleagues. The BDI-II is designed to assess the cognitions associated with depression for psychiatric patients and for non-psychiatric people. The higher the score one receives on the BDI-II, the more depressed that individual is presumed to be. Fannie's BDI-II score was 27, which indicates that she is moderately depressed. Scores of 30 or higher indicate a severe level of depression.

Based on the information being presented by Fannie's self-reports, on Dr. Jack's observations and report, and on Rudy's report, we made our preliminary diagnostic interpretation for Fannie based on the following criteria: Her mood has been depressed almost every day; she shows little interest or pleasure in any or most activities nearly every day; she is sleeping too much and also wakes up in the middle of the night and is unable to fall back to sleep; she has little energy almost every day, and this seems to be worsening; and her appetite has significantly decreased, leading to a weight loss. The following were our initial diagnostic impressions:

Axis I: Major Depressive Disorder, Recurrent, Moderate,   296.32
          Chronic, with Melancholic Features
Axis II: No Diagnosis   V71.09
Axis III: None
Axis IV: Problems with Primary Support Group: Husband
Axis V: GAF = 45 (Current)

We used Recurrent because Fannie's depression occurs on a continuous basis. Moderate was used because Fannie displayed at least five *DSM-IV-TR* diagnostic criteria (but not most or all of the nine criteria) for Major Depressive Disorder, and her ability to function normally was moderately compromised. The Melancholic Features specifier was used because Fannie displayed the following symptoms: Her depressed mood has been worsening over the past year, she often has early morning awakening, she displays psychomotor retardation based on her self-reports and on Rudy, and her weight loss and appetite loss is considered significant.

Treatment Plan
We used Beck's cognitive triad model of depression to treat Fannie in individual therapy. Beck sees the individual as misinterpreting environmental situations and viewing any disappointment as being a major disaster, and, therefore, any hope of succeeding in the future is seen as impossible. We worked with Fannie to get her to change her distorted and dysfunctional thought processes. Fannie spends more time focusing on how bad she feels instead of focusing on the thoughts that are involved with these negative feelings. We also worked with Fannie to get her to focus on the good things in her life and not on the negatives. We expected that by doing so she would eventually feel good about herself. We also wanted her to get more active, so we assigned homework where she had to go outside several times each day and go for walks with Rudy after dinner no matter how tired she was. By getting her active, we suspected that her energy level would increase and that the depressed feelings would lift.

Finally, Fannie was prescribed Zoloft (sertraline), an SSRI antidepressant. The SSRIs are indicated for older and elderly patients because they have a low risk of producing side effects, especially anticholinergic, cardiovascular,

(continued)

and central nervous system effects. One caution is that the older patient (mid-50s and above) might take longer to respond to Zoloft than the average individual. We warned Fannie about this.

After being in therapy for almost 11 months, Fannie was discharged. She was still taking her Zoloft, but she now had new-found "energy, like I've been reborn. I walk a lot, sleep a lot less, and I have energy and interest in activities. My sex life is back to normal and is even over the top at times. In some ways it's as though I was never depressed." Thus, Fannie's prognosis is listed as Good.

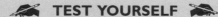

TEST YOURSELF

1. **Affect refers to**
   (a) how one individual impacts on another.
   (b) the physical (facial) display of an individual's present mood.
   (c) one's general emotional feeling over a period of time.
   (d) something that occurs in Bipolar Disorder.

2. **In Dysthymic Disorder**
   (a) the individual has been depressed for many years, and the depressed mood must have been present for at least 2 years.
   (b) the individual's moods fluctuate between mania and depression.
   (c) the individual suffers from hysterical amnesias as described by Freud.
   (d) the individual suffers from mania.

3. **If someone has been diagnosed with Cyclothymic Disorder, that person will present with**
   (a) bizarre hallucinations.
   (b) catatonic behavior and waxy flexibility.
   (c) numerous hypomanic episodes and numerous periods of depression over the course of 2 years.
   (d) ideas of reference and alogia.

4. **Women are at least 2 to 3 times as likely as men to develop unipolar depression.** True or False?

5. **One Freudian concept still accepted today sees depression as**
   (a) anger turned inward.
   (b) caused by unresolved castration anxiety.
   (c) a harbinger of Schizophrenia.
   (d) caused by genital stage fixation.

6. An example of a selective serotonin reuptake inhibitor (SSRI) is

(a) Zoloft (sertraline).

(b) Prozac (fluoxetine).

(c) Tegretol (carbamazepine).

(d) both a and b.

7. Which of the following medications is/are used to treat Bipolar Disorder?

(a) Tegretol (carbamazepine)

(b) Lithium

(c) Depakene (valproic acid)

(d) All of the above are used to treat Bipolar Disorder.

8. The main goal of ECT is to produce permanent brain damage in a selected area to cure the individual's unipolar depression. True or False?

Answers: 1. b; 2. a; 3. c; 4. True; 5. a; 6. d; 7. d; 8. False

Four

ESSENTIALS OF SUBSTANCE-RELATED DISORDERS

Substance-Related (or Substance Use) Disorders have been around since the beginning of time. Alcohol has been mentioned in the Old Testament. Wine has been used in some religious ceremonies for millennia. Sigmund Freud may have been dependent on cocaine, as he suffered significant pain from oral cancer. Most people throughout time have found some way to alleviate pain, either mental or physical, through some type of substance.

For example, you know how ubiquitous Starbucks is, and most readers have probably visited there a few times over the past year. Ask yourself this: Could you truly wake up and start the day without your cup of coffee (or for some, strong tea)? What might your reaction be if you went a few days without this daily habit? What would occur if you did not have your daily cigarettes? What about getting through the day without having your cola drinks? In sum, could you manage this?

If you believe that you are indeed unable to function on a daily basis without your caffeine or nicotine fix, then you know what it is like to be dependent on a substance. The research is still inconclusive on whether caffeine is truly harmful to a healthy individual, but we can say with certainty that anyone who uses too much of any substance (including food) will suffer some kind of consequences.

Let us once again briefly examine a real individual. Mrs. J. is 35-year-old airline pilot for a major commercial carrier. She is a White female and has been married for 6 years. She and her husband have been trying to get pregnant the past year and have had no success. She comes to you and presents the following concerns: She thinks that she may be unable to conceive and, because of this, she has recently begun to "take a nip" now and then of wine. These "wee nips" have progressed to having at least half a bottle a day. "It helps me to relax, especially since my job is so stressful. I'm responsible for all of these lives every time I fly." She tells you that her appetite has decreased somewhat,

and her sleep has not been as rest-
ful as she would like it to be. She is
able to get to work, and she hints
at having had some wine before flying at least once. However, she can
stop whenever she wants. Her main
reason for coming in is to find out
if stress might be causing her to be
unable to conceive.

> ### DON'T FORGET
> You have heard the term *alcoholic*
> used before. For our purposes, the
> term is used interchangeably with *alco-
> hol dependent*; the meaning is identical.
> The term alcoholic has some negative
> connotations, so some professionals
> do not use the term anymore.

Does Mrs. J. seem to have a problem? After all, she can hold down a very
stressful and demanding job, and she told you that she can stop having her
wine whenever she wishes. How would you handle this issue? In fact, is there
an issue at all?

When most psychologists think of Substance-Related Disorders they
think of Alcohol Abuse and Alcohol Dependence. The *DSM-IV-TR* (APA,
2000) has diagnostic criteria for abuse and dependence diagnoses for various
licit and illicit substances. However, because Alcohol Abuse and Dependence
are so prevalent, and in the interest of space, we will limit our discussion to
alcohol and the problems it may cause if misused.

According to the Substance Abuse and Mental Health Services Administration (SAMHSA, 2003), 119 million Americans reported some amount
of alcohol use, and 54 million reported having at least one episode of binge
drinking within the past 30 days of being surveyed (binge drinking means
that, for a male, they will consume five or more drinks in a row on at least one
occasion during the preceding two week period; for a female, four or more
[Wechsler, Lee, Kuo, & Lee, 2000]). These are not statistics of abuse but,
instead, of general use. However, what these data illustrate is how prevalent
alcohol is in our daily lives. Before we define *substance abuse* and *substance dependence,* we need to examine (and explode) some myths.

MYTHS OF ALCOHOLISM AND ALCOHOL ABUSE

Over the years we have had many patients and students ask us about the
following myths, always believing them to be factual (of course a myth is fic-
tion!). You have probably heard of some. Pay particular attention to those that
may be new to you or to those that you thought might have been factual.

Myth: All Alcoholic Dependents Are Street People

This is a common myth perpetuated by the media. In fact, most of the alcoholic dependents that you may see on the street are former psychiatric inpatients who were released from the hospital. Unwilling to take their medications, they end up self-medicating the easiest way they know how—with alcohol. In fact, you will find alcoholics in all walks of life, from the homeless man on the corner to the president of the United States (Ulysses Grant, for one) to the heads of major multinational corporations.

Myth: If I Only Drink Beer I Will Not Become an Alcoholic

This myth is quite amusing, as alcohol is alcohol, no matter how it is brewed. We have also heard people tell us that there is less alcohol in a mixed drink than there is in a 12-ounce can of beer. In fact, that can of beer has the same amount of alcohol as a regular mixed drink or a 5-ounce glass of wine!

Myth: If I Have Too Much to Drink, Some Coffee Will Help Me Sober up

Alcoholics Anonymous (AA) answers this myth: All this does is create a wide-awake drunk, which is true. Additionally, because caffeine dries you out as does alcohol, you will have excessive thirst and will be urinating quite a bit.

Myth: Coffee Will Speed up the Metabolism of the Alcohol and Sober Me up Faster

This is a classic. No matter what one does, alcohol is metabolized at the rate of one ounce of alcohol (i.e., one drink) per hour. Only time will get it metabolized.

Myth: Alcohol Is a Stimulant

In fact, the opposite is true. Alcohol is a central nervous system (CNS) depressant and does not stimulate an individual. This myth is tied to the myth that alcohol enhances sexual functioning and performance. The answer to both of these myths: People *think* that alcohol helps sexual functioning and stimulates the individual, but in fact what it does is loosen inhibitions. Thus, the individual is more "ready and mentally willing" to have sexual relations or to be the life of the party. Alcohol slows reaction time and depresses the CNS functions.

These are some of the more common myths. Did any of them surprise you? Do you dispute any of them?

SYMPTOMS OF SUBSTANCE (ALCOHOL) ABUSE

The *DSM-IV-TR* (APA, 2000) notes that estimates of the prevalence of Alcohol Abuse vary across studies and across geographical areas of the United States. Thus, it is difficult to accurately state how prevalent Alcohol Abuse is at this writing. The *DSM-IV-TR* does note that among adults, anywhere from 66 percent to as many as 90 percent have consumed alcohol at some point in their lives. Binge drinking, which is a serious problem and may be a form of abuse, occurs in about 50 percent of all college men (SAMHSA, 2003). Its peak is at age 21, and it is highest among men aged 18 to 25 (SAMHSA, 2003). Regardless of which study you examine, Alcohol Abuse remains a problem in the United States and is a problem that is not disappearing in the near future.

Generally speaking, the diagnosis of Alcohol Abuse can be applied when alcohol is causing problems in the individual's life. In other words, the individual is experiencing hardships that are directly (or in some cases indirectly) caused by the consumption of alcohol. Let us examine the specific diagnostic criteria.

First, the substance use must lead to "clinically significant impairment or distress . . ." within a one year time frame (APA, 2000, p. 199). *Distress* is a relative term, but *clinically significant impairment* is not. Within this time frame, the individual must be unable to fulfill school, work, or homelife obligations, for example, constant school absences or school-related problems caused by alcohol use (such as vandalism, fights, and so on). A classic example often used in training films shows a wife calling up her husband's employer early

---

CAUTION

When helping professionals treat someone with an alcohol problem, they often have to fight through the denial and some of the myths previously listed. Part of the problem is that the media do not accurately portray alcoholism or alcohol abuse. In fact, we will often see someone who is drunk on television or in the movies and it will be in a humorous scenario. If you placed that individual in another scene—being the driver involved in a fatal auto accident caused by drinking too much—I suspect the audience reactions would differ significantly.

> ## CAUTION
> ....
> Read the diagnostic criteria *very* carefully; you will soon see that getting drunk (or intoxicated) is not one of the listed criteria. Think about the reasons for this as you read on.

in the morning as her husband, hung over yet again and yelling at her, cannot get out of bed because he had too much to drink the night before. Many times helping professionals will get referrals from supervisors, principals, and other authority figures because they witness multiple absences or work-related issues where previously none existed.

Next, the individual will use alcohol in situations that are physically hazardous (APA, 2000). The most common situation here is driving while intoxicated (DWI). Alcohol is the number one cause of all automobile accidents in the United States. Alcohol and driving do not mix. The individual may also operate a hazardous machine while they are under the influence of alcohol. An important aspect of this, not mentioned by the *DSM-IV-TR,* is that the individual *thinks* that he or she is capable of operating a motor vehicle or a dangerous machine as well as he or she could if he or she had nothing to drink! Does our airline pilot fall into this category?

Third, the individual must have "recurrent substance-related legal problems . . ." (APA, 2000, p. 199). This refers to DWIs and any crimes related to Alcohol Abuse. For example, I once had a patient who only committed crimes when he was drinking. In his estimation, the crimes were victimless and petty (he was involved with breaking and entering (B&E), a felony), but he told us that had he not been drinking, he "would never had gotten up the nerve to do the B&Es." Recall when we mentioned that alcohol works to loosen one's inhibitions; many people see this as a positive aspect of alcohol use. As you can see, this can also have a negative aspect.

Finally, the individual will continue to use the substance (alcohol) even though the social and interpersonal problems he or she experiences are either caused by, or exacerbated by, the substance's effects (APA, 2000). This is a variation of *denial,* which is defined in the *DSM-IV-TR* and is a criterion of substance dependence: The individual continues to drink even though they know that they have an ongoing *physiological* or psychological problem that is caused or exacerbated by the continued usage (APA, 2000). The difference is minor, but the substance *dependence* criterion includes a physiological component. A joke heard an at AA meeting might help to illustrate this concept: "So as the

≡ Rapid Reference 4.1

Key Terms to Know

Substance (Alcohol) Abuse: This is when alcohol causes problems (legal or otherwise) in the individual's life—disrupting work, school, or family life.

Binge Drinking: This is when a male consumes five or more drinks in a row on at least one occasion during the preceding 2-week period or when a female consumes four or more drinks during the preceding 2-week period (Wechsler et al., 2000).

Driving While Intoxicated (DWI): This is the legal term for drunk driving. In most states in the United States, a blood alcohol concentration (BAC) of 0.08 is considered legally intoxicated.

Blood Alcohol Concentration (BAC): This is the percentage of alcohol that is in the body as compared to the total blood supply. A BAC of 0.10 is equivalent to about five drinks consumed per hour for an average-sized individual.

Denial: This is a Freudian ego-defense mechanism, often seen in individuals with substance abuse or dependence diagnoses. The individual denies reality; she or he denies that a problem with alcohol exists.

guy was being wheeled into the operating room to have his liver removed because of cirrhosis [alcohol-related liver damage] from drinking a quart of vodka every day for thirty years, he keeps on saying, 'Hey doc, I don't got a drinking problem, I just have a faulty liver!'" Some view denial as a Freudian ego defense mechanism, where the ego does not allow the id impulses to break through into the conscious mind. No matter how solid the evidence, the individual still cannot see that a Substance Abuse problem exists. Thus, he or she continues to use and the problems multiply and intensify.

Finally, the symptoms must never have met the criteria for Substance Dependence for this particular substance (APA, 2000). In other words, you cannot be diagnosed as having Alcohol Abuse and Alcohol Dependence at the same time. For definitions of key terms, see Rapid Reference 4.1.

DON'T FORGET

Legal problems are not the only type of problem that the individual must experience in order to be diagnosed with substance (alcohol) abuse. Relationship problems, problems with children (neglect or abuse), problems at home, school-related problems, and work-related problems also must be considered.

SYMPTOMS OF SUBSTANCE (ALCOHOL) DEPENDENCE

According to Morrison (1995), approximately 1 in 10 people in the United States suffers from Alcohol Dependence. The *DSM-IV-TR* (APA, 2000) does not list a prevalence rate because all Substance-Related Disorders are categorized into a single chapter. What is mentioned, however, are some important statistics that clearly illustrate how lethal Alcohol Dependence (and alcohol intoxication) can be. For example, approximately one-half of all highway fatalities involve either a driver or a pedestrian who is intoxicated. About 10 percent of individuals with substance dependence commit suicide, but this may be related to a Substance-Induced Mood Disorder, most like a depressive disorder (APA, 2000). We can infer that this statistic refers to those who have abused alcohol. Additionally, alcohol crosses the placenta and may produce fetal alcohol syndrome (FAS) in the developing fetus. The fetus may also become physiologically dependent on alcohol and may suffer withdrawal symptoms once born.

Before we examine the diagnostic criteria and symptoms of Alcohol Dependence, we first need to briefly examine FAS and fetal alcohol effects (FAE; a milder version of FAS). Approximately 1.5 out of every 1,000 live births (the baby was alive at the time of delivery) has FAS. Fetal alcohol syndrome's symptoms include growth retardation, small head, narrow eyes, heart defects, and usually some type of intellectual deficiencies. The child most likely will have some form of Mental Retardation (usually Mild) and will usually have some type of learning disability. Fetal alcohol syndrome is the third leading cause of birth defects and is the primary preventable cause of Mental Retardation in the United States (Kaemingk & Paquette, 1999). Clearly, this information is disturbing.

DON'T FORGET

As of this writing, many ob-gyns tell pregnant women that is okay, on rare occasions, to have a drink. Fetal alcohol syndrome becomes more likely when the pregnant woman ingests alcohol on a regular basis to the point of, minimally, abuse.

DON'T FORGET

A visible sign of FAS is the lack of a Cupid's bow. This is the portion of the upper lip that is shaped like the bow of a bow and arrow. Children who have FAS *lack* this physiological feature.

There are many *DSM-IV-TR* (APA, 2000) diagnostic criteria for the diagnosis of Alcohol Dependence. First, the individual must demonstrate a maladaptive pattern of substance use that will lead to clinically significant impairment or distress. This concept is similar to that for substance abuse. In fact, some view substance dependence as being on the same continuum as substance abuse, although at a later stage. This perspective views substance dependence as a chronic disease with a well-defined course. The individual must have three or more of the following symptoms, each of which must have occurred within the same 12-month time frame (APA, 2000):

First, *tolerance* must be present. Specifically, if someone is dependent on alcohol, it will eventually take more alcohol to achieve the same effect. Later on, if physiological damage has occurred, it may take *less* alcohol to achieve the same effect. This is known as *reverse tolerance* and is viewed as a sign that liver damage may have occurred.

Second, *withdrawal symptoms* must be present. This can be noted in one of two ways. First, the characteristic withdrawal signs and symptoms for alcohol must be present. These include delirium tremens (DTs), which is a series of symptoms that includes fever, sweating, trembling, and sometimes hallucinations. Second, the substance (alcohol) or a substance that is closely related (such as a barbiturate or an anxiolytic) is taken to relieve or to avoid the withdrawal symptoms. If this occurs, then the body is in a state where it cannot function normally without alcohol coursing through it. The body is now used to having the substance, and thus the individual is physiologically dependent.

Third, *loss of control* must be present. When this occurs, the substance is often taken in larger amounts or over a longer period of time than was intended, and the individual tries to decrease or control the alcohol use without success (APA, 2000). In other words, once the individual begins to drink, she or he has great difficulty stopping. A classic example is when the individual goes into a bar with the intent to have one or two drinks and ends up closing down the bar.

CAUTION

DTs are not what you might think. The media often portray alcohol-induced hallucinations as pink elephants dancing around the maypole or something else in a similar vein. In fact, the hallucinations may be rather frightening and generally are not too pleasant. The DTs themselves can lead to a seizure, which can cause death.

Finally, *denial* must be present. Recall that denial in substance dependence occurs even though the individual has an ongoing physiological or psychological problem that is caused or exacerbated by the continued alcohol usage (in substance abuse the ongoing problems are social or interpersonal, such as frequent fights with their partner or child abuse while intoxicated; APA, 2000). Here is another good illustration of denial: I had a former patient who came to see us because he had received two DWIs within a 3-year period. Each time he was arrested, his BAC was at least .20, which is equivalent to about 10 drinks in 1 hour. The second time he came in to see us, he believed that the police had set him up and that he was a victim when in fact in his eyes he had done nothing wrong. In his words, he had "a driving problem, not a drinking problem" (Getzfeld, 2004, p. 127). Does this sound like denial to you? It certainly fits the *DSM-IV-TR*'s definition.

The APA (2000) notes that there are two specifiers for Alcohol Dependence:

With Physiological Dependence: Evidence of tolerance or withdrawal
Without Physiological Dependence: No evidence of tolerance or withdrawal (p. 198)

The first of these simply means that the individual demonstrates *either* tolerance or withdrawal, both symptoms of physiological dependence. The second means that the individual does not demonstrate either tolerance or withdrawal. What is interesting is that the individual only need have either tolerance or withdrawal in order to be diagnosed as having Alcohol Dependence. Do you think that because of this, we may be over-identifying alcohol dependent individuals?

Before we conclude this section, we must discuss *blackouts,* which are memory lapses caused by heavy alcohol consumption. Contrary to myths, the person does *not* pass out from drinking. Instead, the individual is unable to remember anything that occurred during a period

CAUTION

It is possible to have alcohol-related blackouts and not be alcohol dependent or an alcohol abuser. However, when a person who does not have a substance-related disorder has blackouts, they often are frightened by them. When individuals who have Substance-Related Disorders have blackouts, they will often make light of them and dismiss them as a normal occurrence. For definitions of key terms, see Rapid Reference 4.2.

≡ *Rapid Reference 4.2*

Key Terms to Know

Fetal Alcohol Syndrome (FAS): This is a condition caused by excessive alcohol consumption that can lead to disabilities in the fetus; typically Mental Retardation, learning disabilities, and physiological problems will be present.

Fetal Alcohol Effects (FAE): This is a condition similar to FAS, but the symptoms are not as severe and not as debilitating.

Delirium Tremens (DTs): These are a series of alcohol-withdrawal symptoms that includes fever, sweating, trembling, and sometimes hallucinations.

Tolerance: This is one critical diagnostic criterion for substance dependence and a sign of physiological dependence. The individual needs more or less of the substance (alcohol) to achieve the same effect.

Withdrawal: This is the other critical diagnostic criterion for substance dependence and a sign of physiological dependence. The individual's body cannot function properly unless the substance is present in the body.

Blackouts: These are alcohol-induced amnesia. They are not a *DSM-IV-TR* diagnostic criterion but not an everyday normal occurrence either.

of particularly heavy alcohol usage. Another way to think about this is to view blackouts as alcohol-related amnesia. Blackouts may occur because the high amount of alcohol consumed prevents new memories from being created (McKim, 2003). Blackouts remain controversial in the addictions field because they are not a *DSM-IV-TR* diagnostic criterion for Alcohol Dependence. However, it must be noted that these experiences are not considered to be normal.

ETIOLOGIES OF SUBSTANCE (ALCOHOL)-RELATED DISORDERS

A person does not begin to drink alcohol one day and then by the end of the first week of use become physiologically dependent. Some AA members will tell you that they were an alcoholic the moment they had their first drink. In theory this sounds good, but in practice and in research this is not possible. Most Substance-Related Disorders follow a pattern, similar to the other disorders discussed in this book. Some theorists see substance abuse and dependence as taking a specific developmental path with various factors influencing whether the individual eventually ends up on that path or they veer off that path and do not develop one of these disorders.

What is generally agreed upon are two key factors. First, the individual (typically an adolescent when alcohol is first used) must have a positive attitude towards alcohol. Certainly the media's portrayal of alcohol use can be partially implicated. Beer ads are targeted at young people, especially young men, with the implication that if you drink beer (especially while on Spring Break), scantily-clad women will flock to you and desire you. Rarely can one find ads in the media that point out the hazards of Alcohol Abuse or Alcohol Dependence or the monetary cost each year.

From that point, the individual will begin to experiment with alcohol, most often with a peer group. For most people this first experience will not be pleasant because alcohol is an acquired taste. If they also have a positive attitude and enjoy the experience, they will probably do their best to drink again, perhaps in a similar situation. According to Li, Duncan, and Hops (2001), early deviant behavior or peer pressure can contribute to increased adolescent alcohol use as the adolescent gets older and progresses through school. Once this has occurred, the individual may begin to use alcohol on a regular basis and will probably continue to enjoy it. Once (if) the individual progresses to heavy alcohol use, the problems may begin to worsen. Blackouts may occur, and grades may begin to fall. Job absences may occur. Auto accidents may enter the picture.

The period of abuse is considered by some professionals to be the most critical period in the development of Alcohol Dependence and is the time period when professional intervention can be most useful. The reason for this is simple. After abusing alcohol for a certain time period, tolerance and withdrawal will eventually take over the individual, and he or she will have thus become dependent on alcohol. The etiology is more complex than this (we will examine more factors in a moment), but professionals who intervene at this point will often work with the patient to make him or her realize that a problem already exists. More critically, they can point out that if the abuse continues, the abuse may become dependence. The idea, as we have noted in previous chapters, is prevention. When intervention occurs as early as possible, the success ratio increases.

How critical are social factors? At the least, these factors can only add to the increase of Substance-Related Disorders. As we mentioned, alcohol-related advertisements often target adolescents; the same can be said for some cigarette ads. (Do you recall the infamous Joe Camel ads backed by a merchandise program? You could purchase Joe Camel gear by mail.) People view these ads and want to be with the in group, so they do what the ads suggest, that is, drink a lot of beer, smoke cigarettes, and so on, unaware of the consequences of abuse.

The context in which alcohol is used also seems to be a factor. In general, cultures and religions that use alcohol in ceremonies (such as Judaism) tend to have lower rates of abuse and dependence than those cultures/religions/societies where there might be pressure to drink someone under the table or to use alcohol as a social lubricant. If drinking is seen as a sin or as a virtue or alcohol is treated as something other than a food or as something to be served with a meal, abuse and dependence are more likely to develop. Alcohol dependence seems to be lower in groups and cultures where alcohol usage involves religious customs and values.

Although they may seems like stereotypes and pejorative statements, Alcohol-Related Disorders are more prevalent among Native Americans and among the Irish or Irish Americans. The reasons for this may appear simple, but they become more complex as one closely examines these populations. For Native Americans, the explanations are straightforward. Being deprived of land that is rightfully theirs and thus being denied stability and the chance at economic success, it is not surprising that Alcohol Abuse and Alcohol Dependence are overrepresented within their communities. The extreme poverty that affects them is also a factor. This leads to stress, which is exacerbated by high unemployment. For the Irish, the pub is the social center of many peoples' lives because their houses and apartments are too small and crowded to get together with friends. Alcohol use goes along with the environment. Also, until recently, unemployment was very high in the Republic (and in Northern Ireland, but not as bad), thus exacerbating the problem.

Psychodynamic etiologies need to be considered, although many professionals discount them. The psychoanalyst would see Alcohol Dependence as a result of anxiety, repressed emotions, neurotic conflict, and as a way to boost self-esteem. In effect, alcohol usage could be seen as working like a defense mechanism, the goal being to deny or distort reality and reduce anxiety. The individual may also wish to correct negativity (thanatos perhaps) so they can gain psychological relief. Additionally, alcohol dependents can be viewed as having an *oral fixation*. Oral traits such as dependence, depression, and the refusal to grow up (regression, if you will) occur due to a fixation in the oral stage. The use of alcohol displays a return to the fixation point to attain anxiety reduction and need gratification. The individual thus has an oral personality, which is associated with babies and young toddlers.

The cognitive behavioral explanation is interesting in its simplicity. One reason that people drink is that alcohol is reinforcing. The effects produced by drinking are pleasurable, thus increasing the likelihood that the individual will drink again. If you are among the 90 percent of the population who has used alcohol at some point in your life, you know that taking even one drink will, at the least, relax you and make you feel warm inside. Alcohol can reinforce positively by changing brain and body chemistry, and it can reinforce negatively, removing inhibitions and anxiety. Modeling may be another causal or etiological factor. The individual may see peoples' anxiety reduced because they are drinking, or their problems might be solved because they were drinking (meeting a woman or a man in a bar while drunk, for example). Modeling, as Bandura pointed out, is an extremely powerful and rapid form of learning.

Cognitively, alcohol may produce an expectancy set; that is, the individual expects good things and good feelings to occur while drinking, even though the final results may not be good at all. This expectancy will lead the person to keep on drinking. An expectancy set is a very powerful molder of behavior. An early experiment by Marlatt, Demming, and Reid (1973) demonstrated how important expectancy can be in determining the amount of alcohol consumed. The researchers discovered that the only statistically significant determinant of the amount of alcohol consumed in their study was the subjects' expectations that they were drinking alcohol. If they expected alcohol to be served, they in fact drank more. If alcohol is seen as desirable, the individual may indeed drink more, perhaps a lot more (Read, Wood, Kahler, Maddock, & Palfai, 2003).

There is a problem that occurs with expectancies and positive reinforcement. The alcohol dependent person will often see and hear of celebrities, sports stars, and so on who have significant alcohol problems yet seemingly never get punished for their behaviors and, in fact, may get rewarded for it. For example, David Wells, a very good baseball pitcher who is valued because he is left-handed and does not walk many batters, has had a long-standing battle with alcohol. While it cannot be determined if he is alcohol dependent or not, he made the famous statement that when he pitched his perfect game (he did not allow a baserunner for the entire game, a rare feat indeed), he was *gassed,* meaning he was drunk. His punishment for this? In winter 2004 he signed a 2-year free agent contract with the Boston Red Sox worth millions! Indeed, Wells's behaviors should not be modeled by others, but how many people would listen to that, especially when they see his yearly salary?

Finally, we will examine biological etiologies, and we will spend most of our time on this topic. One aspect that is well received and widely accepted (and used) is the *disease model,* which sees Alcohol Dependence as a medical condition. In this perspective, the only truly successful way to ensure successful treatment is for the dependent person to totally abstain from alcohol use (not all professionals espouse the total abstinence perspective; since we do, we will support it in this book). The main idea is that this will remove temptation and make it less likely that the individual will drink alcohol again. The less likely you are to use something that has addictive potential, the less likely, over time, you will miss it. The cravings will still appear, and this is acceptable. The disease model removes temptation, for the most part, from the dependent individual. Thus, if a substance causes significant problems in your life, your life will be less complicated and less troublesome if you do not use the particular substance at all. Alcoholics Anonymous espouses the disease model.

How exactly does the disease model work? Mental illness (in this instance Alcohol Dependence) is like a physical illness or a disease. It runs a specific course, does not discriminate, and has identical symptoms for all people who are affected. Like physical illnesses such as various cancers, there is a

DON'T FORGET

Alcoholics Anonymous (AA) has been around for 70 years. Many laypeople think that AA is only attended by chronic alcoholics who sit around, swear, and drink coffee throughout the meetings. Many also think that AA meetings are free group therapy sessions. In fact, AA meetings attract all types (Tobey Maguire, the star of the *Spider-Man* movies, is an active member) from all socioeconomic, racial, and ethnic backgrounds. Alcoholics Anonymous is a support group not led by a helping professional but by a member; no therapy is supposed to take place.

possibility that the individual will relapse. This means that the sober alcohol-dependent individual may return to alcoholic drinking patterns at some point during sobriety. Because relapse is so common, some professionals (the author included) believe that it is unwise to tempt fate by agreeing to controlled drinking. Many alcoholics will tell you the same thing; they expect to return to alcoholic drinking if they drink in a controlled fashion. Alcoholics Anonymous also espouses total abstinence.

Evidence is increasing that a genetic predisposition or a diathesis exists for Alcohol Dependence (McGue, 1999). Identical twin studies have also supported this hypothesis (Tsuang et al., 1998). The ability to tolerate alcohol may also be inherited (Goodwin, 1979). In effect, the individual is allergic to alcohol, and whenever some (or too much) gets into his or her body, negative reactions happen. Of course, you cannot develop an allergic reaction to anything until you are exposed to the substance that causes the allergy. This may explain why some individuals who grow up in alcohol-dependent families consciously abstain from using alcohol. The APA (2000) also notes that people who have a family history of Alcohol Dependence are about four times as likely to develop Alcohol Abuse or Alcohol Dependence as those whose families do not suffer from these problems.

Like many of the disorders that we have (and will) cover, Alcohol-Related Disorders seem to have a familial component. In fact, it is at least three times as likely for a primary biological relative (son, daughter, sibling) to have Alcohol Dependence if a first-degree biological relative has the same disorder (Bierut et al., 1998). Environmental factors can play a role, but when twin studies are examined, this hypothesis is supported. What is interesting is that in many twin studies, the rates of Alcohol Dependence were discovered to be significantly higher for men than for women even though the heritability estimates for the diathesis were similar (McGue, 1999).

Finally, there is a relatively new theory that postulates that serotonin levels in alcohol-dependent individuals are below normal. What occurs is this: The individual drinks to compensate for the abnormally low serotonin levels, and if they become intoxicated, the serotonin levels rise significantly. However, extended drinking further depletes the serotonin levels, and thus the individual must continue to drink to counteract the effects of feeling worse due to the lowering levels. This theory has received some support because individuals who take medications such as Prozac (fluoxetine) and other SSRIs will decrease their alcohol usage voluntarily (see McBride, Murphy, Yoshimoto, Lumeng, & Li, 1993).

In sum, Alcohol- and Substance-Related Disorders have biological, genetic, and environmental components, similar to the other disorders discussed. As is true for many mental illnesses, we cannot pinpoint one specific causal factor ... yet. Perhaps in a few years we will be able to get more specific answers.

> # CAUTION
>
> The theory of subnormal serotonin levels has been used to explain unipolar depression, Bulimia Nervosa, and, perhaps, Schizophrenia. When this concept is used to explain Alcohol Dependence, the evidence is quite spare. Thus, until more evidence is gathered, this theory should remain an intriguing hypothesis that warrants further investigation.

TREATMENT MODALITIES

Before we begin, one needs to realize that successful treatment of Substance-Related Disorders is rather difficult. Comorbidity is common, as is denial. Many individuals are mandated clients, that is, they are being forced into a treatment setting by a legal entity or in order to avoid going to jail or prison. Compliance is thus low, drop-out ratios are high, as are recidivism ratios. The goals of substance-related treatment are also somewhat controversial. As was stated, we believe that all individuals who come into treatment for these disorders should practice total abstinence for the rest of their lives. However, there are some who state that controlled drinking (or controlled usage) is a more realistic goal. Finally, what really constitutes treatment success? Total abstinence? Or should we also emphasize family, interpersonal, work, and medical issues first and *then* concentrate on the alcohol-specific treatment? These are difficult questions and ones with which you may struggle if you see patients with Substance-Related Disorders.

First, let us examine what occurs when an individual is unable to stop drinking on his or her own or if he or she attempts to do so, the physical dangers would be potentially life-threatening. These individuals are substance dependent and need to have the substance (alcohol) removed in a safe fashion, that is, in an inpatient hospital setting. Usually detoxification (or detox) lasts anywhere from 1 to as long as 6 weeks, depending on the severity of the dependence, physical concerns, and so on. Detoxification is the medi-

DON'T FORGET

Using benzodiazepines to help alcohol dependents in detoxification is somewhat controversial, especially because these medicines are also CNS depressants and function similarly to alcohol. Most critically, they are highly addictive. Thus, it is possible that the alcohol dependent can substitute benzodiazepine dependence for Alcohol Dependence.

cal removal or withdrawal of the substance on which the individual has become dependent, in this case alcohol. Detoxification for alcohol and similar substances is gradual; rapid withdrawal (cold turkey) can lead to serious consequences, such as seizures, cardiac arrest, and death. The individual will receive vitamins, nutrients, and benzodiazepines (recall that this is a class of antianxiety medications (anxiolytics); Valium is one type) to prevent serious withdrawal complications.

Not all individuals need detoxification. Whether they do, the next step is to maintain remission, which for many helping professionals means maintaining total abstinence. This is easier said than done. One treatment adjunct that has proven to be somewhat beneficial is the use of medications designed to maintain abstinence. One well known medication is Antabuse (generically known as disulfiram).

Antabuse has been around since 1948. Antabuse prevents the breakdown (metabolism) of alcohol. The patient must take Antabuse regularly. If taken regularly and if the individual remains alcohol free, nothing occurs. However, as soon as the slightest bit of alcohol enters the bloodstream, the individual becomes violently ill. Some of the symptoms (vomiting, heart palpitations, profuse sweating) mimic those of a heart attack. The idea here is that the individual will stop drinking so as to avoid these unpleasant effects. This sounds wonderful in principle; however, treatment compliance is a must in order for Antabuse treatment to work. Some individuals stop taking Antabuse because they wish to have a controlled slip (a planned relapse) where they drink again, or they believe that they can handle the dependence on their own. Research has supported the inconsistent effects of Antabuse treatment (for example, Garbutt, West, Carey, Lohr, & Crews, 1999).

Two newer medications offer some interesting perspectives. Revia (naltraxone) acts as an endogenous opioid (endorphin) antagonist and is FDA approved. When this medication is in the bloodstream and the individual drinks or uses a narcotic, this medicine blocks the highs that these drugs produce. In other words, the effects of alcohol are reduced. Additionally, this drug blocks alcohol's ability to stimulate the endorphins and thus reduces the cravings that typically accompany Alcohol Dependence. As you might suspect, this method is most efficacious with significant treatment compliance (at least 80 percent; Garbutt et al., 1998) and when the individual is involved with some form of psychotherapy. The FDA is currently examining the utility of Campral (acamprosate). This drug appears to reduce the cravings that accompany alcohol withdrawal. We are not yet completely sure of its mechanisms of action and its action sites, but research states that it is quite effective, especially in combination with Naltrexone. Both of these medications in combination appear to enhance relapse prevention potential in alcohol dependent individuals and used together may perhaps be as effective as Revia (Kiefer et al., 2003).

Prozac (fluoxetine) is effective in reducing drinking behavior for dually diagnosed individuals—those who suffer from Alcohol Dependence and major depression (Cornelius et al., 1997). A positive feature of Prozac and some other SSRIs is that it is very difficult to overdose with them.

Alcoholics Anonymous celebrated its seventieth birthday in 2005, which is rather remarkable for a self-help program founded by two recovering alcoholics, Dr. Bob and Bill W. Alcoholics Anonymous has at least two million members in the United States and is represented in at least 100 other countries, thus making AA a worldwide organization. AA can be found in Hong Kong, Tokyo, and Bangkok; throughout Europe, and even on cruise ships (some call the meetings "Friends of Bill W."). The premise of most AA groups is similar. New members introduce themselves anonymously, state that they are alcoholics (or that they

CAUTION

A rule when treating substance dependent individuals is to make sure to determine whether the substance is causing other mental illnesses or whether the mental illnesses would be present once the substance is washed out of the individual's system. Alcohol and other drugs, when abused or worse, can mimic signs and symptoms of some of the other disorders in this book. Thus, seek abstinence first, and then determine with more certainty whether a dual diagnosis is warranted.

think they have problems with alcohol) and that their lives have become unmanageable, and then the new members listen to the senior members who have been sober for awhile. These senior members relate their stories to the night's theme and mention how their lives have improved once they sobered up and abstained from drinking alcohol. These meetings offer emotional support and understanding, a social network, and a crisis network where sponsors (senior members) will make themselves available to newer members who may be at risk for a relapse.

Finally, while AA does have spiritual overtones, it has no religious affiliations. Even though AA has been successful based on testimonials of thousands of recovering members over the decades, it still raises some questions within the research community.

First, long-term follow up of its members is not easy because many drop out, move, or change meetings. Alcoholics Anonymous does not lend itself to traditional research designs. All members are anonymous and thus might be reluctant to divulge any demographic information. It would also be difficult to use placebo controls, random designs, and so forth. Finally, attendance is voluntary and sporadic; this makes statistically significant research difficult to perform.

Performing couples or family therapy is another common treatment option. Many professionals consider Alcohol Dependence to be a family disease, that is, it affects all family members, including the user. Many clinicians come to realize that physical and sexual abuse of family members is rather common in the alcohol dependent's family. The problem is not in getting the family members (also called significant others) to come in to the initial sessions; it is in convincing the significant others to remain in treatment. O'Farrell (1993) noted that couples therapy reduced domestic violence, although establishing a cause-effect relationship would prove to be difficult. Regardless, giving the individual a stronger social support network through his or her family is critical and can only help matters.

We will spend most of this section discussing cognitive behavioral treatments (used alone or together) that still represent the most effective treatment modalities for Alcohol Dependence today. As we mentioned, Alcohol Dependence is seen as a learned response to stressful situations or to anxiety. Alcohol use reduces the anxiety or stress, and thus the drinking is reinforced and will continue. A key aspect is for the individual to recognize the situations or circumstances that precipitate alcohol abuse and either defuse them, properly handle them, or avoid them altogether.

One well-known method, albeit not terribly successful, is aversion therapy. Antabuse treatment is one type of aversion method. Typically,

> **DON'T FORGET**
>
> In Kubrick's *A Clockwork Orange* violence and rape are favored pastimes of Alex, the key character. Beethoven's Ninth is used as an aversive treatment method when Alex finally goes to prison.

the individual is shocked or made extremely nauseous when they think of alcohol, reach for a drink, or actually drink. The problem with this technique is simple: It causes the individual a lot of discomfort, and it may not be terribly successful, lacking research support.

Contingency management techniques, sometimes known as operant or Skinnerian techniques, have also been used with good success (Sisson & Azrin, 1989). The individual and his or her significant others reinforce behaviors that are inconsistent with drinking alcohol, such as avoiding risky situations that could cue drinking behavior or avoiding people that might cue drinking. Social skills training and assertiveness training are also included (assertively refusing to drink at a party, for example). If used properly, these methods are extremely effective.

Relapse prevention training is a relatively new treatment modality (Daley & Marlatt, 1992; Marlatt, Blume, & Parks, 2001). The goal is to teach the patient how to handle relapses or slips and to notice the antecedents—or high-risk situations—so that they can successfully cope with the stresses in these situations. Examples might include situations that create anxiety, stress, or tension; economic troubles; and, relevant in today's times, the fear of another terrorist attack or of a natural disaster like a tsunami or a hurricane. Relapse prevention is based on the notion that the individual can control his or her behavior as long as they continue in treatment and as long as they make an effort to change.

A key feature of relapse prevention is a concept called *abstinence violation effects (AVE)*. Patients are taught that a relapse is not the end of the world or a sign of weakness, and they are taught how to interpret relapses. Individuals may feel a loss of control due to this relapse. The relapse may be as simple as having one drink. They are not to feel guilt or shame because they had a slip. Instead, if they are involved with relapse prevention, they are taught to attribute it to a temporary lapse in control, not a total relapse or a collapse.

Finally, there is the most controversial behavioral modality of all: controlled drinking, first introduced by the Sobells (Sobell & Sobell, 1993). The idea here is that the individual *can* drink on occasion, but not to the point of intoxication; the individual does not need to maintain total abstinence. This concept infers that the alcohol abuser or dependent can control his or her drinking and therefore can make other life changes because of this control. This can be also used in cognitive treatment programs; the individual is taught to notice cues and antecedents that may lead to excessive drinking, they are taught how to cope so as not to drink too much, and they are taught to note the consequences when they either ignore the antecedents or drink too much. Similar to relapse prevention, a slip is not seen as something that is out of the individual's control and is not seen as something that is disastrous in his or her recovery. The relapse is seen as a learning experience and is seen as a sign that the individual needs to become more vigilant. She or he needs to be more alert to cues that might encourage drinking and properly attend to the cues or to the situations.

Needless to say, this perspective remains quite controversial. Some research has discovered that controlled drinking works the best with younger alcohol abusers or those in the very early stages of Alcohol Dependence (in these early stages, withdrawal symptoms are usually not a significant issue; Sobell & Sobell, 1993). The key argument for controlled drinking is that it is very difficult to remain abstinent for the rest of one's life, and in some cases it may not even be necessary! The research has still not been conclusive enough for some professionals to espouse controlled drinking, and more detailed, longitudinal research is needed.

In general, the use of medications to treat Alcohol Dependence is not viable. Even though antianxiety medications (anxiolytics) are used in detoxification procedures, their use on an outpatient basis would be extremely hazardous. These medications produce effects that are similar to those produced by alcohol; for example, muscle relaxation and feelings of calmness. More problematic, they are extremely addictive and are best used for short-term treatment. Additionally, when anxiolytics are taken while alcohol is in the bloodstream, the medications' effects are significantly magnified. The combination may eventually lead to death.

Surprisingly, antidepressants are even more problematic. Antidepressants are not physiologically addictive; however, the TCAs and MAOIs have a very low overdose threshold. This means that the individual does not need to take many pills if she or he wishes to attempt suicide. If alcohol is added to the mix, the combination may become lethal. One advantage of medications like Prozac (fluoxetine) and other SSRIs is that it is very difficult, if not impossible, to overdose on them (Bezchlibnyk-Butler & Jeffries, 2005).

Finally, here is a word about barbiturates and hypnotics, commonly known as sleeping pills. A physiological symptom of Alcohol Dependence (and many other substance dependences) is sleep disruption. If an individual is intoxicated, he or she may pass out and could potentially sleep for many hours. However, the sleep is not quality sleep because the dream state (REM sleep) does not occur when intoxicated. This is one reason why alcohol abusers and dependents, although having been passed out for many hours, do not feel rested when they awaken. In fact, this is one symptom of the classic alcohol-related hangover. The problem really begins in the physician's office.

When alcohol dependents have sleep disruptions, they will go into their primary care physician's office mentioning this as their presenting problem. Sadly, many physicians do not investigate or consider Alcohol- or Substance-Related Disorders to be causes of these sleep difficulties and thus they prescribe barbiturates or hypnotics (such as Nembutal [pentobarbital]). This combination of barbiturates or hypnotics, and alcohol is one of the deadliest drug combinations as both are CNS depressants. Mixing the two can (and often does) lead to a CNS shutdown, respiratory and cardiac arrest; the individual may become comatose and eventually die.

Thus, how can we sum up effective treatment for Substance (Alcohol)-Related Disorders? Of the techniques discussed, the most effective appear to be cognitive, behavioral, or a combination of the two. This is important in today's era of managed care where insurance companies and clinics are looking for rapid results and scientifically measurable treatments. Additionally, Freudian analysis (either short or long term) is not terribly effective and is not favored in many substance abuse clinics, if for no other reason that progress takes too long. However, you need to decide which modality (or modalities) works best for you. See Rapid Reference 4.3 for definitions of this section's key terms.

≡ Rapid Reference 4.3

Key Terms to Know

Alcoholics Anonymous (AA): This is a free self-help and support group for alcohol dependents or abusers and for people who think they may have alcohol problems. It is *not* a therapy group.

Antabuse (disulfiram): This prevents the metabolism of alcohol; if the patient, while on Antabuse, has the slightest bit of alcohol enter the bloodstream, the patient becomes violently ill.

Controlled Drinking: This is the idea that the alcohol abuser or dependent can control his or her drinking and therefore can make other life changes because of this control.

Relapse Prevention Training: This is a modality where the patient is taught how to handle relapses or slips and to notice the antecedents—or high-risk situations—so that they can successfully cope with the stresses in these situations.

Putting It Into Practice

The Case of Robert Tippler

Robert (or Bob, which he prefers) is a 46-year-old Caucasian male who was referred to the clinic by his probation officer Estelle because of his two DWI arrests within the past 2 years. When he was arrested for his DWIs, his BAC was .24 for the first arrest, and .22 for the second, both at least twice the legal limit (a BAC of .24 for an average weight individual represents about 12 drinks in 1 hour). Many individuals would pass out at these BAC levels, so imagine how difficult it would be to operate a motor vehicle and not get into an accident. Estelle was quite concerned about the high BACs; because of this, and because of his two DWI arrests within the past 2 years, Estelle felt that Bob needed treatment for a serious alcohol problem. Thus, he came into our clinic as a mandated potential patient. If he did not follow through with the treatment recommendations, he would be headed off to jail.

Bob appeared to us in the initial intake interview with a flat affect, and he was red-eyed, and he had flushed skin. He answered most of our questions in a forthright fashion, except when the questions involved alcohol usage, at least initially.

We began by asking Bob about the DWIs and about his drinking behavior. "Well, I had to drive home from work, of course, and I often go out with some friends to the local diner. They serve beer, and why shouldn't we have a few once in awhile? Both of those times I messed up. I had more than I had anticipated, and I got caught. That seems to happen quite a bit. What can I say?" In fact, this is known as *loss of control*, which is one *DSM-IV-TR* diagnostic criterion for Alcohol Dependence. Bob also admitted to driving under the influence of alcohol "a number of other times, but I never got caught. I wasn't really drunk, but I had a few beers, maybe six or seven in a couple of hours, nothing over the top. I know I could cut down or stop if I wanted to, especially because the wife wants me to, but it's hard once you've set a pattern, and it does help to get me to sleep."

Bob told us some more. He stated that he would often drink "a lot" to help get him to sleep during the day, and many times he would pass out, which he figured was a good result. He also found that as the years went on, it took more and more beer to get the same effect and that, at times, he would get "shakes whenever I didn't have anything to drink that morning before hitting the sack. I guess it's from being too tired or too much coffee during the night." Whenever it takes more or less of a substance (in this case alcohol) to achieve the same effect, a physiological tolerance has built up. This is another diagnostic criterion for Alcohol Dependence. Getting "the shakes" because he did not drink any alcohol before retiring to bed is a withdrawal symptom. The body has a physiological need for the alcohol, and when it is not present, the body reacts. Many times alcoholics will continue drinking even if they do not want to in order to avoid these withdrawal symptoms. Withdrawal symptoms are another sign of physiological dependence.

We now had enough information to make an accurate diagnosis, but we wanted some further information to make sure. We thus questioned Bob about his history of alcohol usage and his work history to get some more information. "Well, I've been drinking in the mornings for awhile ... at least six years or more. It really helps to relax me and to make it easier to get to sleep. I never hit my wife or kids or nothing, nothing like that. I usually could stop when I want to. Usually I'd drink most mornings, but not all, and sometimes not on my days off."

We questioned him further about his alcohol usage history and about his sleep difficulties. "Well, you see, it's probably because I work swing shifts, but usually I'm at the factory for the graveyard shift, eleven P.M. until seven A.M. Of course that means when I get home it's always daylight, unless it's a cruddy weather day outside. It's hard to get to sleep because of the noise and what have you, and the wife and kids are always at me when I get home. I don't really get too tense about this, but a guy needs his sleep. You know how it is...."

(continued)

Presented with the preceding information, we made our preliminary diagnostic interpretation of Bob, based on the following criteria: He demonstrated tolerance and mild withdrawal symptoms, and he was unable to control his drinking, that is, he could not stop once he started drinking on many occasions. He also had excessively high BACs; each was more than twice the legal limit for intoxication for both of his DWIs, a warning sign by itself:

Axis I:　Alcohol Dependence, with Physiological Dependence　303.90
Axis II:　No Diagnosis　　　　　　　　　　　　　　　　　　　V71.09
Axis III:　None
Axis IV:　Two DWIs with high BACs
Axis V:　GAF = 51 (Current)

Treatment Plan

After consultation with the staff psychiatrist and with the detoxification unit of the local hospital, the clinic decided to admit Bob and to place him into a weekly low-functioning Alcohol Dependence group. This group was designed for individuals who had alcohol problems but were demonstrating denial and resistance, two common aspects with alcohol dependent individuals that tend to ameliorate more in a group setting. We also used Glasser's Reality Therapy in weekly individual sessions with Bob. Reality Therapy is widely used in substance dependence treatment; Bob had to take responsibility for his treatment and not make excuses or look to place blame. Many outpatient substance abuse treatment programs have a standard practice of expecting their patients to maintain total abstinence, and this clinic was no different. This policy caused Bob some difficulties as he experienced three mild relapses. We explained to Bob that a relapse is not the end of the world or a sign of weakness, and we taught him how to interpret relapses.

In addition, a widely accepted treatment adjunct was also used—attendance at AA meetings. Bob was required to go to weekly AA meetings, at first to just sit and observe. He quickly became comfortable speaking in the meetings, always noting at first that "I may have a problem with alcohol, but I'm not sure. I only drink to help me get some sleep." He would often relate to us that, when he said this, he would be approached by other members after the meeting and told "That sounds like a problem or worse to me, guy." A better option than alcohol or sedative-hypnotics (sleeping pills) to help Bob sleep is progressive muscle relaxation techniques. These techniques did seem to help him. He eventually opened up in group therapy and was willing to investigate his alcohol usage. When we brought in his wife for a consultation, she told us (in front of Bob) that she had wanted him to stop his drinking for a few years "before he killed himself or someone else. He's got grandkids for Christ's sake!"

We also used some cognitive behavioral techniques, which can work quickly without going in-depth into his unconscious and upbringing. We decided to get Bob more active when he was home to take him away from his beloved television shows. Additionally, we examined the thoughts that occurred when he was drinking too much, and we worked with him to assess these thoughts and to think about certain situations differently.

Bob managed to stay sober throughout most of his therapy, having occasional relapses but realizing that this was a normal part of "his illness, the sickness that caused me to drink and to almost destroy my life. A man my age on probation!" At discharge after 9 months of intensive outpatient therapy and continued sobriety, Bob received a prognosis of Good, meaning that his continued recovery was a likely probability.

 TEST YOURSELF

1. **Which of the following statements about alcohol or alcohol dependents is true?**
   (a) If I only drink beer, I will not become an alcoholic.
   (b) If I have too much to drink, some coffee will help me sober up because coffee will speed up the metabolism of the alcohol and sober me up faster.
   (c) Alcohol is a stimulant.
   (d) Alcohol slows reaction time and depresses the CNS functions.

2. **The *DSM-IV-TR* specifier "Physiological Dependence" requires the alcohol dependent individual to demonstrate**
   (a) tolerance.
   (b) blackouts.
   (c) denial.
   (d) both a and b.

3. **Loss of control refers to**
   (a) alcohol being taken in larger amounts or over a longer period of time than was intended, and the individual tries to decrease or control the amount without success.
   (b) drinking at a party and going wild, for example, dancing with a lampshade on.
   (c) alcohol usage leading to hangovers, vomiting, and passing out.
   (d) alcohol usage that leads to visual hallucinations, such as pink elephants.

(continued)

4. **An alcohol-related blackout is**

 (a) when the individual passes out from drinking too much alcohol.

 (b) when the individual faints and then quickly recovers from doing a shot.

 (c) when the individual has an amnesic episode caused strictly by alcohol consumption.

 (d) either a or c, depending on how much the person drinks.

5. **The term *binge drinking* means that a male will consume five or more drinks in a row on at least one occasion during the preceding 2-week period or four or more for a female.** True or False?

6. **Alcoholics Anonymous (AA) is**

 (a) a place where alcoholics can drink in anonymity.

 (b) only attended by chronic alcoholics who sit around, swear, and drink coffee.

 (c) a support group led by a member for alcoholics and those who think they have a problem with alcohol.

 (d) none of the above.

7. **If an alcoholic is sent to detoxification (detox), what can she or he expect to occur?**

 (a) Basically they are sent to the drunk tank; they will go to jail until they sober up and are then released.

 (b) They will be hospitalized, and the alcohol will be medically removed from their system.

 (c) They will receive, among other things, benzodiazepines to prevent serious withdrawal complications.

 (d) Both b and c.

8. **If an individual, while on Antabuse, has the slightest bit of alcohol enter his or her bloodstream, she or he will have no reaction.** True or False?

Answers: 1. d; 2. a; 3. a; 4. c; 5. True; 6. c; 7. d; 8. False

Five

Eating Disorders appear to be on the increase in the United States and in other developed countries (Steiner & Lock, 1998; Wickes-Nelson & Israel, 2000). One recent study found that as many as 1 out of 10 girls aged 16 to 18 may have an eating disorder (Goldstein, 1999). The "drive for thinness" affects Hollywood actresses and actors, athletes (gymnasts and cheerleaders are especially susceptible), models, and royalty (the late Princess Diana). Jamie-Lynn DiScala ("Meadow" on *The Sopranos*) and Tracey Gold have battled Anorexia Nervosa, and in June 2004 Mary-Kate Olsen (one-half of the famous Olsen twins) went into a rehabilitation center for treatment rumored to be related to Anorexia Nervosa. Paula Abdul of *American Idol* fame battled Bulimia Nervosa for years, and it threatened to destroy her career.

Let us look at a real-life example. A 34-year-old White female comes to you and tells you the following: She has had problems controlling her weight for a number of years; generally it fluctuates between being 15 to 30 pounds overweight, based on national averages for a 5 foot 6 inch female. She grew up in an upper class household where both parents are professionals. Her father is a prominent surgeon in the community, and her mother is a school principal. She never lacked for anything except for many close friends. She has had boyfriends in the past but nothing "worked out beyond a few months." She would like to get married someday but does not see that happening right now. She describes herself as moody, having some sleep problems, and tells you that her sex drive (libido) is reduced.

Her main concern is that she cannot get her weight to where she thinks it needs to be. She then tells you that at times she will consume 3,000 calories at one sitting, after which she will purge by making herself vomit by sticking a toothbrush down her throat. All of this has been going on for at least 10 years, and these behaviors occur surreptitiously. Is her behavior a cause for concern? Do any of these symptoms sound familiar?

For our purposes, we will examine only Anorexia Nervosa and Bulimia Nervosa, with most of our attention focused on Bulimia Nervosa. Anorexia Nervosa tends to produce more dramatic symptoms and consequences (untreated, it can result in death), but it remains relatively rare outside of certain professions and fields, and it is rare in general. Bulimia Nervosa, however, is much more common. If you work with young girls that range in age from 11 to about 25, it is almost a given that you will come across a female who suffers from Bulimia Nervosa. Bulimia Nervosa also appears to be comorbid with several other *DSM-IV-TR* disorders, specifically Mood Disorders (unipolar depressions) and Borderline Personality Disorder. Ask yourself this: Which comes first, Bulimia Nervosa, or is Bulimia Nervosa a by-product of having a mood or a personality disorder? Perhaps once you have completed this chapter, you will have a better idea.

HISTORY OF EATING DISORDERS

The history of Eating Disorders, according to some, goes back at least a few thousand years. The ancient Romans were known for many accomplishments as well as decadences, and one of those was the orgy. Typically one would go to an orgy, eat as much as possible, and then make themselves vomit. This could be done in a *vomitorium*. Perhaps the Romans were the first bulimics! The idea behind this was to be able to eat as much as possible before the orgy ended. Bulimia Nervosa and Anorexia Nervosa have always been considered to be a by-product of Westernized cultures. In these societies, television and movies heavily influence peoples' ideals as to what constitutes a healthy body shape and a healthy weight. Because of the heavy in-

CAUTION

Bulimia Nervosa (or bulimia for short) is not strictly a female-only disorder. Bulimic men generally are involved in certain sports or in activities or professions where their weight is required not to go above a certain ceiling. For example, male cheerleaders and gymnasts oftentimes face weight requirements (what do you think the situation is for jockeys?).

≡ Rapid Reference 5.1

Key Terms to Know

Eating Disorders: This disorder occurs when an individual (usually female) suffers extreme disturbances in eating behavior caused by an obsessive (and irrational) fear of gaining weight.

Anorexia Nervosa: Literally means a loss of appetite. The individual (again, usually female) refuses to maintain the minimum body weight defined for her height.

Bulimia Nervosa: Literally means the hunger of an ox. The individual (again, typically female) will oftentimes binge on upward of 3,000 calories in a single sitting and then compensate by purging (vomiting, using laxatives) or by restriction (self-starvation).

fluence of these media in the United States and in parts of Europe, Eating Disorders were seen as being confined to these portions of the world. What is most troubling is that Eating Disorders now seem to be more common in Asia (especially in Hong Kong and Mainland China) and in some South American countries. We therefore have a problem that is increasing and does not seem to be leveling off.

Even though Bulimia Nervosa has been around for a lengthy period of time, the actual clinical term was not used until 1979 (Russell, 1979). In fact, Eating Disorders did not attract much research until the 1960s (Vandereycken, 2002). More important, Anorexia Nervosa and Bulimia Nervosa did not appear until the *DSM-III* (APA, 1980). What is interesting is that until the *DSM-IV-TR*, Eating Disorders were listed as a subtype in the category Disorders Usually First Diagnosed in Infancy, Childhood, or Adolescence. For definitions of key terms, see Rapid Reference 5.1.

DON'T FORGET

A curious anecdote is associated with the term *Anorexia Nervosa.* It was coined by Sir William Withey Gull (1816–1890) in 1874. He was a noted physician in England and treated the Royal Family, which included the Prince of Wales, for typhus. Why is his name noteworthy? Some people implicate Gull as an accessory in the Jack the Ripper murders!

SYMPTOMS OF ANOREXIA NERVOSA

We begin with Anorexia Nervosa, as it is the rarer of the two disorders. The *DSM-IV-TR* (APA, 2000) estimates that anywhere from 0.5 percent to 3 percent of women suffer from Anorexia Nervosa. More important, the *DSM-IV-TR* estimates that the lifetime prevalence of Anorexia Nervosa is approximately 0.5 percent, thus reinforcing its rarity. However, estimates have shown that new cases of Anorexia Nervosa have increased since the 1930s (Hoek, 2002). As we will soon see, Anorexia Nervosa is also more common among certain subsections of the female population.

In order to be diagnosed with Anorexia Nervosa, the individual must satisfy four criteria. First, she must refuse to maintain her minimally normal body weight for her age and height. Her body weight must be less than 85 percent of that expected for someone of her age and height (APA, 2000). This criterion can easily be quantified by asking the person to step on a scale.

Next, the individual must have an intense fear of gaining weight or becoming fat, even though they are obviously seriously underweight (APA, 2000). This fear becomes crippling, so much so that the woman's daily focus is on not gaining any weight and, more important, continuing to lose even more weight. You have no doubt seen pictures of anorectic women or perhaps have seen them when they appear on daytime talk shows such as *Oprah*. These women are literally human skeletons, yet they continue to mention how they need to lose weight and how they see themselves as appearing fat. One of my past clients saw herself as morbidly obese even though she weighed 96 pounds and was 5 feet 8 inches tall! This inability to see one's body as it truly is in a full length mirror has fascinated clinicians for many years.

Denial of the seriousness of the low body weight or the disturbance in how one's weight or shape is experienced is the third criterion (APA, 2000). We have already discussed these points, but the clinician needs to remember that *denial* appears to be a key component of Eating Disorders. This can be denial of the

CAUTION

Many people think that anorectics are unwilling to step on a scale or keep careful track of their weight. On the contrary, because they are obsessed about their weight, they keep a constant vigil of their weight loss and, more important to them, their weight gain. In fact, in many psychologists' experiences, it is the *bulimic* women who are afraid of stepping on the scale.

seriousness of the problem or denial of the woman's actual shape and seriousness of her low weight.

For some psychologists the fourth criterion, *amenorrhea,* is the most fascinating. Here the woman (who must already be menstruating) will have to miss at least three consecutive menstrual cycles (APA, 2000). Some anorectic women use amenorrhea as a yardstick that their extreme weight loss is succeeding,

> # DON'T FORGET
>
> Denial was mentioned in Chapter 4 as being a key component in Substance-Related Disorders. In fact, working with the patient to help them break through their denial is often one of the most difficult aspects in treating an eating disorder. Might this imply that Eating Disorders and Substance-Related Disorders are somehow connected?

as if they are menstruating, their body weight is too close to normal.

There are other overt signs that may indicate the presence of Anorexia Nervosa. Usually the woman will have a low body temperature; have cold intolerance; have cold extremities (hands and feet); and report fatigue and episodes of dizziness, constipation, periodic vomiting, and shortness of breath. The woman's hair may be thinning (due to lack of nourishment), and a coating of fine body hair might be noticed on her extremities (known as *lanugo*). Lanugo occurs as the body's natural defense against a lack of weight to defend against cold temperatures (some suspect that evolution made these coats of hair unnecessary). Her eyes may appear to be sunken, and she may have puffy cheeks, similar to a chipmunk. Do not forget that the woman will most likely be unable to see any of these overt characteristics herself (APA, 2000).

The *DSM-IV-TR* lists two subtypes of Anorexia Nervosa. Recall that these subtypes are used to help clinicians further classify disorders and to help them make more appropriate treatment plans:

Restricting Type. During the current episode of Anorexia Nervosa, the person has not regularly engaged in binge eating or purging behavior (i.e., self-induced vomiting or the misuse of laxatives, diuretics, or enemas).

Binge-Eating/Purging Type. During the current episode of Anorexia Nervosa, the person has regularly engaged in binge eating or purging behavior (i.e., self-induced vomiting or the misuse of laxatives, diuretics, or enemas; APA, 2000, p. 589). (The binge-eating/purging type used to be called *bulimiarexia.* That term is now archaic.).

DON'T FORGET

Anorexia Nervosa took the lives of two women who lived in the public eye. Karen Carpenter (1950–1983) was a very successful folk singer who teamed with her brother Richard to form The Carpenters, a very popular group in the 70s. Christy Henrich (1972–1994) was a world and Olympic-class gymnast who died of multiple organ failure at the age of 22. She weighed approximately 61 pounds when she died; she was 4 feet 10 inches tall. It was reported that Henrich suffered from Anorexia Nervosa and Bulimia Nervosa.

Typically, psychologists will see an even split between the two subtypes (Garfinkel, Kennedy, & Kaplan, 1995). One study discovered that anorectics who purged to lose the weight or to maintain their weight loss suffered from more psychopathology than those who use restrictive methods to maintain weight loss (Garner, Garner, & Rosen, 1993). Regardless, both subtypes are extremely dangerous, as is Anorexia Nervosa itself. In some extreme instances, it leads to death.

SYMPTOMS OF BULIMIA NERVOSA

Bulimia Nervosa is more common in the United States than is Anorexia Nervosa; the *DSM-IV-TR* estimates that anywhere from 1 to 3 percent of women have this disorder. The rate of occurrence in men is one-tenth compared to females (APA, 2000). As you can see, Bulimia Nervosa is about 2 to 6 times more common than Anorexia Nervosa. Still, when the percentages are examined, Bulimia Nervosa does not *appear* to be a common disorder.

CAUTION

As with any epidemiological information, the preceding statistics must be interpreted cautiously. This is especially critical when examining disorders that include denial as a key component (not necessarily as a diagnostic criterion). Women with Eating Disorders tend to be secretive and generally do not actively seek out help. Thus, we can only consider these percentages rough estimates, and we should expect the actual percentages to be higher.

Bulimia Nervosa is diagnosed by using five criteria. As we list and discuss each criterion, ask yourself the following: How normal are these behaviors? In fact, bulimic women see nothing wrong with exhibiting the symptoms we are about to discuss.

First, the individual (woman for the remainder of this discussion) must have recurrent episodes of binge eating over which she believes she has no control. A *binge* is defined as eating within a specific time period an amount of food that is significantly larger than most people would eat during that time period and under similar circumstances. For example, most people tend to overeat at affairs, holiday parties, and at buffets. However, most people would not eat 13 donuts, 2 slices of cake, and many chocolates at one sitting. Bulimic do not see binges as unusual; however, if this is so, why do they typically binge in secret?

Binges are not enough to diagnose someone as having Bulimia Nervosa. For the author, the following two criteria are critical. The woman must engage in recurrent inappropriate compensatory behavior, in other words, self-induced vomiting; misuse of diuretics (drugs that increase urine discharge), laxatives, or enemas (these are all examples of *purging* behaviors); fasting; or excessive or unusual amounts of exercise (such as exercising at least 3 hours a day; APA, 2000). The *DSM-IV-TR* does not behaviorally define *excessive* or *misuse*, which can be somewhat problematic.

Next, the binging and purging (or other compensatory behavior) must occur at least two times per week over a 3-month period. The time frame here is much narrower than many of the disorders discussed in this book. Thus, more women should be receiving the diagnosis of Bulimia Nervosa, and research does indeed support this (Lucas, Crowson, O'Fallon, & Melton, 1999). This smaller time frame also allows more women to get treated for Bulimia Nervosa that, if left untreated, may lead to death.

The woman must next have her body weight and shape unduly influence her self-evaluation (APA, 2000). In other words, she thinks she is overweight no matter what her shape and weight. What is interesting is that bulimic women often do not examine themselves naked or only wearing underwear in a full-length mirror because they are afraid of what they might see. They also do not often weigh themselves because they are even more afraid of the weight that will appear on the scale. These women place extreme and excessive emphasis on body weight and shape. Much of what they do each day is centered on their diet and their weight. Their sense of self-worth and self-esteem is linked too closely to appearance and weight. Does this criterion fit anyone you know?

Finally, this disturbance (Bulimia Nervosa) does not occur solely during episodes of Anorexia Nervosa (APA, 2000). Helping professionals need to distinguish between Bulimia Nervosa and Anorexia Nervosa; at times that may be difficult. It is critical to differentiate, however, as treatment modali-

DON'T FORGET

In the United States, it seems to be rather common for young women, especially, to be overly concerned with their weight and their physical appearance. You probably know some women who always watch what they eat even though they do not appear to have a weight problem or are not on medically ordered food restrictions. Thus, is the fourth criterion, the woman's self-evaluation is overly influenced by her body weight and shape, a reasonable diagnostic criterion given the current situation in the United States?

ties (especially medical interventions) differ significantly.

The *DSM-IV-TR* (APA, 2000) divides Bulimia Nervosa into two subtypes. The first is the *purging type,* which is characterized by the regular misuse of laxatives, diuretics, enemas, or self-induced vomiting. The *nonpurging type* is characterized by individuals who compensate by fasting or excessive exercise but *not* by the misuse of laxatives, diuretics, enemas, or self-induced vomiting. The purging subtype is more common and is associated with more psychopathology, especially unipolar depression (Garfinkel et al., 1996; Getzfeld, 1993). Those who have the purging subtype also are more likely to come from dysfunctional families; this often includes child sexual abuse. For definitions of key terms, see Rapid Reference 5.2.

≡ Rapid Reference 5.2

Key Terms to Know

Amenorrhea: Amenorrhea is when a menstruating woman misses at least three consecutive menstrual cycles and is a diagnostic criterion for Anorexia Nervosa (APA, 2000).

Lanugo: Lanugo is a coating of fine body hair that might be noticed on an anorectic's extremities; this occurs when the anorectic is severely undernourished and underweight.

Binge: A binge is eating within a specific time period an amount of food that is significantly larger than most people would eat during that time period and under similar circumstances; this occurs in Bulimia Nervosa and may occur in Anorexia Nervosa.

Purge: A purge occurs after binging; the individual must engage in recurrent inappropriate compensatory behavior, such as self-induced vomiting, misuse of diuretics (drugs that increase urine discharge), laxatives, or enemas. A purge can only occur if the food is somehow forced out of the body.

ETIOLOGIES OF EATING DISORDERS

Unlike many of the other disorders discussed, Anorexia Nervosa and Bulimia Nervosa each seem to have specific causal factors that are unique to each disorder. We will begin by examining Anorexia Nervosa, as it is the rarer of the two disorders. Researchers generally agree that the specific causes of Anorexia Nervosa are not yet known, but they do agree that sociocultural factors play a key role in its etiology as well as in the etiology of Bulimia Nervosa. Let us first examine some of these factors.

Hsu (1990), a well-known researcher in the eating disorder field, discovered some of the following key social characteristics of anorectic women. Anorexia Nervosa is more common in industrialized societies, where thinness for women is seen as an ideal. A more rounded figure is preferred in nonindustrialized societies. Interestingly, in some of these societies, a more rounded body equates with greater wealth. Why is this? If you have a more rounded body, you can obviously afford more food, or afford food in general. This body shape may also imply that the woman is more capable of bearing children, perhaps many children.

As we stated previously, Eating Disorders are much more common among young women than among young men (Hsu, 1990). They tend to strive for high achievement and come from high achieving backgrounds and usually are middle-to upper-middle class Whites. Hsu and others (Wildes, Emery, & Simons, 2001) noted that Eating Disorders such as Anorexia Nervosa may now be crossing racial boundaries. Upper-middle class African Americans may now be grasping on to the concept that thin is in and is an ideal.

What women are doing in the United States (especially young women) are making themselves into what they perceive—and more important, what the media tell them—is an ideal woman. She is rail thin and has little definition.

DON'T FORGET

Marilyn Monroe is still seen as a sexual icon throughout the world, and many people remain obsessed with her. But did you know that by today's standards she would be considered obese? In fact, Monroe's dress size varied from a size 14 to a size 16—plus sizes today. In Ruben's time, women of her shape or larger were considered desirable and sexy (thus the term *Rubenesque*). Today such women appear in comedies, but not on the model's catwalk.

The helping professions can therefore partially implicate the media for the increase of Eating Disorders.

There are a number of psychological causal factors of Eating Disorders. One trait that appears to be common among anorectics is that they tend to be perfectionistic and have obsessive-compulsive tendencies. In addition, anorectics also struggle for control and for perfection with their bodies and, therefore, in their lives. Perhaps the lack of eating (in effect, this might be a type of highly restrictive diet) can be viewed as a way to gain control over their lives and as a way to gain a sense of independence. The anorectic may feel that her weight, and thus her appearance, is the only thing that she can control without parental or other outside influence or interference. Oddly, anything less than perfection is considered to be failure, especially by anorectics.

Hilda Bruch (1982) stated that this issue of trying to gain control is at the core of Eating Disorders, especially Anorexia Nervosa. She discovered in her research that girls and women with Eating Disorders were extremely conforming and very eager to please people, especially their parents. She saw this struggle for control as crossing over into their eating. Their eating behavior and diets were one way in which these women could gain some control from their parents. For an anorectic to succeed at this, she must lose far too much weight and become skeletal. However, this is a sign that she has regained a certain amount of control and has thus attained success. The situation is a bit different for bulimic women as they will always attempt to gain total control over their weight and eating. The difference is that they will always fail.

Bruch (1982) and others (Leon, Fulkerson, Perry, & Early-Zald, 1995) also discuss a curious aspect of Eating Disorders that is known as *introceptive awareness*. This means the individual lacks awareness of internal cues such as various emotional states as well as hunger. This is not surprising as many women who have Eating Disorders also have a comorbid mood disorder, and some believe that being unable to recognize internal cues of sadness, happiness, or anger may indeed be a warning sign of an impending mood disorder. As was stated, Bulimia Nervosa appears to be associated with Major Depressive Disorder and other forms of unipolar depression (Strober & Bulik, 2002). In addition, some research has discovered that bulimic women do not know when they are sated. In fact, their body chemistry may not signal when they are in fact full, and thus they end up binging (Getzfeld, 1993; Mitchell, Laine,

Morley, & Levine, 1986). For whatever reason, cholecystokinin (CCK) levels appear to be dysfunctional in bulimic women. This chemical tells the body when it is full. Mitchell et al. (1986) discovered that these levels are too low in the bulimic women they examined, but they were unable to hypothesize why this was so.

Bruch (2001) also examines psychodynamic perspectives on Anorexia Nervosa. Bruch noted that that girls with Anorexia Nervosa may have problems separating from their families, and they also may have difficulty establishing an identity separate from their family. These young girls are seen as avoiding adulthood and its responsibilities and independence by manifesting Anorexia Nervosa. An interesting perspective views Anorexia Nervosa as the girl's desire to remain just that—a prepubescent girl. Once the weight loss becomes severe, the girl may stop menstruating; her breast size will decrease as will her hips. In fact, this may be an extreme form of regression, a Freudian ego defense mechanism. Finally, Getzfeld (1999) hypothesized that anorectic girls may be engaged in a slow form of suicide, slowly disappearing and wasting away.

Body dissatisfaction is a key factor in both Bulimia Nervosa and Anorexia Nervosa. However, the anorectic is much more concerned with her appearance and is totally dissatisfied with her body shape to point of pathology. In other words, she will continue to starve herself even when her weight is dangerously low "just to lose a bit more" and to appear ever thinner. This can also be seen as culture specific because most Westernized countries (like the United States) place a very high value on a reed-thin body. It has come to the point where Hollywood and fashion designers consider a size 8 to be too large.

Learning theorists view Anorexia Nervosa in a simpler fashion. The chronic weight loss is reinforced by society's demands for rail-thin women and young girls. If an anorectic is complemented on her thin appearance, this will positively reinforce her starvation, and the cycle will continue. She is punished by society when she gains weight and is not noticed or is criticized by significant others for her weight (including her family and friends and, of course, herself).

Finally, we will examine familial factors. Like many of the disorders in this book, Eating Disorders tend to run in families and thus *may* have a genetic component (Hudson, Pope, Jonas, & Yurgelun-Todd, 1983; Strober, Freeman, Lampert, Diamond, & Kaye, 2000). Female relatives are affected more so than are male relatives. Hsu (1990) hypothesizes that certain traits, such as poor impulse control and emotional instability, might be inherited. In other words, the tendency to react poorly to stressful situations and having poor coping skills might be inherited, thus leading to poor coping mechanisms such as an eating disorder. At the least, stress appears to be a precipitating factor in the onset of eating binges.

The major problem with attempting to understand the etiologies of Anorexia Nervosa is that so much still remains a mystery for those in the helping professions. Research continues to try to identify specific causal factors. Once this has occurred, the helping professions should be able to identify more effective treatment modalities.

There are many possible etiologies of Bulimia Nervosa. Like many other mental illnesses, the causes are often multiple and varied. A key causal factor of Bulimia Nervosa remains society's emphasis on a woman's weight and appearance; this was also mentioned as a key factor with Anorexia Nervosa. How many supermodels have truly lifelike bodies? Women and young girls see this, and they see how someone like Cindy Crawford has two children and does not look any different. The same can be said for actresses who have children and then appear on camera 3 weeks later as though they were never pregnant. Imagine the images that these instances portray.

Stice (1994) discovered that Eating Disorders are less common in non-Western countries such as those in parts of Asia and Africa. This has changed recently as Eating Disorders have risen in some of these countries, especially

CAUTION

The View is a highly rated morning television talk show that has also been deemed very influential among women. This show, cohosted by five extremely bright women, had a live segment (in 2005) in which summer swimwear was modeled. All of the models were rail thin, and one appeared to have a pasty white, sickly appearance. One of the models, however, was a plus-size model. Star Jones Reynolds, one of the cohosts and a plus-size woman, noted how real she appeared. What struck this viewer was that out of all of the models, only the plus-size model wore dark sunglasses, hiding her face. This implied that she was ashamed of something. What might a young woman viewing this show think?

in China and in Japan. These countries are extremely *trend conscious,* meaning that if something is trendy, many young people will go along with that trend.

Which psychiatric disorders, if any, appear to be comorbid with Bulimia Nervosa? Common disorders among bulimic women include Alcohol Dependence, Mood Disorders, and Anxiety Disorders. Some researchers hypothesize (and aver) that childhood sexual abuse may contribute to an individual's vulnerability to manifest Bulimia Nervosa. This view is not universally held and is often disputed. What can be stated with a degree of certainty is that Mood Disorders, specifically unipolar depression, appear to be comorbid with Bulimia Nervosa (Getzfeld, 1993).

Most women suffering from Bulimia Nervosa have a history of extreme or very rigid dieting (Hunicutt & Newman, 1983; Patton, Selzer, Coffey, Carlin, & Wolfe, 1999). In addition, these women exercise often, and they tend to be extremely restrictive as to what they actually eat. In some instances, these women will not eat much in public; binging almost always occurs in private, if possible, as does purging.

Female athletes, especially in sports where weight gain is considered a reason to be thrown off of a team or squad, are much more susceptible to Eating Disorders such as Bulimia Nervosa. Ballet dancers are particularly at risk, where gaining as little as 5 pounds can be considered a career-ending situation (Abraham, 1996; Garner, Garfinkel, Rockert, & Olmsted, 1987). Oftentimes female ballet dancers are publicly mocked, berated, and humiliated if they gain too much weight. One way to look at this is that ballet requires precise control, and bulimia (and anorexia) will often involve control issues.

The behavioral explanation, as you might surmise, is rather simplistic. The purging or nonpurging behaviors are reinforced by the extreme fear of gaining weight. As weight is lost through these techniques, these techniques then become reinforcers, making it more likely that the purging behaviors will continue. Purging especially leads to relief and to anxiety reduction, thus further reinforcing the purging behavior.

Some research has discovered that Eating Disorders may have a familial component, especially among females (Strober et al., 2000). Some researchers believe that women who develop Eating Disorders do so to punish their families for being too harsh, too demanding, or too cold and distant. What can be said with some certainty is that bulimic and anorectic women gener-

> **DON'T FORGET**
>
> The FDA approved the prescription of Prozac (fluoxetine) for the treatment of Bulimia Nervosa in 1996. This was a critical decision as it supported the connection between unipolar depression and Bulimia Nervosa.

ally have issues with their parents and families, and their families have a significant amount of intrafamilial conflicts (Fairburn, Welch, Doll, Davies, & O'Connor, 1997; Getzfeld, 1993).

Cognitive factors have been touched on briefly. Bulimic women tend to be perfectionists and to never go off of their diets; if they do and they gain even 1 pound, they see themselves as total failures and will often try even harder to control their eating. Bulimic women also exaggerate and distort the consequences if they do gain any weight.

Finally, what about potential biological etiologies for Bulimia Nervosa? Low levels of serotonin activity have been linked to Bulimia Nervosa, especially to binge eating of carbohydrates. Low serotonin levels have also been associated with impulsive behavior, of which binging and purging should be included. Research has demonstrated that there is a link between low serotonin levels and the presence of Mood Disorders, specifically unipolar depression. A link has also been posited between Bulimia Nervosa and Mood Disorders (depressions), but many in the field are unsure which condition manifests itself first (Getzfeld, 1993). This link can be substantiated by the fact that antidepressants that work to increase serotonin activity in the brain will, in many instances, reduce or eliminate bulimic symptoms (Getzfeld, 1993; Johnson, Tsoh, & Varnado, 1996).

TREATMENT MODALITIES

Like Substance-Related Disorders, the successful treatment of Anorexia Nervosa and Bulimia Nervosa is difficult and can be quite frustrating. Women who have Anorexia Nervosa are much more likely to relapse than those who have Bulimia Nervosa. Some treatment professionals prefer to say that these women, while in treatment, are recovering, the implication being that these disorders are controllable but not curable. We will follow this line of thinking in this chapter.

As with the Substance-Related Disorders, the ego defense mechanism of

denial is a key component and becomes a major treatment obstacle.
Because of this, compliance tends
to be rather low, and recidivism and
drop-out rates tend to be high. This
is more prevalent with Anorexia
Nervosa.

Anorexia Nervosa's treatment
includes two foci. First, the initial
goal is usually to get the individual
to gain back a certain amount of
weight to attempt to normalize her

CAUTION

While by our definition Eating
Disorders (and other disorders
discussed previously and to follow)
are incurable, this does *not* mean
that they are untreatable. What this
does mean is that the patient needs
to realize that his or her disorder is
chronic and that he or she always
needs to be on the alert for potential relapse cues.

eating patterns. The weight gain should be gradual, with a target being about
2 to 3 pounds per week. There are several reasons for this. Psychologically,
rapid weight gain might spook the woman, and she might drop out of treatment. In effect, the treatment goal would be acting as a punisher! The APA
(2000) also notes that if weight gain is rapid, the individual might suffer from
constipation, abdominal pain, and bloating. The reason for this? The human
body cannot tolerate rapid weight gain. In more extreme instances, the anorectic needs to be force-fed. This is especially true when denial is extremely
strong with the individual. This aspect of treatment typically takes place on
an inpatient unit so that the weight restoration can be medically controlled
and supervised.

The second goal of treatment is to work on the psychological, social, and
environmental issues that may either have caused or are somehow maintaining the disorder and thus are interfering with recovery. Many studies note
that family therapy appears to be one of the more successful treatment modalities for Anorexia Nervosa. Family therapy seems to be most successful
with young girls who have only had Anorexia Nervosa for a relatively short
period of time. The core problem is presumed to be the parents' disagree-
ments (and perhaps denial) of the adolescent woman's desire for autonomy.
Mealtimes and thoughts about food and weight are presumed to be dysfunctional within the anorectic's family and are focused upon in treatment. Family attitudes toward body shape are also discussed. Any underlying conflicts
will be discussed as well.

Cognitive interventions focus on replacing the negative thoughts that maintain the Anorexia Nervosa. For example, the anorectic might think, "I can still lose more weight. Cripes, I look like Santa Claus or a Sumo wrestler. I'm too bloody fat." The psychologist would attempt to replace these thoughts with positive thoughts that emphasize a positive outlook and work on the concept that weight and thinness should not serve as the sole reference and determinant of the woman's self-worth. We would also work on getting the individual to emphasize the nonphysical aspects of herself, turning focus away from the body and its shape.

A somewhat newer modality is the *feminist perspective,* which focuses on getting the woman to pursue her own values and roles and not be blindly driven by (or into) those that society thinks she *should* have or those that society thinks she should demonstrate (Fallon, Katzman, & Wooley, 1994). Finally, Bruch (1982) would work on increasing the woman's introceptive awareness, as we have already mentioned.

Psychoanalysts might take an interesting perspective on Anorexia Nervosa. Freud and other analysts might state that Anorexia Nervosa is a form of regression. In effect, by losing so much weight, they lose their curves and breasts, and they contract amenorrhea. Thus, they physically appear to be prepubescent, and physiologically they, in fact, become prepubescent. Freud and other analysts might also point to these women having unresolved Electra complexes, thus leading to dysfunctional relationships with their fathers. This eventually leads the woman to seek some semblance of control in her life, and her eating behavior is, for her, the best solution. In addition, by starving herself and slowly committing suicide, she is also indirectly getting back at her family, especially her father (Getzfeld, 1999).

Self-help groups can also prove to be useful. The American Anorexia Bulimia Association (AABA; http://www.aabcinc.org), is a national nonprofit organization that functions similarly to AA, the most prominent self-help group. These support groups do not provide therapy but instead offer support for the individuals who attend; attendance is anonymous. Additionally, there are no membership fees or costs.

Most professionals agree that medications should not be used in the treatment of Anorexia Nervosa as they tend to be rather ineffective. Because many anorectics are severely underweight, potential medication side effects could be more pronounced, leading to significant complications. For example,

TCAs may lead to heart arrhythmias, which can potentially lead to cardiac arrest. Antidepressants in general seem to be ineffective in treating Anorexia Nervosa (Bezchlibnyk-Butler & Jeffries, 2005; Vitousek, 2002).

Fortunately, the treatment of Bulimia Nervosa is much more effective. This may be due to several reasons. Bulimia Nervosa is more common and thus may have led to more research being conducted. Medications, specifically antidepressants (especially the SSRIs like Prozac and Zoloft) have proved to be quite effective in reducing or eliminating the symptoms. Some helping professionals also believe that the degree of pathology with bulimic individuals is not as severe as is that with anorectic individuals. For example, when some bulimic women come into treatment, they realize that something is not right with their behaviors. Anorectics will tell you that they need to lose even more weight as they have difficulty standing up without feeling lightheaded because they are so malnourished.

Standard practice when treating Bulimia Nervosa suggests using the treatment modalities of individual and family therapy (Eisler et al., 1997). One well-researched and quite effective modality is cognitive behavioral therapy. This modality typically focuses on teaching ways to resist the binge-purge impulses and notice the warning signs. Christopher Fairburn (1985), a major researcher in the field of bulimia, created a three-step approach to treat Bulimia Nervosa. First, an eating plan is set up where many small meals a day are eaten, with no more than 3 hours between any meal. This planned eating schedule will eliminate the bouncing back and forth between periods of overeating and purging (or restriction) that occur with Bulimia Nervosa (Fairburn, 1985). Next, the psychologist will examine the dysfunctional cognitions (or beliefs) that the bulimic has about her appearance and dieting behaviors. Cognitive restructuring may be used at this point. Finally, the psychologist will prepare her for potential relapses and instruct her how to handle them. She or he will also work with the individual to help her develop realistic beliefs and expectations about eating and weight-related issues. Research has demonstrated that these techniques lead at least one-third of bulimic individuals to eliminate the bulimic symptoms (Agras, Walsh, Fairburn, Wilson, & Kraemer, 2000).

Interpersonal therapy may also be effective. The goal here is to focus on the individual's current relationships, with particular focus on the family.

Communication and problem-solving skills are worked on in order to improve the individual's interpersonal relationships. Fairburn, Jones, Peveler, Hope, and O'Connor (1993) examined this modality but not as an experimental variable. They instead set out to measure the effectiveness of their cognitive behavioral methods, and they decided to use interpersonal therapy as a placebo treatment. What was most interesting is that, initially, interpersonal therapy was not nearly as effective as cognitive behavioral therapy. However, in a longitudinal follow up 12 months later, many in the interpersonal group continued to improve. Those who received cognitive behavioral therapy remained stable over the course of the 12 months. What was most interesting was that those in the third condition, behavioral therapy, deteriorated, and many dropped out of their treatment group. Fairburn et al. (1993) recommend interpersonal therapy as a secondary line of treatment for Bulimia Nervosa.

We will conclude this section by examining which medications might be effective in treating Bulimia Nervosa. Research has discovered that antidepressant medications are quite effective in reducing bulimic symptoms (see, for example, Wilson et al., 1999). These can be SSRIs, such as Prozac (fluoxetine), Zoloft (sertraline), and Paxil (paroxetine), or standard TCAs, such as Norpramin (desipramine). Another class of antidepressants, MAOIs, have also proven to be somewhat effective. Drugs in this class include Nardil (phenelzine) and Parnate (tranylcypromine). There is a problem with this subclass of antidepressants. If the individual is taking MAOIs, she needs to be on a tyramine-free diet. This means that they need to avoid foods that contain tyramine such as aged cheeses, some beers, fava beans, and sauerkraut. As you might imagine, it is not easy to tell a bulimic to watch what they eat while they are binging. One possible side effect of being on MAOIs while ingesting tyramine foods is death.

Antidepressants alter the brain's chemistry, and SSRIs inhibit the reuptake of serotonin, leading to a buildup of serotonin at neuronal synapses in the brain. Serotonin is involved in the regulation of appetite, mood, sleep, and sex drive. All of these are disrupted in bulimic individuals as well as depressed individuals. Because antidepressants are quite effective in reducing bulimic symptoms, there is a hypothesized relationship between bulimia and depression. The problem, however, is determining which causes which:

bulimia or depression? Apparently the two disorders are related, but this relationship, and the causal relationship between the two, is still under investigation. Psychotherapy remains the most important treatment modality, but using antidepressants as a treatment adjunct appears to be effective and appears to lead to a higher success ratio (Walsh et al., 1997).

In sum, what can be confidently stated about the treatment of Anorexia Nervosa and Bulimia Nervosa? First, treatment success is more likely and is greater for Bulimia Nervosa than for Anorexia Nervosa. Anorexia Nervosa generally does not respond well to treatment, leaves the individual more prone to relapse, and has a higher mortality rate. Bulimic individuals have greater success at maintaining an appropriate weight for their size and, in general, have fewer relapses (Keel & Mitchell, 1997). Antidepressants have been effective in reducing or eliminating bulimic symptoms, while no effective medication(s) exist—yet—for the treatment of Anorexia Nervosa. Finally, as was stated anecdotally, the bulimic woman's pathology does not appear to be as severe as that of the anorectic woman. They tend to follow through more often with treatment and are often more willing to be introspective and cooperative in therapy. Regardless, both remain fascinating disorders that hopefully will continue to attract research, and hopefully even more effective treatment modalities, in the future. For definitions of key terms, see Rapid Reference 5.3.

≡ Rapid Reference 5.3

Key Terms to Know

Feminist Perspective: This perspective focuses on getting the anorectic individual to pursue her own values and roles and not be blindly driven by (or into) those roles that society thinks she should have, such as being rail thin.

The American Anorexia Bulimia Association (ABBA): This is a national support group for anorectics and bulimics; it functions similarly to AA.

Interpersonal Therapy: This is a treatment modality for Bulimia Nervosa; the goal is to focus on the individual's current relationships, with particular focus on the family.

Putting It Into Practice

The Case of Lisa Dieter

Lisa is a 25-year-old Caucasian female who is a graduate student in the helping professions at a major university. Lisa came to us as a voluntary self-referral because "her eating and dieting issues have been causing her stomach to be extremely upset lately. I have no idea what's going on, but my ex-boyfriend told me that my eating habits are weird. Well, maybe, but they still work for me." In addition, Lisa's dentist also strongly suggested that she come in to see us as he noticed that the enamel on many of her teeth displayed significant erosion; this was not from decay. He suspected that she had an eating disorder, and he wanted her to be evaluated.

We asked Lisa about her dental problems. Dentists are often the first professionals to discover a bulimic individual because they (more than anyone else) look at the backs of a person's teeth. Constant purging (vomiting) will erode the enamel of the tooth's back. "Yeah, I've got teeth problems, but I eat lots and lots of sweets. I just need to cut down on the sweets is all."

Lisa openly described her weight control techniques to us and was proud of the fact that they worked quite well. Lisa has been making herself throw up (or purge) since she was "twelve years old, give or take a year or so, but certainly no younger than eleven. At first I used a toothbrush or the old finger-down-the-throat technique, but now I can do it on demand, only if I think about it. It's helped me to control my weight, and I only do it, like, four times a week, although when I began I was only doing it about twice a week. I realized that the more often I did this, the better my weight would be, so I increased the number of times per week. Hey, it's healthier than cigarettes, and I still eat—a lot, which means that I can't have a disorder, because in those you only starve yourself. I know all about that. So many of my friends eat a ton and then vomit it back up. It's how we stay in shape. What grad student has time to go to the gym every day?"

We can already see that Lisa's binges and purges fulfill three *DSM-IV-TR* diagnostic criteria for Bulimia Nervosa: The binges and inappropriate compensatory behavior (i.e., the purges) are present and occur regularly, and both binges and purges have occurred at least twice a week for at least 3 months.

Lisa told us that she would normally eat about 3,400 calories at one time (this is a binge), but "I get the hungries, just like anyone. My body is abnormal, as it gets hungrier than most. I'm big, pretty big butt really, but I'm not morbidly obese, not yet anyway." We asked Lisa, who is 5 feet 7 inches what she weighed, and she told us "probably about one hundred thirty-five now if I looked. I haven't checked since this morning. I'm still not in the best of shape, and that makes me feel like crap." Bulimics will be preoccupied with their body weight and shape, as Lisa demonstrates.

Finally, Lisa's family fits the classic eating disorder profile. Her father is an executive who earns in the high six figures, and her mother is a nurse who works in the emergency room. "I get tons of pressure to succeed, not to let my parents down. They expect at least a doctoral degree from me, and I'll tell you, I've already had enough of school. My master's degree will be it." Typically bulimic individuals come from high achieving white-collar, professional families.

Thus, Lisa binges and purges approximately four times a week and has been doing so for many years, and she sees nothing odd about these actions. In fact, we can safely state that Lisa is in denial about her eating problems as these actions are obviously unusual for many people. Based on her regular binging and purging lasting for at least 13 years and her preoccupation with her weight and body shape, we arrived at the following diagnoses:

Axis I: Bulimia Nervosa, Purging Type   307.51
Axis II: No Diagnosis   V71.09
Axis III: None
Axis IV: Discord with Parents
Axis V: GAF = 60 (Current)

Treatment Plan

We concluded that Lisa was bulimic because her binge-purge cycles occurred at least twice a week for at least 3 months; this was corroborated by Lisa. In addition, Lisa told us that she saw nothing wrong with her bulimic behaviors as a method of weight control. We admitted Lisa to the clinic; she agreed to engage in therapy with us even though she saw nothing wrong with her behavior. We then engaged Lisa's parents in family therapy with her and also engaged Lisa in individual therapy to work on her bulimia. We asked her to keep an eating diary, keeping careful track of what she ate each day and when, and if she binged or purged. The time of day is critical as possible situational cues could be setting off her binge-purge cycles. We also asked Lisa to weigh herself, initially at least once a week and then more often. We needed to find out if her weight was fluctuating, and we also wanted her to get in touch with her actual weight and with her body. Most of Lisa's binges consisted of junk food, ice cream, and other high carbohydrate foods. This is typical for most bulimic individuals.

We also used a cognitive treatment modality, focusing on teaching Lisa ways to resist the binge-purge impulses and helping her to notice the warning signs. We mentioned that she should not be alone after eating so as to forestall any binging or purging behaviors. We discussed dieting and how binging

(continued)

and purging do not lead to successful weight control. We also supplied photos of teeth badly damaged by binging and purging. Lisa was quite shocked when she saw these photos as she "had no idea that's what can happen. No wonder my dentist was concerned."

Following Fairburn (1985), we set up an eating plan where Lisa would have many small meals a day, with no more than 3 hours between meals. This planned eating schedule will eliminate the bouncing back and forth between periods of overeating and purging that occur with Bulimia Nervosa and with Lisa. Finally, Lisa was given Prozac (fluoxetine), an SSRI antidepressant that helps to alleviate (and in some cases eliminate) the binge-purge cycle and symptoms. Once the medication took effect, it worked extremely well for Lisa, who reported only three binge-purge episodes in a 5-month period, "all occurring when I was totally, like, stressed out. Usually it's guys, school, or the parents."

Lisa was making good progress until her parents dropped out of therapy, leaving Lisa in individual therapy. She remained on her Prozac and continued to avoid binging and purging until the end of the academic year arrived. Her boyfriend graduated and moved to Europe, and Lisa could not afford to visit him. Upset by this, she did poorly on her finals and was told she had to repeat some of her major requirements. She then stopped taking her Prozac and told us "I'll come back during the fall semester. I don't have time for analysis right now." Once the fall arrived we received a letter that she had dropped out of the university. That was the last we heard from her.

🐟 TEST YOURSELF 🐟

I. Amenorrhea
  (a) refers to a woman who is already menstruating missing at least three consecutive menstrual cycles.
  (b) is used by some anorectic women as a sign of success.
  (c) is a *DSM-IV-TR* diagnostic criterion for Anorexia Nervosa.
  (d) is all of the above.

2. In a binge episode
  (a) the individual must engage in recurrent inappropriate compensatory behavior, such as self-induced vomiting or misuse of laxatives.
  (b) the individual eats, within a specific time period, an amount of food that is significantly larger than most people would eat during that time period and under similar circumstances.
  (c) one only sees its presence in Bulimia Nervosa.
  (d) one sees none of the above.

3. **In a purge episode**
   (a) the individual must engage in recurrent inappropriate compensatory behavior, such as self-induced vomiting or misuse of laxatives.
   (b) the individual eats, within a specific time period, an amount of food that is significantly larger than most people would eat during that time period and under similar circumstances.
   (c) one only sees its presence in Bulimia Nervosa.
   (d) one sees none of the above.

4. **Most bulimics are significantly underweight and are considered human skeletons.** True or False?

5. **Which of the following medications can successfully treat the symptoms of Bulimia Nervosa?**
   (a) Prozac (fluoxetine)
   (b) Zoloft (sertraline)
   (c) Thorazine (chlorpromazine)
   (d) Both a and b

6. **The primary goal of treating an anorectic individual is**
   (a) to get the individual to gain back a certain amount of weight to attempt to normalize her eating patterns.
   (b) to put her on Prozac immediately to get her to eat.
   (c) to use psychodynamic treatment to help her resolve her parental conflicts.
   (d) to support her anorectic behaviors as the reasons for them are valid.

7. **Typically, Bulimia Nervosa is comorbid with**
   (a) Schizophrenia, Disorganized Type.
   (b) Bipolar I Disorder.
   (c) unipolar depression.
   (d) PTSD.

8. **Bulimia Nervosa and Anorexia Nervosa are disorders unique to the United States.** True or False?

Answers: 1. d; 2. b; 3. a; 4. False; 5. d; 6. a; 7. c; 8. False

Six

ESSENTIALS OF SEXUAL AND GENDER IDENTITY DISORDERS

When many people first see the term *Sexual Disorders,* most people have the immediate association of impotence, technically called *male erectile dysfunction.* The second most common association is most likely Female Orgasmic Disorder, which is still popularly (and incorrectly) called *female frigidity.* One of the problems with these disorders is that many individuals are reluctant to discuss sexual issues with helping professionals. What goes on in the bedroom (or elsewhere) is to remain there. Compounding this issue is the fact that some helping professionals still remain uncomfortable discussing sexual issues with patients. If you fall into either of these two categories, hopefully you will become more comfortable after reading this chapter.

The *DSM-IV-TR* (APA, 2000) lists the prevalence rates of sexual and gender identity disorders as ranging from 3 percent for those suffering from male dyspareunia (painful male intercourse) to 33 percent for female hypoactive sexual desire disorder. The disparity is interesting but not terribly surprising, given what we just stated. Agreed, Male Erectile Disorder is more readily discussed today, simply because of Viagra (sildenafil citrate). However, just as many jokes have been made about Viagra and male erectile dysfunction as have been made about the current U.S. president. Instead of properly addressing how debilitating this condition can be, many people choose to joke about the matter. This again shows our discomfort in discussing these topics.

Sexual and gender identity disorders are divided into four categories in the *DSM-IV-TR.* We will focus on two of these categories: *Sexual Dysfunctions,* whose key characteristic is a disturbance in sexual desire; and the *Paraphilias,* sometimes known as *fetishes.* The Paraphilias are characterized by sexual urges that involve unusual objects or activities. The other two categories are Gender Identity Disorder, which occurs when the patient is uncomfortable with his or her assigned sex, and Sexual Disorders Not Otherwise Specified (APA, 2000). Typically, the last category is used until one of two events occurs: The helping professional gathers enough additional information in order to make a more definitive diagnosis, or the helping professional cannot gather enough information to make a conclusive diagnosis. By using the Not Otherwise Specified category, the helping professional can at least ensure that the patient qualifies for services, if not insurance reimbursements.[1]

SYMPTOMS OF SEXUAL DYSFUNCTIONS

Sexual Dysfunctions can be subdivided into three categories. Interestingly, having a diagnosis in one category can cause problems in either (or both) of the other two categories! Sexual Desire Disorders include Sexual Aversion Disorder, where the individual reports fear, anxiety, or disgust at the prospect of a sexual encounter. This may indeed be an aversion to all sexual activity (such as intercourse, fellatio, cunnilingus, as well as kissing and fondling), or it may be limited to the genitalia. In this case, the aversion may be focused on vaginal or anal penetration, genital secretions, and so on.

Sexual Arousal Disorders tend to be more common, or at least better known by the general public. These occur during the arousal phase of sexual excitement (as defined by Masters and Johnson). For men this means that they cannot get an erection or they are unable to maintain an erection until intercourse has been obtained (i.e., penile insertion). This is known as *erectile dysfunction* (or ED).

For women, inhibited sexual arousal means that the vagina is not properly lubricated for penile insertion. While insertion can occur without vaginal lubrication, it would most likely be quite painful. The problem becomes exacerbated if the woman continues to attempt to have intercourse without the proper lubrication. She may eventually develop

> **DON'T FORGET**
> ....
> Erectile dysfunction is commonly known as impotence. Psychologists do not use this term because it is technically incorrect, and because it is considered pejorative.

---

[1] For the remainder of this chapter only, we will presume that whenever the word *couples* is used, these couples are heterosexual.

CAUTION

There are many physiological conditions that can lead to a Sexual Desire Disorder. For example, diabetes may cause nerve damage and nerve deadening in the genitalia, thus leading to decreased sensitivity and therefore making it difficult to achieve orgasm.

Hypoactive Sexual Desire Disorder, where sexual desire may be completely suppressed. Usually the individual will report the problems to the psychologist, but both members of a couple may also report the problem. However, each member may view the problem differently. It is the role of the psychologist to accurately determine what is actually occurring and to devise the most effective treatment modality.

The second group includes *Orgasmic Disorders*. For men, this manifests itself as *Premature Ejaculation* or as delayed or absent ejaculation. For women, this manifests itself as delayed or absent orgasms after normal sexual excitation. Premature Ejaculation is typically defined as the male being unable to delay ejaculation long enough for the female (assuming heterosexuality) to achieve orgasm through intercourse. We prefer to generalize this and expand the definition as follows: The male cannot delay ejaculation long enough to either achieve intercourse (intromission) or cannot delay long enough for the woman to achieve a reasonable amount of pleasure. Some clinicians believe that this is the most common type of male sexual dysfunction, and we are inclined to agree. However, ED has received a lot more publicity, and now it is seen as okay to discuss this with a medical doctor or with close friends. We attribute this to the tremendous amount of press that Viagra (sildenafil citrate) has received in the past few years.

CAUTION

Premature Ejaculation can have a variety of causes which will be examined a bit later in this chapter. What psychologists need to remember is that, regardless of the cause(s), Premature Ejaculation can lead to ED, most likely because of the psychological problems it can create. At the least, the male may feel sexually inadequate, and if this preoccupies him in the midst of sexual behavior, ED could occur.

A less common problem for men is *Retarded Ejaculation*, which is exactly as it sounds. Ejaculation is inhibited in males, even though they will respond to sexual stimuli and to sexual stimulation, and they will achieve an erection. Once again, physical causes need to be ruled out by a medical doctor before successful psychotherapy can be performed. Women suffer from *Female Orgasmic Disorder*, which is defined as either being unable to attain orgasm or having a delay in achieving orgasm following sexual stimulation or sexual excitement. Clinicians should again keep in mind that any physiological causes need to be ruled out before psychotherapy can begin. Clinicians also need to remember that other *DSM-IV-TR* diagnoses may contribute to this condition. For example, people who suffer from unipolar depression may have sexual difficulties, ranging from a lack of desire to mechanical problems (ED) or Orgasmic Disorders.

The last category of sexual dysfunction include the Sexual Pain Disorders. Women, and to a lesser degree men, can suffer from Dyspareunia (Not due to a General Medical Condition). This is defined as experiencing pain in the genitals (penis or vagina) before, during, and after sexual intercourse. A related condition that affects only women is called Vaginismus (Not due to a General Medical Condition). Intercourse is difficult or impossible because the outer part of the vagina (typically the outer third) experiences involuntary muscle contractions. Thus intromission of the penis into the vagina becomes difficult if not impossible. For definitions of key terms, see Rapid Reference 6.1.

≡ *Rapid Reference 6.1*

Key Terms to Know

Sexual Dysfunctions: This is a subcategory of Sexual Disorders; a key characteristic is a disturbance in sexual desire.

Paraphilias: This is a subcategory of Sexual Disorders, sometimes known as fetishes; it is characterized by sexual urges that involve unusual objects or activities.

Gender Identity Disorder: This is a subcategory of Sexual Disorders; a key criterion is that the patient is uncomfortable with his or her assigned sex.

Erectile Dysfunction (ED): ED occurs when the man cannot get an erection or the man is unable to maintain an erection until intercourse has been obtained (i.e., penile insertion); it is sometimes known as impotence.

Premature Ejaculation: This is when the male is unable to delay ejaculation long enough for the female to achieve orgasm through intercourse.

Dyspareunia: This is a sexual pain disorder; it is defined as experiencing pain in the genitals (penis or vagina) before, during, and after sexual intercourse.

Vaginismus: This is a sexual pain disorder; intercourse is difficult or impossible because the outer part of the vagina (typically the outer third) experiences involuntary muscle contractions, making intromission of the penis into the vagina difficult if not impossible.

SYMPTOMS OF THE PARAPHILIAS

The Paraphilias involve special sexual practices such as sadism and masochism, the use of special sexual devices and props, and unusual masturbatory practices. Most of the Paraphilias are acted upon alone (they usually involve masturbation) or with a consenting partner and, while seemingly unusual to the layperson or average individual, usually cause no harm to the primary individual or to other people. However, if the partner is nonconsenting or is not of a legal age or if the sex practices involve force, then the Paraphilias can indeed cause harm, in some cases serious harm.

Some hypothesize that unusual sexual practices stem from boredom of traditional sex (or boredom with the partner) or out of curiosity. The famous sports broadcaster Marv Albert once noted that when he was involved with transvestic behaviors, he was in a "curious period" of his life. In this instance, curiosity almost destroyed a storied career. The same can occur to anyone who engages in the Paraphilias.

The *DSM-IV-TR* (APA, 2000) states that the essential features of a Paraphilia include sexually arousing fantasies, sexual urges, or behaviors that involve one of the following three categories: nonhuman objects (such as phallic-shaped objects); the suffering or the humiliation of one's partner (sadism or masochism, to name two; the suffering may be real or may be simulated); and repetitive sexual activity involving children or other nonconsenting adults over a period that lasts at least 6 months (p. 566). The *DSM-IV-TR* considers the duration of the fantasies that must be evident for at least 6 months (this time period, as you have seen, is consistent across most *DSM-IV-TR* diagnostic categories) and the level of distress or physical or psychological malfunctioning or impairment that these fantasies or urges cause.

CAUTION

The *DSM-IV-TR* notes (as do we) that diagnosing Paraphilias becomes more difficult when we examine cultures other than that of the United States. That is, what is considered to be deviant in one culture or society might be more acceptable in another culture.

Fetishism

Fetishism involves using nonliving objects to obtain sexual arousal. Some of the more commonly used objects are a woman's underpants, bras, stockings, shoes, boots, or dresses. Typically the individual (almost always male) will masturbate while holding or rubbing the object. He may also ask his partner to wear the object during sexual encounters. What is more interesting is that in the absence of the fetish object, ED may occur. The *DSM-IV-TR* states that Fetishism is not diagnosed when the individual limits the use of clothes to cross-dressing (as in Transvestic Fetishism) or when the fetish object is stimulating because it has been designed for that said purpose, like a vibrator. Fetishes usually begin in adolescence, and once they have been diagnosed they usually follow a chronic course. Most individuals involved with fetishes do so alone, and they generally do not voluntarily go into psychotherapy. Finally, although fetishes have been around for centuries, the cause of this behavior remains unknown.

Sexual Sadism and Masochism

Sexual Sadism involves real acts where the individual gets sexual excitation from the psychological or physical humiliation of the receiving individual, or the victim. These urges must have been recurrent for at least 6 months. Achieving sexual excitation or orgasm depends on the other individual being humiliated or receiving pain (APA, 2000). Some of the individuals are bothered by these fantasies, which may occur during sexual excitation and sexual activity but otherwise are not carried out; thus, they remain fantasies. However, the partner (victim) may be terrified of the anticipated act, especially if it involves total control and domination. In other instances, the sexual sadist will have a partner who willingly acts with him or her; she or he may suffer from Sexual Masochism. Finally, some sexual sadists may act out their fantasies on unwilling partners or victims. Typical sadistic fantasies involve dominance over the partner or victim, and the sadistic fantasies were most likely present during the individual's childhood. Usually the sexually sadistic activities appear during early adulthood,

CAUTION

The *DSM-IV-TR* (APA, 2000) takes care to note that if Sexual Sadism is severe and is associated with Antisocial Personality Disorder (to be discussed in Chapter 8), the sexually sadistic individual may either seriously injure or kill the victim or partner.

and the disorder is usually chronic in its course. In general, the sadistic acts increase in severity over the years.

Sexual Masochism is very different from Sexual Sadism, yet oftentimes the two are linked. During sexual excitation or during sexual contact, the individual is humiliated, beaten, bound, or otherwise involved in receiving pain or suffering. For the masochist, she or he is typically bound, that is, tied up or unable to escape the situation. Like Sexual Sadism, some sexual masochists are bothered by their fantasies, and they may appear, but are not acted upon (i.e., acted out), during sexual activity. In this situation the fantasies usually involve rape without any possibility of escape. Some may act on these fantasies privately; usually these would include self-mutilation, sticking themselves with pins, or giving themselves electric shocks. Finally, if a partner is involved, the acts might include restraint, blindfolding, spanking, whipping, cutting, and humiliation (such as being urinated or defecated on, being forced to act like a dog, and so on; APA, 2000).

Two other interesting examples of Sexual Masochism are *infantilism* and *hypoxyphilia*. Infantilism involves the victim's desire to be treated as an infant and to be wearing diapers. Hypoxyphilia is a dangerous act. The victim achieves sexual arousal by oxygen deprivation. This can occur via strangulation, using a plastic bag or a mask, to name a few methods. Of course, mistakes here can lead to serious injury, brain damage, or death (APA, 2000).

As with Sexual Sadism, this Paraphilia usually has its onset during early adulthood with the fantasies present during childhood. The urges must have been recurrent over a 6 month time frame. Sexual Masochism tends to be chronic once it appears, and the acts may increase in severity, eventually leading to serious injury or to death. Both Sexual Sadism and Sexual Masochism are not well understood, and their etiologies remain unclear.

DON'T FORGET

Based on the *DSM-IV-TR*'s definition of Sexual Masochism, it appears that individuals who have multiple piercings or tattoos may indeed be masochists, if not sexual masochists. Do these individuals get sexual excitation when they are getting tattooed or pierced?

Pedophilia

While many of the Paraphilias are part of the common vernacular and are often discussed, usually in humorous fashion, Pedophilia is a different story. Pedophilia has received a tremendous amount of press the past few years, with good reason. A number of Catholic priests have been found to have sexually abused young children, usually boys. Michael Jackson, who was found Not Guilty of charges involving Pedophilia and child molestation, is another example of a trusted entertainer who, regardless of the court's verdicts, many still believe sexually abused young boys. Pedophilia scares many parents, but like many of the disorders that receive a lot of press, it is misunderstood.

Pedophilia involves sexual activity (not necessarily intercourse) with a pre-pubescent child. The *DSM-IV-TR* states that the child is typically age 13 or younger. The pedophile must be at least 16 and must be at least 5 years older than the child or children, and he or she must either have acted on these sexual urges *or* have been very distressed by them. Usually pedophiles are attracted to children who fall within a specific age range. Some prefer males, some females, and some both. Generally, those that prefer females usually prefer those who are 8 to 10, and those who prefer males prefer the boys to be slightly older. The *DSM-IV-TR* reports that female victims are more common than male victims.

Pedophiles may limit their activity to exposing themselves to the child (sometimes known as *flashing*), touching and fondling the child gently, undressing the child and looking at him or her, or masturbating in front of the child. The behaviors may become more serious and more severe. If this occurs, the pedophile may perform oral sex on the child or attempt to penetrate the child's vagina, anus, or mouth with a foreign object, their fingers, or their penis, all the while using force.

Pedophiles are not the typical "dirty old men in raincoats" who hang around playgrounds and school yards. In fact, they tend to be in their 30s or 40s, are most likely law-abiding citizens, and are often respected in their communities and in the workplace. They usually know their victims, either through friends of the family or through relatives. The pedophilic behaviors usually begin when the child is young and continue until the pedophile is discovered or until the relationship ends for whatever reason(s). A crucial fact is that not

CAUTION

Many pedophiles do not experience significant distress. The APA (2000) notes that experiencing distress about having pedophilic fantasies, urges, or exhibiting pedophilic behaviors is *not* necessary in order to receive a diagnosis of Pedophilia. The APA states that individuals who have a pedophilic arousal pattern and who act on these fantasies or urges with a child qualify for the Pedophilia diagnosis.

all child sex offenders or abusers can be diagnosed with Pedophilia. Pedophiles are sexually aroused by children but display little or no sexual arousal toward adults. We will examine this distinction later on in this chapter.

Pedophiles will explain their behavior when caught (as they rarely voluntarily seek or enter treatment) by stating that their behaviors have educational value for the child or that the child is somehow deriving sexual pleasure from the behaviors. They may even rationalize that the child was sexually provocative and thus was asking for it.

Pedophiles will attempt to lure in children by nonviolent means if they do not know them. They may try to win the trust of the child's mother, perhaps even marry the child's mother, or take in foster children. In extreme instances, they may abduct children. The pedophile may also threaten the child in order to ensure that no disclosure of his activities occurs. The pedophile is usually very attentive to the child's needs so that trust, loyalty, and affection are gained.

Pedophilia usually begins in adolescence, but it may also onset during middle age. The course of the disorder is chronic, and the frequency of the pedophilic behaviors usually increases with increased stress. The recidivism rate for pedophiles who prefer males is twice as high as for those who prefer females. See Rapid Reference 6.2 for definitions of key terms regarding the Paraphilias.

≡ Rapid Reference 6.2

Key Terms to Know

Fetishism: This is a Paraphilia; it involves using nonliving objects to obtain sexual arousal.

Sexual Sadism: This is a Paraphilia; it involves real acts where the individual gets sexual excitation from the psychological or physical humiliation of the receiving individual, or the victim.

Sexual Masochism: This is a Paraphilia; during sexual excitation or during sexual contact, the individual is humiliated, beaten, bound, or otherwise involved in receiving pain or suffering.

Pedophilia: This is a Paraphilia: it involves sexual activity (not necessarily intercourse) with a prepubescent child; the child is typically age 13 or younger; the pedophile must be at least 16 and must be at least 5 years older than the child or children; they must either have acted on these sexual urges or have been very distressed by them.

ETIOLOGIES OF SEXUAL DISORDERS

The Sexual Response Cycle

William Masters, a gynecologist (1915–2001), and Virginia Johnson, a psychologist (1925–), were two sex researchers who examined sexual behaviors of 694 human subjects in a controlled laboratory setting (1966, 1970). Their research was landmark work because, if for no other reason, sexual behavior was scientifically studied; their work also gave support and credence to the treatment of Sexual Dysfunctions and began to attempt to remove their stigma. Masters and Johnson divided the human sexual response into four phases:

1. *The Excitement Phase.* In this stage, the initial signs of sexual arousal begin.
2. *The Plateau Phase.* Physical arousal now intensifies.
3. *The Orgasmic Phase.* Climax (orgasm) and release of sexual tension occurs.
4. *The Resolution Phase.* The individual returns to lower levels of sexual tension and arousal (1966).

Masters and Johnson also noted that humans have a point during the plateau phase called, for lack of a better term, the point of no return. It is at this point that orgasm is inevitable and is irreversible. This is critical because this point is often used as the focal point of certain types of treatments, especially treatments for Premature Ejaculation and for anorgasmic women. We will examine the importance of this period momentarily.

There are many physiological and psychological conditions that can cause Sexual Dysfunctions. Most psychologists and other clinicians view Sexual Dysfunctions as being caused by a combination of physical and psychological factors. In many instances the causes are psychological, but psychologists must rule out any potential physiological causes before treatment proceeds.

DON'T FORGET

William Masters and Virginia Johnson were married in 1971. Johnson started out as Masters's research assistant. In 1993, Masters and Johnson were divorced. This also ended their more than 30-year collaboration in sex research and sex therapy. Masters retired in 1994 and passed away from complications due to Parkinson's Disease in 2001.

Some researchers note that early traumatic sexual experiences can lead to Sexual Dysfunctions. If a woman were a victim of rape or of date rape, she might have a negative viewpoint toward sexual contact later on. It is also possible (and needs to be investigated) that the man or woman (or both) may no longer be physically or emotionally attracted to each other. What may happen is that the partners have difficulty expressing this, so they suffer in silence. This can lead to further communication problems or may foster them if they do not exist.

Feelings of low self-esteem may contribute to sexual dysfunction. Viewing this from the cognitive perspective of Albert Ellis, he would probably state that irrational beliefs and attitudes may lead to Sexual Dysfunctions. For example, the individual might believe that they *must always* be ready to have sex, and they will always orgasm and will always enjoy sex. A woman might also believe that because she has gained some weight since giving birth, she is ugly and unattractive, and she must always be thin and therefore desirable. Thus, by expecting and demanding perfection each time, failure is guaranteed, thus increasing low self-esteem.

Some individuals may feel uneasy about being naked or about showing a partner his or her body. Low self-esteem goes along with this. The individual may have been raised in a background where nudity is considered dirty or wrong, or he or she may have been mocked by his or her parents or caretakers, thus feeling shameful about being nude. Related to this, the individual may worry about being rejected or being criticized during sexual relations. Again, the individual may believe that he or she has to be the superlover, capable of multiple orgasms or, for the male, being able to have intercourse for endless periods of time before ejaculating. If these scenarios do not occur, he or she will be rejected or criticized. The individual may have difficulty expressing him- or herself emotionally or may have difficulty expressing warmth. He or she may be afraid to let go and to cede control, which can lead to a fear of being dominated.

Sex (and intercourse) involves many aspects and can lead to many psychological issues. Sexual intercourse itself can be mechanical, but having an orgasm in the presence of only one (presumably) individual is very personal and intense and involves letting go of inhibitions and ceding control for a few moments.

In order to function sexually, the mind needs to be relatively stress and tension-free, not the easiest task in today's complex world. If you are attempt-ing intercourse while worrying about the impending deadline for your next book, chances are that the encounter will be brief, not be pleasurable, or not occur at all. If the partner cannot achieve an erection, the heterosexual woman might get anxious and upset, exacerbating his situation and thus making a disorder of ED somewhat more likely to occur.

Physiological conditions, such as undiagnosed diabetes, may cause nerve damage and nerve deadening in the genitalia, thus leading to decreased sen-sitivity and therefore making it difficult to achieve orgasm. Undiagnosed hormonal imbalances can also lead to sexual dysfunction. Chronic fatigue syndrome can leave an individual so exhausted that they have little desire for sex (sex does take a physical effort, contrary to some popular myths). Hyper-tension and cardiac issues can also lead to sexual dysfunction. The individual may be so stressed about getting aroused or having an orgasm that it may not occur. The individual fears that this would lead to a stroke or a heart attack, especially if this has already occurred with him or her.

Alcohol usage is interesting. We know that alcohol lowers inhibitions and therefore loosens social restraints; however, it actually interferes with sexual performance because it is a CNS depressant. What is interesting is that even though your desire to have sex increases, physically your performance will suffer. In other words, "The mind is willing while the body is unable." Look-ing at Substance-Related Disorders, chronic Alcohol Dependence can lead to liver and neurological damage. This can cause fertility problems for both men and women, which may be related to the increase of Premature Ejacula-tion in alcohol dependent men. Illicit substances such as cocaine and mari-juana have reputations of increasing sexual performance and sexual desire. Cocaine is an anesthetic and can delay ejaculation, especially if rubbed on the penis; its ability to physically increase sexual desire is questionable.

Psychotropic medications may decrease sexual desire and can cause ad-ditional problems. Antidepressant medications, specifically the SSRIs, can lower sexual desire and cause arousal problems (Bezchlibnyk-Butler & Jef-fries, 2005). Tricyclic antidepressants may also disrupt desire and arousal.

Sexual orgasmic problems have similar etiologies. Premature Ejaculation may lead the man to feel anxiety and may make him feel sexually inadequate (not manly enough to be able to control himself, immature, and so on). He may experience anxiety as he becomes more and more sexually aroused; this

CAUTION

Bernie Zilbergeld (1939–2002), a psychologist and sex researcher, made a distinction between a male's ejaculation and a male's orgasm (1999). Zilbergeld stated that ejaculation is the physical expulsion of seminal fluid, while orgasm is the physiological and psychological pleasure response that occurs, usually during sexual contact.

anxiety may set off the ejaculation and the involuntary orgasm. Again, a physical examination is required to rule out any potential physiological causes that could either be causing or contributing to this problem.

We also discussed Retarded Ejaculation, where a man's ejaculation is inhibited. Physical injuries may again be responsible for either causing or contributing to this problem. Psychological factors that might contribute include ambivalence (or displeasure or dislike) toward the partner or, perhaps, being raised in a very strict religious background that makes the individual feel guilty about having sex. More interestingly, suppressed anger may also lead to this condition. The anger may be directed at the partner; thus, sex (or the withholding of sex) can be used as a weapon.

For women who have Female Orgasmic Disorder, organic factors again need to be ruled out before treatment can occur or continue. If a woman suffers from undiagnosed diabetes or has pelvic cancer, the ability to orgasm remains. Most researchers believe that once a woman learns how to orgasm, she rarely forgets and rarely loses this ability (if something were extremely relaxing and pleasurable for you, would you forget what needed to be done to bring about these feelings?). What *can* lead to this disorder is poor sexual communication, which is not that unusual. Other situations might include difficulties with the woman's partner and their relationship. If the woman suffered from some type of sexual trauma (such as rape), this could also lead to an orgasmic disorder.

One key issue is that the woman may either not be receiving adequate sexual stimulation during said encounters, or the stimulation may be incorrect. The best way to handle this situation is to focus on proper communication between the partners and to make sure that the woman knows and understands her own body. Many times a woman is unaware of her own body's reactions or possible reactions, or she simply does not know her anatomy. All of these things can lead to orgasmic disorder. A critical concern is that a good portion of a woman's genitalia is hidden and is a bit difficult to access. Thus, if

≡ Rapid Reference 6.3

Masters and Johnson's Human Sexual Response Cycle

Excitement Phase: This is the first phase of human sexual response; the initial signs of sexual arousal begin.

Plateau Phase: This is the second phase of human sexual response; physical arousal now intensifies.

Orgasmic Phase: This is the third phase of human sexual response; climax (orgasm) and release of sexual tension occurs.

Resolution Phase: This is the fourth phase of human sexual response; the individual returns to lower levels of sexual tension and arousal (1966).

she is unaware of her genitalia and its structure, it is difficult if not impossible for her to communicate to her partner how to pleasure her to orgasm.

Female Orgasmic Disorder may affect how a woman views her body. She may see it as being dysfunctional because it cannot produce what all of her friends are experiencing (and perhaps exaggerating). Her self-esteem may be affected as well; this may lead to further relationship difficulties. See Rapid Reference 6.3 for a discussion of Masters and Johnson's human sexual response cycle.

DON'T FORGET

Lonnie Garfield Barbach is a clinical social psychologist who wrote an excellent book on female sexuality, *For Yourself: The Fulfillment of Female Sexuality* (2000). In it she writes how many women do not know their own bodies and discusses self-exams of female genitalia using a mirror. We have found this to be an excellent educational activity for women.

ETIOLOGIES OF THE PARAPHILIAS

As we have mentioned, the Paraphilias are poorly understood, and we are not entirely sure what causes Pedophilia and most of the other Paraphilias, such as Sexual Sadism and Sexual Masochism. In addition, the Paraphilias are chronic conditions. When a mental illness is chronic, some in the field (your author included) suspect or search for a biological or biochemical (neurotransmitter, hormone, etc.) etiology. So far, nothing has yet been discovered for the various Paraphilias. Researchers have identified that the Paraphilias are often characterized by repetitiveness. That is, their sexual deviations are repetitive and are involuntary in nature.

Freud would probably see the Paraphilias as a result of unresolved conflicts that occurred during the oral, anal, or phallic stage of development. We suspect that he would see the difficulties occurring during the phallic stage, when heterosexual urges are repressed by the ego. The child desires the opposite sex parent, but this cannot be openly expressed. Thus, the urges are repressed. If the Oedipus or Electra complexes are not properly resolved, the individual may become fixated in the phallic stage of development. Thus, problems may develop because of these scenarios.

The behavioral perspective has some merit and is quite interesting. Sexual deviations (note that some call them options or variances because deviations can be considered to be pejorative) are viewed as being learned in a fashion similar to other behaviors—through reinforcement, punishment, modeling, generalization, and conditioning. The Paraphilia is learned by the individual because in some way it has been reinforced.

One way of interpreting this perspective is by examining the nature of the individual's early sexual fantasies. What may occur is that the individual, through reinforcement via classical or operant conditioning, now associates previously neutral objects with reinforcement. Let us presume that we are seeing an individual that has a fetish for women's shoes, not an uncommon occurrence. Holding and fondling women's shoes produces sexual excitation for the individual and may lead to orgasm. What has occurred, based on the behavioral perspective, is that previously neutral objects have now taken on a reinforcing value. This occurred because the shoes were repeatedly presented while the person was sexually aroused. We can generalize this concept to Pedophilia. Early sexual fantasies, such as having sexual intercourse with little boys or girls, may be paired with sexual arousal and excitation caused by masturbation. This may occur by accident, but the sex drive and its rewards are quite powerful. What then occurs is that the sexual arousal and orgasm (if the fantasies and behaviors lead to this) are associated with the pedophilic fantasies. The sexual arousal and possible orgasm both reinforce the fantasies, so the fantasies of having sex with little girls and boys continues.

We previously mentioned how researchers have identified that the Paraphilias are often characterized by repetitiveness and by involuntariness. You thus might wonder, "Hmmm. Is there any relation between the Paraphilias and OCD?" David Barlow (2002) attempted to examine this possible connection. He posits that many individuals with a Paraphilia have an uncommonly high sex drive. For example, some of the men that he examined and interviewed were found to masturbate as often as four times a day, which in reality is a high number of episodes. Based on these data, Barlow hypothesized that this may be a compulsion used to suppress the obsessions, and therefore the Paraphilias may be related to OCD. Thus, the act of trying to suppress the obsession may in fact increase the compulsion's intensity and frequency.

The Paraphilias can also be viewed from the cognitive perspective. This viewpoint is rather simple, as it views the Paraphilias as substitutes for more socially and sexually appropriate ways to function in everyday society. This perspective would also examine the individual's interpersonal life and, if appropriate, marriage.

Finally, the biological perspective examines the heritability of the Paraphilias and the role (if any) of hormonal functioning. This perspective examines abnormal hormonal functioning, which is presumed to be present in the Paraphilias. In this case, hormone levels are presumed to be abnormally high. Chromosomal abnormalities are also examined as are possible parts of the brain being examined for malfunctions. The critical problem is that we are not sure which comes first. That is, do these abnormalities cause the Paraphilia, are they related to (correlated with) them, are they a result of the Paraphilia, or do they have no relation and perhaps no impact on the Paraphilias? In sum, we are not certain.

Another perspective sees individuals with Paraphilias engaging in their actions because they were sexually abused in childhood. This viewpoint sees these individuals as attempting to reverse the situation in order to achieve a sense of power, dominance, and control. This is to reverse the shame, humiliation, and subversion they experienced as children. By sexually abusing children, they will get, if nothing else, a sense of power.

Generally speaking, the interactionist perspective, seeing the Paraphilias as a combination of heredity, biology, and environment, seems to hold the most promise. This perspective works for some in the helping professions because no one treatment modality is better than another in successfully treating the Paraphilias. We strongly suspect that if treatment occurs, this approach will have a greater percentage of success than the other approaches mentioned.

The major dilemma in psychology is that people with Paraphilias rarely seek out a psychologist's help, especially voluntarily. Because of this the research that *has* been conducted is often specious or flawed. For example, most of the data we have are based on single case study designs (N = 1), which have significant methodological flaws. Research performed without any control groups or control subjects leads to results that are empirically difficult to support.

TREATMENT MODALITIES FOR THE SEXUAL DISORDERS

The most common sexual complaint for women who seek therapy is the inability to reach orgasm. According to Heiman (2000), 25 percent of women studied had significant difficulty reaching orgasm. Psychologists need to remember that Sexual Disorders (not the Paraphilias) usually involve a combination of psychological, physiological, and interpersonal factors and interactions; all of these areas usually contribute to the manifestation of the sexual disorder. We have found that these individuals, whether male or female, suffer from tremendous guilt, shame, self-doubt, anxiety, or embarrassment about their conditions. We have also found, somewhat surprisingly and certainly rather distressingly, that many of these individuals lack information about sexuality and sexual functioning. Therefore, we believe that sex education is one modality that is extremely effective and is mandated.

The first step in effectively treating a sexual dysfunction is to get a detailed medical history and a history of the symptoms of the apparent dysfunction. If the patient has

CAUTION

In order to properly and effectively provide sex education, the clinician needs to be comfortable having candid discussions surrounding these topics. It is therefore critical that the clinician know his or her values before attempting to work with patients who present Sexual Dysfunctions. Thus, if using words such as *penis* and *vagina* or educating a woman about her internal anatomy by using sketches is upsetting to you, you might need to refer anyone with a sexual dysfunction to another clinician.

not had a physical, she or he needs to be referred to a general practitioner or an ob-gyn. We tend to err on the cautious side and thus strongly urge a complete physical, specifically mentioning to the patient that they need to bring up their sexual dysfunction with the doctor as well as all of the symptoms they are experiencing. The psychologist also needs to get a complete alcohol and drug usage history, family history, as well as a history of the patient's sexual development. Research supports psychological and interpersonal relationship therapy (sometimes called couple's or marital therapy) as being the most effective treatment modalities for Sexual Dysfunctions.

In addition, the therapist needs the patient to discuss what occurs during sex, specifically what physical acts occur, for example, only vaginal intercourse, anal intercourse, and so on. Examining the patient's fantasies during sex also proves to be helpful. Finally, we should also examine their expectations that occur during sexual encounters. Generally speaking, a man's expectations do not usually match up with the experiences of his partner, especially if she is female ("Was it as awesome for me as it was for you?" [Long pause] "No. . . .").

With the Sexual Dysfunctions, couple's therapy is the preferred modality as Sexual Dysfunctions affect both members of the couple. This also allows the psychologist to ascertain how each feels about the other outside of their sexual encounters. The couple may just not be in love with each other any more, and they may, in fact, not even be in like with each other. Thus, Sexual Dysfunctions and problems would not be unexpected. Clinicians can also examine how their relationship may have changed since they first met or since they first became a couple as well as any sexual behavior changes that may have occurred. Couple's therapy should also examine how the couple communicates. Some people say that sexual problems are not physical or psychological but have their basis in poor communication between the partners. Poor communication thus translates into poor sexual behavior.

Two other aspects can be examined in couple's therapy. First, is

DON'T FORGET

Some clinicians prefer making sure that if an individual patient is requesting sex therapy that the patient's therapist be of the same sex. This is more important if the patient is a victim of Sexual Abuse. However, this scenario is by no means mandated, nor is it agreed upon by all in the field.

CAUTION

Popular myth states that men are always ready for sex, having an erect penis whenever they see a woman, and are always able to orgasm. They are thus superhuman. However, women desire sexual encounters as much as men, if not more so. For many women, sex may not always equal intercourse, fellatio, or cunnilingus (see Zilbergeld, 1999). Cuddling and foreplay may be enough.

one partner more interested in having sex than the other and, second, which partner is more invested in sex therapy (or psychotherapy in general)? We believe in the concepts of balance and homeostasis: If something is out of balance within an individual, a family, or a couple, problems will generally onset. In this case, if the woman desires sex three times a week and her husband is too tired for more than even once every 2 months, a problem exists. Psychologists should not seek even, exact matches between a couple (this is unrealistic), but ideally there will be a give and take or a situation where the desires and wishes are closely aligned, but not identical.

In an ideal situation, the clinician will also see each member of the couple individually. Not everyone agrees with this approach, but let's briefly examine why it is a prudent approach. One partner might not want to discuss masturbation, for example, in front of the other partner. Popular myth tells us that once you are sexually involved with a partner, masturbation is no longer necessary and is a sign of a dysfunctional relationship. One partner may be embarrassed about his or her fantasies. It is not uncommon for a partner (or both) to be fantasizing about having sexual contact with someone other than their current partner while engaging in sex. Finally, one partner might now find the other partner sexually unattractive for many reasons but may not feel comfortable—yet—expressing this in front of the other partner.

Masters and Johnson emphasized couple's treatment, not just treating the afflicted individual. Logically, this means that both members are affected by the patient's Sexual Dysfunctions, not just the patient him- or herself. Masters and Johnson used male and female cotherapists in an intensive atmosphere. The couple would typically meet with them every day for at least 2 weeks. Education and homework assignments are critical components. Homework assignments are used often with behavioral treatment modalities (imagine having homework where the primary goal is sexual stimulation or pleasure!). The homework is designed to get the couple to focus primarily on their sexual sensations. The therapy includes sex education, including much information on sexual anatomy. Many believe that the education provided during treatment is itself quite beneficial, and we agree.

Masters and Johnson would also emphasize communication between both partners, including

> **CAUTION**
>
> Do not be surprised when you discover that many men and women are quite uninformed when it comes to their genitalia. Make sure *you* are well informed before you disseminate information.

nonverbal communication. They believe that communication is often the best treatment modality for couples with sexual concerns and dysfunctions. Masters and Johnson (and other researchers) believe that in heterosexual couples seeking psychotherapy, the male will take the lead in making sexual advances. Thus, intercourse occurs only when the man expresses interest. In their view, many women still believe that they will be rejected by the male if they take the lead during sex.

Masters and Johnson are perhaps best known for their technique of *sensate focus*. These techniques allow the couple to focus on sexually pleasuring each other without intercourse; each member must focus on his or her own pleasure, not on the partner's. The premise here is that these couples cannot think and feel sensually because they place too much pressure on consummating intercourse. Masters and Johnson (and Zilbergeld) believe that focusing primarily on intercourse and orgasms is the primary cause of many Sexual Dysfunctions. They are taught to realize that touch, exploring and caressing their partner's body, can be exciting as well. The goal is to make sure that sensate focus is experienced under conditions unlike that of when they have intercourse, that is, without the accompanying stress, anxiety, and possible resentments.

What about prohibiting intercourse, which typically is mandated during the early sessions? Masters and Johnson believed that by doing so, the tension that probably is occurring in all aspects of their relationship (sexual and nonsexual) would be reduced. In addition, this intercourse prohibition would also be effective in treating possible performance anxiety, which could lead to ED or to other Sexual Dysfunctions.

As you might imagine, Masters and Johnson also worked with couples who had Premature Ejaculation problems. This concern is usually more upset-

CAUTION

Not all therapists agree with the intercourse ban. Some prefer to deemphasize it during sensate focus and not to ban it entirely. Perhaps banning it makes it more tempting, especially when the early goals of sensate focus are basically extended foreplay, according to some psychologists.

ting to the woman than to the man. There are several reasons for this. The woman might view herself as a failure because her partner cannot control himself. She might see herself as unattractive as Premature Ejaculation indicates (irrationally) that the male wants to get this over with as quickly as possible because he cannot stand even touching her. Finally, women take longer to orgasm and take longer to be sexually warmed up. If the male is ejaculating even before intromission, she probably will be frustrated and angry but might not express these feelings as the male will also be quite upset.

The *squeeze technique* can be used to treat this problem. The woman will squeeze the penis several times during the early stages of intercourse. She will use her entire hand and will hold the penis firmly, applying pressure but not (of course) hurting the male. This method reduces the ejaculatory reflex and helps to teach the male how to retard his ejaculation.

If a woman has an orgasmic disorder, several different steps are taken, but the end goals are the same. First, the woman's own views and ideas about intercourse are explored as these might be causing her orgasmic dysfunction. Then homework is assigned to both members of the couple; in this case the homework is designed to get the woman to orgasm. She should start out by exploring her own body and by masturbating. It is best to have her partner present, but she may be alone if she prefers. As she becomes more comfortable with masturbation and ideally reaching orgasm (or getting close), the male will then participate, stimulating and kissing her. The critical aspect here is that the woman needs to clearly communicate her reactions, desires, and dislikes to the male.

Masters and Johnson reported a very high success rate with their techniques. As with all research, their results can be questioned. They were never really clear how *success* or *failure* were defined, and they were not clear as to how the couples were either selected or rejected for their programs. Regardless, their techniques are still widely used today, and they are effective. At the least, Masters and Johnson deserve acknowledgment for their groundbreaking work and for spending a lot of time emphasizing a woman's needs during sexual encounters.

Helen Singer Kaplan (1979) believed that men and women who had Sexual Desire Disorders and that men who had ED had more deep-rooted problems that may be caused by unconscious conflicts. Thus, she preferred to use Masters and Johnson's approaches along with psychodynamic techniques to root out these conflicts. She might work one on one with one of the partners, or she might see them together. She also stated that when Sexual Dysfunctions were based on mild anxieties and conflicts, traditional methods would be effective.

Let us use an example. A woman, Rose, comes to you because she is unable to orgasm, and her vaginal lubrication is minimal to nonexistent. This is upsetting to her husband, Nat, who has threatened to leave her, have an affair, or hire a prostitute. Masturbation is just not enough. He blames her inability to orgasm on himself, but he has had enough. In addition, this lack of lubrication makes their intercourse sessions very infrequent and is harming their ability to get pregnant. Rose tells you that she is uncertain if she wants children, and she may not want them at all.

Kaplan and Freud would focus on unresolved penis envy in Rose. Rose is fixated in the phallic stage and is thus punishing Nat for having a penis. The punishment is that he cannot have intercourse, and the phallus cannot bring Rose pleasure. Freud and Kaplan would also say that she has been unable to overcome penis envy and mature psychologically and emotionally beyond the phallic stage. In sum, she cannot transfer her sexual feelings from her clitoris (some do consider this a phallus) to her vagina, thus preventing orgasm through intercourse (Kaplan, 1974). This viewpoint is controversial and is lacking in strong research support.

We mentioned cognitive behavioral approaches. Ellis would focus on irrational beliefs as possibly causing Sexual Dysfunctions, as we previously discussed. Relaxation and modeling techniques would be used. For example, books and DVDs, as well as various devices (vibrators and so on), would be introduced. One focal point is fantasies. Fantasies can increase the pleasure of sexual encounters, and, in fact, people often do fantasize during sexual encounters as well as during masturbation. Some of the more common fantasies might surprise you. They include being overpowered and giving up to the aggressor, having an imaginary partner, and reliving a previous sexual encoun-

DON'T FORGET

While anal intercourse may be a sexual turn off for many people, it does occur, and rather often, with heterosexual couples. The anus has many nerve endings that some people find pleasurable when stimulated. It is also physiologically impossible to get pregnant through anal intercourse. Unprotected anal intercourse is very risky.

ter. One fantasy that is surprising to most people is being involved in a sexual encounter where the acts are usually regarded as being deviant or repulsive. Usually this includes anal intercourse.

Systematic desensitization also works well in treating Vaginismus. Typically the woman's partner is given phalluses of slightly increased size. Either he (or the woman) inserts the smallest phallus into her vagina. When the vagina comfortably accommodates that size, the next size is then inserted. Eventually the vagina's muscles are expected to relax enough to accommodate a very large phallus and will thus be able to accommodate the partner's penis.

Finally, we will examine pharmacotherapy for Sexual Dysfunctions, and for that we only need to look at one medication—Viagra (sildenafil citrate). Viagra was an immediate hit, so much so that within 3 months of its introduction in 1998, it became the most widely prescribed medication in the United States! Viagra does not directly cause erections, but it does positively affect the penis' response to sexual stimulation and thus enhances a male's ability to achieve an erection (Fuller & Sajatovic, 2000). Viagra does not produce an immediate erection, contrary to myth, nor does it

CAUTION

Would a medication be warranted (or spark interest if one existed) for treating female sexual dysfunctions? Perhaps; however, research indicates that for many women, psychological factors contribute more to sexual dysfunctions than do physiological factors. Thus, focusing on communication, education, and the woman's relationship with her partner would be the most helpful at the present time.

increase a male's desire. However, psychologically a male's desire *may* increase as he is now more likely to attain an erection. Viagra also does not produce 100 percent acceptance; some research reports indicate that only one-third to one-half of the men were satisfied with Viagra's results (Pallas, Levine, Althof, & Risen, 2000). Certainly some of this dissatisfaction can be attributed to general practitioners who did not consider any psycho-

≡ *Rapid Reference 6.4*

Sexual Dysfunction Treatment Modalities

Sensate Focus: Sensate focus allows the couple to focus on sexually pleasuring each other without intercourse; each member must focus on his or her own pleasure, not on the partner's; the premise is that the couple cannot think and feel sensually because they place too much pressure on consummating intercourse.

Squeeze Technique: This technique is used to treat Premature Ejaculation; the partner squeezes the penis several times during the early stages of intercourse; this method reduces the ejaculatory reflex and helps to teach the male how to retard his ejaculation.

Viagra (sildenafil citrate): This prescription medication does not directly cause erections, but it does positively affect the penis's response to sexual stimulation and thus enhances a male's ability to achieve an erection.

logical factors that can contribute to ED. Viagra, like all medications, can produce side effects that are unpleasant and may impact Viagra's effectiveness. Viagra usage, as a rule, directs focus to a male's erection. Thus, the net results of sexual encounters may be compromised: Delayed or Premature Ejaculation, Dyspareunia, or other Sexual Dysfunctions. See Rapid Reference 6.4 for definitions of treatment modalities for Sexual Dysfunctions.

TREATMENT MODALITIES FOR THE PARAPHILIAS

As has been mentioned, the Paraphilias are notoriously difficult to treat because although they receive much mainstream press, they remain relatively rare. In addition, the paraphiliacs keep their behaviors hidden from the general population. Behavioral techniques have been proven effective. Generally, this means aversive conditioning; these methods are most effective when the treatment programs are created with the problems that are specific to the patient. Aversive conditioning is not without its critics as the administration of some pain is generally involved. A more critical problem is that aversive conditioning does not lead to the acquisition of new or adaptive behaviors. Instead, it only leads to avoidance behaviors that may end up strengthening the Paraphilia.

Freudians would view the Paraphilias as a result of unresolved castration

> **DON'T FORGET**
>
> Avoidance behaviors are one explanation for phobia's etiologies. The individual avoids the phobic situation, and, by doing so, the avoidance response is reinforced.

anxiety and an unresolved Oedipal Complex, both occurring in the phallic stage of psychosexual development. Vaginal intercourse—when the penis vanishes inside of the vagina—is seen as a type of castration. All of this occurs unconsciously. Therefore, the individual compensates by displacing his sexual arousal into safer venues, such as children, animals, or leather. The concept is interesting, but research support is generally nonexistent. Finally, Freudians would also attempt to identify unconscious thoughts, wishes, and desires in the individual's fantasies that contribute to his or her Paraphilias. Treatment compliance with the Paraphilias is quite poor, as you can imagine. However, in the end, conventional psychotherapy, psychoanalysis, or counseling have not been proven to be effective in successfully treating the Paraphilias.

Cognitive treatment methods attempt to teach the individual interpersonal skills and will also use a slight variation of aversive techniques known as *covert sensitization*. The individual is asked to imagine potential negative consequences if he or she continues thinking about Pedophilia or if he or she continues to commit pedophilic acts. The goal is to create anxiety toward the desire to sexually abuse children. Covert sensitization appears to be somewhat effective in treating Pedophilia and Sexual Sadism.

The biological perspective attempts to suppress the pedophilic and deviant sexual urges; a secondary goal is to suppress sexual responsiveness (erections while involved in a Paraphilia, for example) as well. Treatment may be surgical (castration) or hormonal. Outcomes are measured based on physiological responses, psychological responses, and by examining the individual's sexual activity.

Hormonal medicines such as Depo-Provera or Provera (medroxyprogesterone acetate) have been used successfully with repeat sex offenders. These medications reduce testosterone levels and also reduce the sex drive. Typically Depo-Provera is used when the pedophile's sex drive is uncontrollable and thus dangerous. Antiandrogen medicines such as Androcur (cyporterone) are designed to reduce sexual desire and sexual fantasies by reducing testosterone levels. The problem here is that once the usage is stopped, the sexual fantasies and the sexual arousal both return. When the term *chemical castration* is used, Androcur is the medicine that is involved with this method. The pedophile needs to be on any of these medications for a lengthy duration because relapse is common once these medications are discontinued. A rather significant side effect of these medications is that the individual is more prone to developing liver disease or liver cancer from long-term usage (Bezchlibnyk-Butler & Jeffries, 2005).

In sum, what can we say about successful treatment modalities of the Paraphilias, specifically Pedophilia? We can safely state that no single method is overwhelmingly effective in treating this disorder, and most modalities do not show great efficacy alone or when used together or as a whole. We can also state that the immediate future does not bode well for successful research into, and successful treatment of, the Paraphilias. The reason is simple: As we stated previously, many paraphiliacs do not seek psychological or medical help. These individuals remain hidden, in general seeing little wrong with their behaviors and thus little reason to seek out our help. Research needs to continue, and the debate will continue: Should the paraphiliacs (especially the pedophiles) be rehabilitated if possible (or at the least worked with in therapy), or should they be incarcerated and removed from the general population and mainstream society as rehabilitation is not possible and society needs to be protected? We cannot answer this here, and we will not attempt to even try. Research needs to continue into these troubling, and yet fascinating, disorders.

Putting It Into Practice

The Case of Bernard Quick

Bernard is a 29-year-old Hispanic male who stands 5 feet 11 inches tall and weighs 190 pounds.[2] Bernard came to us voluntarily with his wife because he was having sexual problems. Specifically, he was ejaculating too early, at times even before vaginal intercourse had occurred. He told us, "You have to understand, this has been occurring for far too long now and is causing problems for me and for my wife. We're trying to get pregnant with our

[2] Please be advised that Bernard uses some strong language when he describes his situation

(continued)

first child, and this makes it impossible. I come too fast, and there's no hope of me ever getting close to having intercourse with her. I'm afraid that the marriage might not last." Bernard's wife Paula told us that "he'll come with me only pulling him close to me, not even on top of me. A simple naked hug sometimes does it. This is driving me nuts. He says it has nothing to do with me or my weight gain, but I wonder. Sometimes I think he doesn't want to have sex with me, so he comes like a shot to avoid it. Let me tell you, I am not happy at all."

We asked Bernard to relate the history of his condition to us. "We've been married for six years, so I'm used to Paula now. It only got worse about nine months ago, when the sex occurred only once a week because of our jobs. My job also sent me back to school to get my MBA. I never had this problem before with Paula or with my old girlfriends, except for the first few times I had sex. But then I was a young teenager, and I could not control anything then." Paula then interjected, "Yeah, blame it on our jobs. Are you cheating on me? Is that it? Or do you see me as some kind of fat cow, totally repulsive?" Paula corroborated Bernard's timeline.

We then asked when they really made the decision to actively try to get pregnant. Bernard said, "That really began about six months ago, but the condom came off about one year ago. We had no luck for the first six months, so we increased the intercourse, but we've still had no luck. We saw Paula's ob-gyn and told him the whole story, and he suggested I get my problem taken care of first before we decide that we can't get pregnant through regular methods. I also need to tell you that I'm also worried about our marriage, and the anxiety this causes me makes it hard to sleep at night because I lay awake worrying about this."

We can see that Bernard demonstrates recurrent ejaculation with minimal sexual stimulation before penetration and surely before he desires to ejaculate. We can rule out that intercourse is a new experience for him, that this is due to the excitement of having a new partner, that this is due to his age, or that this is due to less frequency of intercourse thus leading to more rapid ejaculation. The latter occurs because the male gets overexcited about having intercourse as it happens infrequently. Additionally, Bernard's Premature Ejaculation is causing him and Paula extreme psychological distress and threatens to harm or end their marriage.

We also received a report from Bernard's general practitioner because we wanted to be sure that the Premature Ejaculation was not due to an underlying physical condition or to some medications he might be on. When we received the documents, nothing remarkable was noticed, so we were able to rule out physiological problems or medication as causal factors. Finally, we asked Bernard about his alcohol and illicit drug usage. "I have a drink every now and then, and sometimes I do have a few too many beers when we barbeque. Other than that, nothing. I tried pot, coke, LSD, and hash a few times as an undergrad, but I haven't used that stuff since I graduated." Paula corroborated all of this information.

Based on Bernard's ejaculating before penile insertion into Paula's vagina, on the length of time this has been occurring, and on the fact that his marriage is endangered and his self-esteem is being harmed, we had enough information to make a diagnosis. Bernard's Premature Ejaculation is causing him sleep difficulties at night, but this symptom is insufficient to provide a diagnosis of Generalized Anxiety Disorder, so a rule out is not necessary:

Axis I: Premature Ejaculation, Acquired Type, Situational   302.75
          Type, Due to Psychological Factors
Axis II: No Diagnosis   V71.09
Axis III: None
Axis IV: Problems with Primary Support Group: Paula (wife)
Axis V: GAF = 70 (Current)

We used the Acquired subtype because Bernard's Premature Ejaculation developed after a period of normal sexual functioning. His Premature Ejaculation is limited to his encounters with Paula (if he is being honest, that is), so his Premature Ejaculation is situational, not generalized to all sexual encounters. Finally, we ruled out the Premature Ejaculation being caused by an underlying medical condition, by prescription, over the counter or illicit substances, or by alcohol, so he received a Due to Psychological Factors subtype.

Treatment Plan

We used couple's therapy, where a primary goal is to improve communication between a couple, to both perform therapy and to provide education to Paula and Bernard. In couple's therapy we taught Paula and Bernard two widely accepted behavioral modalities to treat his Premature Ejaculation: the squeeze technique and the stop-start, or pause, technique. In the squeeze technique, Paula would squeeze Bernard's penis several times during the early stages of intercourse. She will apply pressure around the upper shaft of the penis; by this method, the ejaculatory reflex is decreased, and Bernard also learns how to retard his ejaculation. In the pause technique, Bernard's penis would be stimulated, ideally by Paula, until he is highly aroused and feels like he is nearing ejaculation. Once he reaches this point, Paula would pause until his arousal abates, and then she would commence stimulation again. This sequence would be repeated a few more times until ejaculation occurred, the idea being that Bernard would now get more penis stimulation than he has in a while. Eventually they would have intercourse, with Bernard pausing whenever he got too highly aroused. Some clinicians

(continued)

have used SSRIs such as Prozac to treat Premature Ejaculation because these medications appear to reduce arousal or orgasm; however, the research is inconclusive on its efficacy.

We also worked on Bernard's anxiety as he was pressuring himself to get Paula pregnant. We spent a lot of time on education, discussing with him how long it takes the average couple to conceive and how often intercourse needs to occur. We also worked with him and Paula to help them understand that they needed to concentrate on pleasuring each other and themselves, and the pregnancy will hopefully occur.

Within about 4 months, Bernard and Paula were enjoying prolonged intercourse because of the behavioral methods they employed. At last report they were still married ("usually happily, but not always"), he was still able to maintain sexual intercourse, and they were still trying to get pregnant.

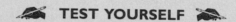

🗡 TEST YOURSELF 🗡

1. **Sexual Dysfunctions**
    (a) are commonly known as *fetishes*.
    (b) have the key characteristic of a disturbance in sexual desire.
    (c) include frigidity and Pedophilia.
    (d) always have a psychological etiology.

2. **The Paraphilias**
    (a) are commonly known as *fetishes*.
    (b) include Sexual Sadism and Sexual Masochism.
    (c) usually affect women.
    (d) Both a and b.

3. ***Dyspareunia* is defined as**
    (a) experiencing pain in the genitals before, during, and after sexual intercourse.
    (b) intercourse being difficult or impossible because the outer part of the vagina experiences involuntary muscle contractions.
    (c) a Paraphilia.
    (d) a sexual deviation.

4. *Vaginismus* is defined as

   (a) experiencing pain in the genitals before, during, and after sexual intercourse.

   (b) intercourse being difficult or impossible because the outer part of the vagina experiences involuntary muscle contractions.

   (c) a Paraphilia.

   (d) a sexual deviation.

5. **Pedophiles tend to be in their 30s or 40s, are most likely law-abiding citizens, and are often respected in their communities and in the workplace.** True or False?

6. **One common treatment modality for Premature Ejaculation is**

   (a) the squeeze technique.

   (b) rubbing a topical anesthetic on the penis.

   (c) having the male go through extensive analysis to discover the unconscious reasons behind his Premature Ejaculation.

   (d) prescribing Viagra (sildenafil citrate).

7. **When Viagra (sildenafil citrate) is used, it results in**

   (a) directly causing erections.

   (b) positively affecting the penis's response to sexual stimulation, thus enhancing a male's ability to achieve an erection.

   (c) immediately causing a physiological increase in the male's sexual desire.

   (d) all of the above.

8. **Conventional psychotherapy, psychoanalysis, or counseling have been proven to be effective in successfully treating the Paraphilias.** True or False?

Answers: 1. b; 2. d; 3. a; 4. b; 5. True; 6. a; 7. b; 8. False

Seven

ESSENTIALS OF SCHIZOPHRENIC DISORDERS

Schizophrenia (technically known as *Schizophrenic Disorders*) is the most debilitating mental illness, affecting anywhere from 0.5 percent to 1.5 percent of the U.S. population (APA, 2000). Schizophrenia knows no barriers: It affects people of all races and socioeconomic classes; however, APA lists certain factors that increase the chances of developing Schizophrenia (2000). One's chances are increased if the person has one or more of the following characteristics: they are single, they come from a Westernized or industrialized nation, they come from a lower socioeconomic status (SES) (note that APA does not list defining criteria for lower SES strata), they live in an urban area, they had problems while in utero, they were born during the winter, or they had recently experienced some extreme stress (p. 313). Some researchers have discovered that ethnic minorities (in the United States, specifically African American and Puerto Rican individuals) are more likely to be diagnosed with Schizophrenia. This may be due to bias and to stereotyping (Lewis, Croft-Jeffreys, & Anthony, 1990). Schizophrenia is problematic in that oftentimes it does not respond well to treatment. We are also not certain as to what causes Schizophrenia; thus, finding a highly effective treatment or cure has evaded the helping professions.

When we discuss Schizophrenia with students, more questions are asked and greater interest is generated than when any other *DSM-IV-TR* category is discussed. During these discussions, many myths and misconceptions have arisen. It is important to discuss these common myths, which are often perpetuated by the media, before we continue.

First, Schizophrenia does not refer to a split personality (generally known as *Dissociative Identity Disorder* (DID), previously known as *Multiple Personality Disorder*). The split in Schizophrenia is best seen as a break or a *split* from reality. Second, many people think that all schizophrenics are homicidal maniacs—serial killers like Jeffrey Dahmer, Jason from the *Friday the 13th* movie series, "Leatherface" from *The Texas Chainsaw Massacre*, and so on. In fact, most schizophrenics are more of a danger to themselves than to others and some may attempt suicide.

Next, it is a myth that the Schizophrenic Disorders only affect senior citizens and older individuals. In fact, the average age of onset occurs between the late teens and early 30s, with onset before adolescence rare (APA, 2000). Thus if someone is diagnosed initially with Schizophrenia at age 70, other diagnoses must be considered first or in addition to Schizophrenia. Finally, many myths abound about the etiologies of Schizophrenia. First, Schizophrenia is not caused *solely* by any of the following: a bad upbringing (by parents, caretakers, or guardians), lower SES, prenatal brain damage, bad chromosomes, or environmental toxins. Some people consider all of these etiological perspectives plausible. A popular viewpoint today sees Schizophrenia as Schizophrenias, that is, as a group of disorders or as a series of diseases that have many etiologies but end up as a Schizophrenic Disorder. This perspective is logical because we do not know for sure—yet—what causes Schizophrenia, how to prevent it, or how to treat it with significant efficacy.

HISTORY AND CHARACTERISTICS OF SCHIZOPHRENIC DISORDERS

The history of Schizophrenia begins with two prominent names in psychology. Emil Kraepelin (1856–1926), a German psychiatrist, adopted the term *dementia praecox* to classify a group of disorders that had as their common feature intellectual and cognitive deterioration early in life, probably beginning during adolescence. *Dementia* refers to the severe intellectual deterioration, while *praecox* refers to the early or premature onset of this disorder. Kraepelin stated that this disorder could be differentially diagnosed from other mental disorders because the individual's cognitive functions deteriorated over time, unlike other disorders such as unipolar depression. Interestingly, there is no present evidence to support this contention of progressive brain deterioration, and we certainly have the technology available to track any brain degeneration. Oddly, if brain degeneration has occurred, it is usually the result of long-term usage of antipsychotic medications (Cohen, 1997).

Eugen Bleuler (1857–1939; *not* to be confused with Breuer, who worked closely with Freud when Freud first began his psychology career), first used the term *Schizophrenia* in 1911. Bleuler was a Swiss psychiatrist and Kraepelin's contemporary. Bleuler agreed with some—but not all—of Kraepelin's concepts about the disorder. He did not believe that dementia praecox always ended with the individual experiencing cognitive and intellectual deterioration, and he also did not believe that this disorder always had its onset in late adolescence. He thus used the term Schizophrenia, which literally means "split mind" or "splitting of mental associations." Bleuler felt that this was the distinguishing characteristic of Schizophrenia, that is, a thought disorder where the thoughts and thought processes are disorganized, the individual "splits off" from reality (their intellect is split off from external reality), and where the individual does not demonstrate coherence or logical links between his or her thoughts and emotions. You now see where the confusion, and the myth, that Schizophrenia refers to DID (Multiple Personality Disorder) has its origins! Note also that DID was until recently a much rarer diagnosis than any of the Schizophrenias.

Schizophrenic disorders are known today by the diagnostic criteria established in the *DSM-IV-TR* (APA, 2000). Interestingly, the diagnostic criteria in the *DSM-IV-TR* are more restrictive than Bleuler's original definition of Schizophrenia; he placed less emphasis on the presence of hallucinations and delusions, perhaps the two most dramatic symptoms of these disorders. The *DSM-IV-TR* does include *negative symptoms* in its diagnostic criteria. Negative symptoms are those symptoms that, as a rule, do not respond well to treatment and to many medications. Negative symptoms are responses, behaviors, or functions that are deficient or absent in a schizophrenic individual's behavior and thus refers to a loss or reduction of normal functions. Some examples include *anhedonia* (a loss of pleasure in all activities), poverty of speech, significant cognitive impairment, and flat or blunted affect. An individual who is mentally healthy (however we quantify this concept) is expected to be emotional, able to communicate with his or her speech, and react appropriately (or at all) to environmental events. By definition, a schizophrenic who has negative symptoms has deficits or is lacking in these behaviors. Another way to view negative symptoms is that these behaviors that are normally present have deteriorated, so nothing new is *added* as far as behaviors are concerned.

Positive symptoms, on the other hand, refer to behaviors that *have been added* to an individual's normal behavioral repertoire and include delusions and hallucinations as well as psychomotor agitation, bizarre behavior, and minimal cognitive impairment. A somewhat related classification system refers to Type I or Type II Schizophrenia. Types I and II have symptoms that are similar to positive and negative symptoms, respectively, but they include more emphasis on biology and on medication efficacy. Type I schizophrenics respond well to antipsychotic medications, have normal-sized brain ventricles (the fissures or gaps in the brain), and have evidenced abnormalities in their limbic system (sometimes called the *old brain* because primitive emotions are housed here). Type II schizophrenics do not respond well to medications (or their responses are inconsistent or unpredictable), they may have enlarged ventricles, and abnormalities have been evidenced in their frontal lobes.

Keep in mind that most schizophrenic individuals demonstrate both positive and negative symptoms during the course of their Schizophrenia. Also note that in general individuals who demonstrate significantly more negative symptoms than positive symptoms have a much poorer prognosis in therapy, including response to medications (Bezchlibnyk-Butler & Jeffries, 2005). For definitions of key classification terms, see Rapid Reference 7.1.

≡ *Rapid Reference 7.1*

Key Terms to Know

Negative Symptoms: These are responses, behaviors, or functions that are deficient or absent in a schizophrenic individual's behavior; The term refers to a loss or reduction of normal functions.

Positive Symptoms: These are behaviors that have been added to an individual's normal behavioral repertoire and include delusions, hallucinations, psychomotor agitation, bizarre behavior, and minimal cognitive impairment.

Type I Schizophrenics: These individuals respond well to antipsychotic medications, have normal-sized brain ventricles, and have evidenced abnormalities in their limbic system.

Type II Schizophrenics: These individuals do not respond well to medications (or their responses are inconsistent or unpredictable), may have enlarged ventricles, and abnormalities have been evidenced in their frontal lobes.

GENERAL SYMPTOMS OF SCHIZOPHRENIC DISORDERS

The *DSM-IV-TR* lists three specific criteria for Schizophrenia. Specifically within Criterion A, several active symptoms are listed. The patient must have at least *two* of these during a 1-month period (with one major exception to this rule discussed in a moment); during this 1-month period, the criteria must be present for a significant period of time. We will examine each of the symptoms within Criterion A, and then we will examine Criteria B through F as wholes.

First, *delusions* may be present. Delusions can be seen as false beliefs that are held in spite of their impossibility of occurring or being so. Thus, no matter how absurd the delusion, the schizophrenic individual will hold fast to that belief. Typical delusions include thought insertion into the patient's head; the delusion that the patient's thoughts are being broadcast to other people; or that the patient's thoughts, behaviors, and feelings are being controlled by mysterious, unseen, external forces beyond his or her control. Delusions have several defining characteristics. First, the individual experiencing delusions will defend his or her beliefs with tremendous conviction and certainty, even when he or she is presented with contradictory evidence. The individual will also be preoccupied with his or her delusions; during active psychotic episodes, many delusional patients cannot help but talk and think about their delusions. Last, the delusional patient cannot see others' perspectives when it comes to examining his or her delusions. Even though others may view the patient's delusions as ridiculous, the patient cannot see their point of view. Delusions also tend to be quite personal, and in clinical settings they may be fragmented. This means that the delusions themselves are not always consistent and coherent beliefs. For example, a patient might talk about his bones melting and then talk about being a morphodite.

The most well-known criterion

CAUTION

The APA (2000) makes an important statement at the end of Criterion A that some people may miss. The APA specifically states that "only one Criterion A symptom is required if delusions are bizarre or hallucinations consist of a voice keeping up a running commentary on the person's behavior or thoughts, or two or more voices conversing with each other" (p. 312). Make certain not to forget this critical point.

for Schizophrenic Disorders, and perhaps the most fascinating, is *hallucinations,* which are defined as sensory experiences that are not caused by any external stimuli. In other words, the individual senses things (voices, visions) even though there are no stimuli in the environment to cause the sensory receptors in the brain to react. Most schizophrenic hallucinations are auditory; the individual hears voices in his or her head that are not really there. Typically these voices will comment on the schizophrenic's behavior or will give the schizophrenic individual commands (command hallucinations). Oftentimes two or more voices will be arguing with each other inside of the schizophrenic's head. They may even hear the voice of God or Christ talking to them. Tactile hallucinations (feeling like bugs are crawling on you, for example) are less common than auditory and visual, but they can still occur.

The third active symptom under Criterion A is disorganized speech; this often includes frequent derailment or incoherence. The latter simply refers to the inability of the individual to make sense in his or her speech. Some signs of this might include using words in unusual ways (or perhaps making up words), making irrelevant responses to questions, and having no connection between the ideas expressed. At times the connections between thoughts or sentences are arbitrary and difficult to follow. Note that *all* speech of schizophrenic individuals is not incoherent, just some of it, or certain parts during a discourse. Rules of grammar are often followed, and the words used by schizophrenics are usually not pieced together randomly. In essence, their speech at times conveys little meaning.

There are several types of verbal disruptions that occur with schizophrenic individuals. You may have heard these terms, but they are worth repeating. *Tangentiality* refers to replying to a question with a response that is irrelevant (e.g., "So, Rose, how are you today?" "Well, sweet, I maybe, that frogs live on lily pads. . . ."). As you can see, this reply makes no sense, and it is impossible to comprehend the speaker's intentions. When a schizophrenic individual shifts topics too abruptly, this is called *loose associations* or *derailment.* Finally, *perseveration* refers to repeating the same word or phrase over and over again. People who do not have Schizophrenia are guilty of all of the above verbal disruptions at times, but schizophrenic individuals present these subsymptoms many times during a discourse.

Grossly disorganized or catatonic behavior is the fourth active symptom listed in the *DSM-IV-TR.* This includes inappropriate affect, which refers to emotional expressions (facially) that do not match the experiences being verbally related or experienced or lack of adaptability to emotional expressions. For example, when an individual is describing the horror, repulsion, and abject fear for her life when she was being sexually molested by her brother and father when she was 8-years-old, she giggles uncontrollably. Her relating of this event is inconsistent with the nature of the situation she is describing. The reverse of this also holds true. If an individual is describing a situation where he or she felt extreme joy and happiness, yet they are teary eyed or more often unexpressionless, this is also considered inappropriate affect.

Unusual motor behavior is also evident in some schizophrenic individuals. *Catatonia* refers to marked muscular rigidity and immobility, but what is less well known is that it can also refer to opposite actions, excitement, and overactivity, usually while the patient is performing an endless task or ritual. They may be rocking back and forth for hours on end or rubbing their hands together for hours in the same fashion. We might also see these patients displaying either reduced or awkward movements, or, in the extreme, the patient may assume a very unusual posture or remain standing and stiff for a long period of time. If someone who did not have Schizophrenia assumed one of these frozen positions for a long period of time, she or he would feel pain and probably not be able to remain still. Catatonic individuals, however, can remain still and at times can be posed (called *waxy flexibility*) and remain frozen in the new position. Typically catatonic individuals will resist any attempts to alter their positions no matter how painful they might appear to be to other people. Finally, catatonic individuals may also demonstrate reduced responsiveness to their surroundings; this is called *stuporous state*. They do not respond to questions, yet their conscious awareness of events that are occurring in their environment remains. Thus they know what is going on around them, but they are unable (or choose not) to respond.

The last active symptom under Criterion A is the general classification of negative symptoms, such as affective flattening, alogia, or avolition (APA, 2000). We previously discussed negative symptoms, but we want to focus specifically on the terms mentioned here because they are some of the examples given by the *DSM-IV-TR*. First, affective flattening is also known as *blunted affect;* this refers to an individual's restriction of his or her nonverbal emotional responses, usually seen on the face. The way to tell if this is occurring is to look at their facial expressions. They are not happy, but then they are not sad either. They do not demonstrate signs of emotion or of feelings. Their faces often appear to be expressionless and blank, devoid of emotion (and anecdotally, color as well. That is, if the individual is Caucasian, for example, his or her face appears to lack color from a normal blood flow). Their voices tend to be monotones and lack the various pitch and tone changes you would expect to hear when normally conversing with someone. They generally are not concerned with environmental events and generally are not too concerned for themselves either (Andreasen & Black, 1995).

We already discussed *anhedonia,* which refers to the inability to experience pleasure. This is also a classic symptom of unipolar depression. This, specifically, is a lack of pleasurable feelings when involved in activities that used to bring the individual pleasure or when they are interacting with people whose company they previously enjoyed. What is most interesting is that people who suffer from anhedonia may also be unable to experience pleasure from physical sensations as well, such as touch and taste. Thus, a marvelous meal or a stupendous dessert would be lost on someone with anhedonia. Herbener and Harrow (2002) note that social and physical anhedonia appears to be a chronic feature with schizophrenic individuals, and it may also be a precursor to Schizophrenia's eventual onset.

Alogia is a speech disturbance that literally means "speechlessness." One form of alogia is called *poverty of speech,* or *poverty of content.* The amount of speech of these individuals is greatly reduced. In effect, they do not have much to say. *Thought blocking* is another form of alogia. What occurs here is that the individual's train of thought, and therefore their speech, is interrupted before he or she can conclude that thought or idea.

Avolition refers to a lack of volition, or a lack of will, as well as indecisiveness and ambivalence. These individuals are apathetic and do not work toward their personal goals and are unable to work independently. They might sit around all day, not properly grooming themselves for an unusually lengthy period of time. Oftentimes avolition is accompanied by apathy, where the schizophrenic individual socially withdraws from interpersonal relationships, social

CAUTION

Thought blocking, a form of alogia and a negative symptom of Schizophrenia, is not the same as *thought stopping,* a behavioral treatment technique used in the treatment of OCD.

situations, and from life in general. Many times social isolation and apathy are the first symptoms to develop and may be a signal that something is not right with the individual. It is possible that social isolation may also work as a coping strategy to avoid stimulation that could lead to, or increase, disorganization (Andreasen & Black, 1995). See Rapid Reference 7.2 for some *DSM-IV-TR* Criterion A Symptoms for Schizophrenia.

Criterion B also examines the individual's social and occupational functioning to see if either of these two areas is dysfunctional. Specifically, the *DSM-IV-TR* looks at the individual's overall functioning at work, in interpersonal relations, or his or her involvement in self-care (or lack of involvement). One or more of these areas needs to be significantly below the level the individual presented before the onset of the disorder. If Schizophrenia's onset is in childhood or adolescence, a failure to achieve an expected level (based on their age and intellectual ability) of interpersonal, academic, or occupational achievement is sought. In sum, his or her social and occupational functioning needs to be on a steady decline during the disorder.

≡ *Rapid Reference 7.2*

Some *DSM-IV-TR* Criterion A Symptoms for Schizophrenia

Delusions: Delusions are false beliefs that are held in spite of their impossibility of occurring or being so; no matter how absurd the delusion, the schizophrenic individual will hold fast to that belief.

Hallucinations: Hallucinations are sensory experiences that are not caused by any external stimuli; the individual senses things (voices, smells, visions) even though there are no stimuli in the environment to cause the sensory receptors in the brain to react.

Tangentiality: This means replying to a question with a response that is irrelevant.

Loose Associations (Derailment): This is when the schizophrenic individual shifts topics too abruptly.

Perseveration: Perseveration means repeating the same word or phrase over and over again.

Alogia: Alogia is a speech disturbance that literally means "speechlessness".

Avolition: Avolition is a lack of volition (or will), as well as indecisiveness and ambivalence.

Criterion C looks at the duration of Schizophrenia. The schizophrenic behaviors (or symptoms) need to be presented (evident) continuously for at least 6 months. The *DSM-IV-TR* notes that this 6-month period must include at least 1 month of symptoms (or less if successfully treated) that meet Criterion A symptoms, and they may include periods of prodromal or residual symptoms. Helping professionals might see only negative symptoms during these prodromal or residual periods, or they may see Criterion A symptoms. If this is the

> **DON'T FORGET**
>
> The helping professions look at an individual's ability to hold down a steady job as one sign of a potentially mentally healthy individual.

> **DON'T FORGET**
>
> It appears that Criteria C and D are in homage to Kraepelin, who saw dementia praecox as having a marked impairment in functioning as well as a chronically debilitating and declining course.

case, two or more Criterion A symptoms are required although they may be in an attenuated form, such as odd beliefs or unusual perceptual experiences (APA, 2000, p. 312).

Criterion D includes some rule-out conditions or disorders. To rule out a disorder means that we can safely state that the symptoms are not indicative of another mental or physiological illness that is somehow related to the condition in question, in this instance Schizophrenia. Active-phase symptoms (Criterion A symptoms) must appear in the absence of a Major Depressive Episode or a Manic Episode. Thus, we need to exercise caution when diagnosing Schizophrenia because we might be seeing a mood disorder, most likely unipolar depression, mania, or Bipolar I Disorder. The second part of this criterion is somewhat more difficult to quantify. Specifically, the *DSM-IV-TR* notes that if symptoms of depression or mania are present during a schizophrenic's active phase (when they are actively hallucinating or actively delusional, for example), the total duration of the depression or mania must be brief relative to the duration of the active and residual periods of the Schizophrenic Disorder.

Criterion E looks to rule out the symptoms (again, most likely Criterion A's active symptoms) as being caused by either a Substance-Related Disorder (such as Alcohol or Substance Dependence), due to the individual's taking

CAUTION

Did you also know that *olfactory* hallucinations are not unusual with individuals who suffer from certain subtypes of seizure disorder (archaically known as *epilepsy*)?

a prescription medication (either due to the medication's effects or to its side effects), or due to a general medical condition.

Finally, Criterion F mentions Pervasive Developmental Disorders (Autistic Disorder falls into this category). Specifically, "if there is a history of Autistic Disorder or another Pervasive Developmental Disorder (such as Asperger's), the additional diagnosis of Schizophrenia is made only if prominent delusions or hallucinations are also present for at least a month (or less if successfully treated; APA, 2000, p. 312).

SUBTYPES OF SCHIZOPHRENIC DISORDERS

The *DSM-IV-TR* lists five subtypes of Schizophrenia. The patient's subtype diagnosis is based on their state during their current (or most recent) psychological and psychiatric intake interview. The most common subtypes today are the paranoid and the undifferentiated types. We will not discuss the last subtype—Schizophrenia, Residual Type. This classification is used for individuals who have experienced Schizophrenia and are now considered to be recovering or in remission. Their prominent symptoms are not present, but they still demonstrate milder signs of Schizophrenia. What we usually see with these individuals is that they are still demonstrating negative symptoms or some mild residual positive symptoms, such as odd beliefs or eccentric behaviors. The prominent positive symptoms, such as bizarre delusions and hallucinations, are no longer presented. Usually individuals who are residual types are in transition from active psychosis to remission, or they may be between psychotic episodes. They may also remain in the residual state for years if not decades.

Individuals who suffer from Schizophrenia, Paranoid Type will have delusions and extreme suspiciousness that increases during the course of the disorder. They frequently have interpersonal problems. Their delusions most often are of persecution; the individual complains of being watched, poisoned, or influenced by devices planted by enemies or aliens. They become increasingly suspicious of relatives and close friends. Paranoid schizophrenics do not prominently present with disorganized speech, disorganized or catatonic behavior, or flat or inappropriate affect. Because of the general lack of negative symptoms, there is a somewhat higher level of functioning for this type of individual, and they should respond better to interventions.

This does not mean that working with paranoid schizophrenics is easy. In fact, they can be difficult patients because of their strong delusions and because command hallucinations may be present. That is, they may respond to a command from a voice to commit a violent act because someone is out to get them. Because their paranoid features become part of their personality, and, more important, because negative symptoms are not a prominent feature of this subtype, these individuals often blend in well with society. These individuals can be dangerous at times, but all of them are not violent, crazed individuals as often portrayed in the media.

Schizophrenia, Catatonic Type is characterized by extreme psychomotor disturbances that may either involve immobility and stupor to excessive amounts of motor activity that does not seem to be connected to the environmental events surrounding the individual. This individual might refuse to speak and may demonstrate waxy flexibility (or catalepsy). At the opposite extreme, these patients may also show extreme psychomotor excitation and excitement, where they are talking and shouting continuously. The excessive motor activity is apparently purposeless and is not influenced by the environment or by environmental events surrounding the individual. Patients who demonstrate extreme excitement and agitation need to be carefully monitored because they can easily harm themselves or other people.

What is not well known to the general public is that a catatonic schizophrenic can also demonstrate *echolalia* or *echopraxia*. Echolalia is the senseless repetition of a word or phrase just spoken by another person. The repetition is pathological, apparently senseless and parrot-like. Echopraxia refers to the repetitive imitation of movements of another person (APA, 2000). Catatonic individuals need to initially present symptoms that qualify for a diagnosis of Schizophrenia before they can be diagnosed with the catatonic

CAUTION

Individuals have a Delusional Disorder when they have well-defined delusional systems that are paranoid in nature *and* the rest of their behavior is typical and is well-integrated. Thus, they have paranoid delusions but otherwise behave appropriately. Their delusions are not considered bizarre and could possibly occur, such as being poisoned by a jealous lover or being followed. Delusional Disorder is ruled out when an individual demonstrates negative symptoms as well as hallucinations, disorganized speech, or catatonic behavior.

subtype. Other rule-out diagnoses include substance-induced conditions, a Manic Episode or a Major Depressive Episode, or a general medical condition that can be causing the symptoms.

Individuals with Schizophrenia, Disorganized Type, generally do not respond well to treatment. They present with disorganized speech, extremely disorganized behavior, and with flat or inappropriate affect. All of these criteria must be present before this diagnosis can be made (APA, 2000). These individuals will be active, but their behavior will seem aimless and pointless, and they may demonstrate a disregard for proper decorum and social conventions. For example, they may masturbate in public or defecate in inappropriate places. If hallucinations or delusions are presented, their content is usually bizarre and poorly organized. What is of greatest importance is that these individuals often demonstrate symptoms at an early age and may not have adapted well to developmental and environmental changes even before the symptoms appeared.

Finally, there is the diagnosis of Schizophrenia, Undifferentiated Type. This category exists for patients who do not fit into the Catatonic, Paranoid, or Disorganized types. To receive this diagnosis, the individual needs to have symptoms present that fit into Criterion A but do not meet the diagnostic criteria for Paranoid, Disorganized, or Catatonic Schizophrenia. Generally these individuals present with disorganized behavior or speech as well as with either hallucinations or delusions (APA, 2000). See Rapid Reference 7.3 for *DSM-IV-TR* Schizophrenia subtypes.

≡ *Rapid Reference 7.3*

DSM-IV-TR Schizophrenia Subtypes

Paranoid Type: Individuals will have delusions and extreme suspiciousness that increase during the course of the disorder; delusions most often are of persecution; they do not prominently present with disorganized speech, disorganized or catatonic behavior, or flat or inappropriate affect.

Catatonic Type: This type is characterized by extreme psychomotor disturbances that may either involve immobility and stupor or excessive amounts of motor activity that does not seem to be connected to the environmental events surrounding the individual; individuals may display waxy flexibility.

Disorganized Type: This type is characterized by disorganized speech, extremely disorganized behavior, and flat or inappropriate affect; all must be present before this diagnosis can be made (APA, 2000).

SOME RELATED PSYCHOTIC DISORDERS

The *DSM-IV-TR* lists several disorders that have prominent psychotic features but differ from Schizophrenia. Schizophreniform Disorder has criteria that are identical to Schizophrenia's Criterion A, but there are two significant differences. First, the total duration of the illness is at least 1 month but less than 6 months. This includes *all* phases of the episode: prodromal, active, and residual phases. Second, social and occupational impairment during the episode (that is, during some part of the illness' duration) is not required even though it may occur. In addition, this diagnosis is also made when the individual has been symptomatic of possible Schizophrenia, but the episode has lasted less than 6 months (APA, 2000).

Schizoaffective Disorder can be diagnosed when an individual demonstrates symptoms of both Schizophrenia and a severe mood disorder, either bipolar or unipolar. This disorder is controversial because it is not a subtype of Schizophrenia but is listed in the Schizophrenia chapter in the *DSM-IV-TR,* and it also shares the same numerical code type (295.xx). The individual, during an uninterrupted period of the illness, demonstrates symptoms that qualify for a diagnosis of Major Depressive Episode, Manic Episode, or a Mixed Episode *with* symptoms that fit Criterion A's active-phase schizophrenic symptoms. The critical criterion is Criterion B: The individual must, for at least 2 weeks, have demonstrated delusions or hallucinations in the absence of prominent mood symptoms. In other words, the hallucinations or delusions must have occurred while the individual was not demonstrating symptoms of a severe mood disorder. See Rapid Reference 7.4 for definitions of related psychotic disorders.

CAUTION

If the individual has been symptomatic for less than 6 months, Schizophreniform Disorder is diagnosed, but with the qualifier of Provisional. This implies that it remains uncertain if the individual will recover from the episode within the 6-month time frame. If the episode persists beyond 6 months, the diagnosis is changed to Schizophrenia.

DON'T FORGET

If delusions and hallucinations are present only during a depressive episode, the diagnosis is Major Depressive Episode with psychotic features.

≡ Rapid Reference 7.4

Some Related Psychotic Disorders

Schizophreniform Disorder: There are two significant differences from Criterion A for Schizophrenia: The total duration of the illness is at least 1 month but less than 6 months, and social and occupational impairment during the episode is not required even though it may occur.

Schizoaffective Disorder: This disorder is diagnosed when an individual demonstrates symptoms of both Schizophrenia and a severe mood disorder, either bipolar or unipolar.

ETIOLOGIES OF SCHIZOPHRENIC DISORDERS

Not surprisingly, entire volumes have been written about the etiologies of the Schizophrenic Disorders, and with good reason. Over the decades, researchers and theorists have produced a number of fascinating etiological theories on the Schizophrenic Disorders. What is most interesting is that even though research has produced volumes of information in support or refutation of an etiology, we still are somewhat hazy as to the true, research-supported causes of the Schizophrenic Disorders, especially when it comes to knowing the exact details of causal factors.

Genetic Influences

No discussion of Schizophrenia's etiologies can begin without considering genetic influences. Indeed, research into genetic causal factors has produced more research than any of the other mental disorders. We can say with relative certainty that a gene or genes somehow play a role in making certain people vulnerable to developing Schizophrenia. The research is just too strong to discount this possibility (Bassett, Chow, Waterworth, & Brzustowicz, 2001).

From a historical perspective, Kallman (1938) produced a landmark study on the families of individuals with Schizophrenia. Kallman, in examining over 1,000 family members of schizophrenic patients and the patients themselves, discovered two important factors. His first point is that the more severe the parent's Schizophrenia, the more likely the parent's children would develop Schizophrenia. His second point is more important. Kallman hypothesized and concluded that individuals do not inherit a genetic predisposition for the various subtypes of Schizophrenia but instead the genetic predisposition is inherited for Schizophrenia as a whole, which may manifest itself differently from that of the parent.

Other studies have pointed to familial components related to the etiology of the Schizophrenic Disorders (Kendler et al., 1993). Gottesman (1991) concluded that the more genes an individual shares with someone who has a Schizophrenic Disorder, the more likely that individual will also develop it. For example, you have about a 48 percent chance of contracting a Schizophrenic Disorder if your identical (known as a monozygotic [MZ]) twin also also has it, and if your fraternal (dizygotic or DZ) twin has Schizophrenia, you have about a 17 percent chance of developing Schizophrenia. Genetically, MZ twins share 100 percent of their genetic information; thus, they are identical inside and outside (MZ twins come from one fertilized egg). Dizygotic twins come from two eggs fertilized at the same time. Cannon, Kaprio, Loennqvist, Huttunen, and Koskenvuo (1998) studied Finnish twins and discovered that MZ twins had an average concordance rate of 46 percent, while DZ twins had only a 9 percent concordance rate for Schizophrenia. What we can conclude from Cannon et al. (1998) and other research is that genetic factors do play a role, and a rather powerful one, in the development of Schizophrenia. We can thus state that the more genes that two family members have in common, the greater the risk of the individual developing Schizophrenia.

What is more interesting is that if Schizophrenia were to only have a genetic cause or causes, we would expect the concordance rates to either be at or near 100 percent. Because they are not close to 100 percent, these studies provide strong evidence for environmental factors in developing Schizophrenia. Thus, the problem with family studies is simple: Where does the genetic influence end and the environmental influence begin? This is a difficult question to answer; attempts have been made, but the results have not pointed to any one aspect with relative certainty. One way to approach this chicken or egg problem (one that is all too common in psychology and in psychiatry) is to use adoption studies.

The Genain Quadruplets

The Genain quadruplets are a genetic rarity—four identical twin sisters who all developed Schizophrenia before age 25. The odds of this occurring are about once in 1.5 billion births! All four were brought up in the same household, all four developed Schizophrenia, yet all of the Genain's Schizophrenias differed in their chronicity, outcome, and severity. The Genains were a classic example of how important the environment is in regard to Schizophrenia. Some critical information is that their father, at the least, may have had an alcohol problem, was reported to have sexually molested at least two of the twins, and perhaps also had OCD. The question remains: Did growing up with an incestuous father lead to the development of a mental illness, or was it the genetics?

Adoption Studies

Adoption studies need to be longitudinal to provide the most conclusive evidence. Typically, adoption and twin studies most often occur in Scandinavia because extended families are relatively common, and, more important, their record keeping for marriages, psychiatric illnesses, and adoptions are very comprehensive and current. Separating hereditary from environmental influences is done through what is called the adoption method. Concordance rates for Schizophrenia are compared for the biological and adoptive relatives of people who have been adopted from their biological families at an early age (ideally this occurs at birth) and have later developed Schizophrenia. Conclusions point to one of two factors. If the concordance ratio is greater among the schizophrenic's biological relatives compared with the patient's adoptive relatives, a strong genetic or hereditary influence is suggested and presumed (some would say proven, but research has not been that conclusive for either viewpoint yet). If the reverse is true, then support is offered for an environmental influence.

A study conducted in Denmark by Rosenthal et al. (1975) revealed that 3 out of 39 high-risk adoptees (children who had at least one biological parent with Schizophrenia) had Schizophrenia, which amounts to 8 percent. The conclusions one can make from this and similar studies are that genetic factors play a moderate role in the development of Schizophrenia. What some later studies have revealed is that parental inadequacy and disturbed communication within a family unit both have an impact on the development of Schizophrenia for both control and index (those people studied who became schizophrenic) cases. Tienari and colleagues (1994) conducted an adoption study in Finland. They gathered data on 20,000 women who received psychiatric inpatient treatment at some point during a 10-year period of time. They then culled 171 women who had Schizophrenia. They then sought out women who had given birth to a child who was given up for adoption before the child reached age 4. The child had to be adopted by a nonrelated Finnish family. Tiernari et al. (1994) concluded that growing up in a healthy family environment served as a protective factor for high-risk adopted children. An additional finding was that the index children were less likely to be psychologically healthy and were also more likely to have some type of psychosis (not necessarily Schizophrenia) compared to the control children. The summation is clear: Genetic transmission of Schizophrenia at the least increases the likelihood of developing the disorder, but growing up in a disturbed and disruptive family environment probably plays a critical role in increasing the individual's vulnerability. This provides evidence as well for the diathesis-stress model of mental illness.

Prenatal and perinatal causal factors of Schizophrenia have also been investigated. Research has revealed that schizophrenic individuals are more likely to have experienced problems while they were in their mother's womb and are also more likely to have suffered some type of birth trauma. Prenatal problems specifically implicate the mother contracting some type of illness or infection. Some studies have noted that pregnant women who had influenza during the *second* trimester were more likely to produce a child who had Schizophrenia (Huttunen & Niskanen, 1978).

One explanation of how influenza might be involved is that the flu interferes with proper neural development, which is especially critical during the second trimester. The hypothesis is that this improper neural development some-

DON'T FORGET

Many schizophrenic individuals have no close relatives (first- or second-degree biological) that have had Schizophrenia. Still, Kendler and Diehl (1993) discovered that the average risk of developing Schizophrenia in first-degree relatives of index cases is 4.8 percent. While this may not seem like a lot, this is nine times *greater* than the rate for normal control cases.

how leaves the individual more vulnerable to developing Schizophrenia later on in life. Perinatal trauma that may increase one's vulnerability include extended labor, breech delivery (the baby does not properly turn and comes out bottom or feet first and is thus born or delivered bottom end or feet first), the use of forceps (at times these clamps are placed around the baby's head to help the baby leave the birth canal), and the umbilical cord being wrapped around the baby's neck before or during birth. The latter condition leads to *anoxia,* where the oxygen supply to the brain is either impaired or cut off. Of course, if the cord is wrapped too tightly, the baby might be asphyxiated. Cannon, Jones, and Murray (2002) examined birth records of mothers whose child or children later developed Schizophrenia and found they experienced more perinatal complications than average. Research remains unclear as to whether these complications somehow interact with genetic factors. There are two possibilities. First, these prenatal and perinatal complications produce neurological abnormalities during fetal development that lead to the development of Schizophrenia regardless of genetics or a biological family history. The other possibility is that a fetus that is genetically predisposed to developing Schizophrenia is more likely to suffer neurological damage from prenatal or perinatal complications.

One interesting fact that researchers have seen over the years is that, for whatever reason, individuals who are more likely to develop Schizophrenia are born in the winter and early spring (e.g., McGrath & Welham, 1999). This *seasonal birth effect* is now a fact and is no longer considered a hypothesis. One possible explanation for this effect is diseases and viral infections. Influenza season peaks during the winter months; of course, during these months the weather gets colder in most parts of the United States, and people are more likely to stay indoors. Diseases and infections breed well indoors where the environment may be moist, which is typical during colder months when people use humidifiers to moisten

CAUTION

It is critical to note that the previously mentioned prenatal and perinatal complications do not necessarily *only* increase the likelihood that an individual will develop Schizophrenia. The complications mentioned can also lead to the development or presence of cerebral palsy, Mental Retardation, learning disabilities, and perhaps Attention Deficit/Hyperactivity Disorder (ADHD) among other conditions.

indoor air. Additionally, influenza is spread by contact and by droplets and is highly contagious, a problem when one person is sick and is stuck indoors with many others. Thus, if a pregnant woman gets the flu, which can increase her child's chances of developing Schizophrenia, she most likely contracted the flu during the colder months of the year. Torrey, Bowler, Rawlings, and Terrazas (1993) performed research that revealed a strong positive correlation between the occurrence of stillbirths (the fetus is dead upon delivery) and live births of individuals who became schizophrenic. The critical point is that both stillbirths and schizophrenic individuals occurrences were elevated during winter months. They hypothesized that a common infection probably exists in both the stillbirths and in the individuals who were at a higher risk for Schizophrenia. This infectious agent produces either a stillbirth or somehow produces neurological damage or neurological changes that increase the person's vulnerability to Schizophrenia.

Anatomy and Physiology

The Dopamine Hypothesis
The dopamine hypothesis provides a fascinating perspective and is one that continues to command attention. It also produces tremendous controversy in psychology and in psychiatry. *Dopamine* is a neurotransmitter that is involved with motor movement (specifically smooth controlled movements like walking in a steady gait); cognitive and frontal lobe functions like memory, attention, and problem solving; and providing feelings of enjoyment and reinforcement to motivate us to do, or continue doing, certain activities. Dopamine is released by naturally rewarding experiences such as food, sex, and the use of certain drugs such as amphetamine. One interesting concept is that the dopamine pathways may somehow be pathologically altered in addicted individuals.

Dopamine is released when unpleasant or aversive stimuli are encountered; dopamine neurons are fired when a pleasurable activity is expected, regardless of whether it actually happens. Thus dopamine may be involved with desire and not, perhaps, with pleasure. Antipsychotic medications such as Thorazine (chlorpromazine) that are known to reduce dopamine activity have also been demonstrated to reduce people's desire for experiencing pleasurable stimuli, but they do not reduce the person's actually liking the stimuli.

The dopamine hypothesis is rather simple: Too much dopamine activity at certain synaptic sites in the brain is responsible for causing Schizophrenia. Alternate viewpoints of the dopamine hypothesis posit that the schizophrenic individual's dopamine receptors for some reason have become hypersensitive and thus the dopamine neurons fire off when they should not be doing so, or the schizophrenic individual has too many postsynaptic dopamine receptors. Some researchers offer support for this hypothesis because of the effectiveness of the typical antipsychotic medications (such as Thorazine and Mellaril) in reducing schizophrenic hallucinations by blocking postsynaptic dopamine receptors. In other words, these medications are effective, in part, because they decrease the dopamine buildup in the brain.

There are some significant problems with this theory. First, typical antipsychotic medications are not only used to treat Schizophrenia. They can also be used to treat other Psychotic Disorders, can be used to treat some forms of mania, and in very mild dosages can be used to treat Anxiety Disorders. Thus, dopamine blockers are not only used to treat Schizophrenia although this is their front-line indication. Another problem is simpler: There are schizophrenic individuals who do not respond to typical antipsychotic drugs that will decrease dopamine levels. Thus, if this hypothesis were the sole explanation for Schizophrenic Disorders, all individuals should respond to a degree to these medications (of course allowing for some variance and error).

The time factor is also an issue. Specifically, the drugs will work quickly when used properly, that is, the dopamine receptors will be effectively blocked within a few hours, but any behavior change with a schizophrenic individual will occur over time, at the least in a few weeks. Thus, we would expect to see immediate or extremely rapid improvement in schizophrenic individuals who take these medications (all things being somewhat equal again) if excessive dopamine activity were the sole cause of Schizophrenia. However, these medications usually do not produce therapeutically effective results rapidly. As you will also see in the next section, many medications work not by stifling excessive dopamine activity but reducing it to unusually low levels, which often produces significant side effects such as tremors and Tardive Dyskinesia.

Thus, what can we conclude about the dopamine hypothesis? We can state with confidence that dopamine is probably somehow involved with Schizophrenia; however, we do not yet know how it is involved. Other neurotransmitters such as serotonin have been implicated. Newer medications such as Clozaril (clozapine) work well with schizophrenic patients who do not respond well to typical antipsychotics such as Thorazine. It is possible that somehow serotonin and dopamine pathways in the brain interact or are dysfunctional, thus leading to the development of Schizophrenia. We can state that once conclusive evidence is found, neurotransmitters, most likely dopamine and serotonin, will be implicated in the etiology of Schizophrenia.

The neuroanatomy of schizophrenic individuals is also intriguing. Magnetic resonance imaging (MRI) investigations seem to reveal that schizophrenic brains are affected in a number of different ways. Many MRI studies revealed that the total volume of brain tissue in the schizophrenic individual's brain has decreased when compared with average brain masses. Another consistent finding is that schizophrenic individuals have enlarged lateral ventricles in their brain, ranging from slightly to moderately enlarged. Ventricles are gaps or cavities in the brain that contain cerebrospinal fluid. In other words, there is more fluid in a schizophrenic's brain than one would expect when compared to a normal individual, thus decreasing the actual brain matter as a result. These differences are thought to be due to the effects of having Schizophrenia and are not thought to be due to treatment with antipsychotic medications. These structural changes do not worsen significantly as the Schizophrenia progresses. The changes seem to occur early on during the course of the Schizophrenia and perhaps do play a role in Schizophrenia's development (Cannon, 1998).

As you might expect, there are problems with these findings. Ventricles enlarge naturally with age. Additionally, enlarged ventricles can also be seen in other conditions such as traumatic brain injuries (TBIs) and Alcohol Dependence. Finally, enlarged ventricles occur in about one-third of schizophrenic individuals, and, if this is indeed a true causal factor, we would expect this number to be much larger.

The temporal lobes have also come under scrutiny with MRI scans. Specific parts of the limbic system have been found to be of decreased size when contrasted with nonschizophrenic brains. Specifically, the hippocampus, the amygdala, and the thalamus have all been found to be reduced in size. These structures are involved with emotion regulation as well as with the integration of cognition and emotion. The hippocampus is also involved with LTM.

The decrease in size is especially evident on the brain's left side, where the language functions are housed. Shenton (1996) asserts that schizophrenic individuals who demonstrate the greatest amount of disorganized language may be most likely to have a size decrease in the temporal lobe structures.

We again need to exercise caution when interpreting these findings. Many individuals who have neurological and other psychological disorders demonstrate brain structure and function changes that are similar to those reported in the preceding. Current research has yet to find a specific lesion in the brain that is associated with the development or presence of Schizophrenia. The MRI studies also do not prove that a patient has Schizophrenia or any other mental illness just because she or he has enlarged ventricles or an undersized hippocampus. Differences have been identified in some studies, but they do not predict the presence of Schizophrenia. Alzheimer's and Huntington's Disease also show neurostructural abnormalities; does this mean that these disorders are linked to the Schizophrenic Disorders? All we can state with certainty is that in some schizophrenic individuals enlarged ventricles have been discovered, and in some schizophrenic individuals certain limbic system structures are smaller than average. All of the MRI hypotheses thus need to be viewed with caution.

One final physiological theory that is relatively new involves dysfunctional eye tracking, also called Smooth Pursuit Eye Movement (SPEM) dysfunction (Holzman, 2000). It has been discovered that schizophrenic individuals have trouble tracking a moving target visually (such as a pendulum) while their head is held still. What occurs is the following: Instead of tracking the pendulum smoothly, in a series of smooth, unbroken waves, the schizophrenic individual demonstrates a disruption of this smooth tracking ability by demonstrating a series of rapid eye movements. The schizophrenic individuals demonstrate abnormal patterns of SPEM. About 50 percent of the close relatives of the schizophrenic individual demonstrate the deviant eye-tracking patterns (Avila, McMahon, Elliott, & Thaker, 2002), which suggests that poor SPEM performance may be correlated with an increased likelihood of developing Schizophrenia. Additional research has demonstrated that SPEM is stable over time and that SPEM can be influenced by genetics. Most interestingly, SPEM dysfunction has been discovered in individuals who demonstrate symptoms of Schizotypal Personality Disorder, which some consider a prodromal Schizophrenia (Iacono & Clementz, 1993).

≡ *Rapid Reference 7.5*

Key Terms to Know

Dopamine: Dopamine is a neurotransmitter involved with motor movement; cognitive and frontal lobe functions like memory, attention, and problem solving; and providing feelings of enjoyment and reinforcement to motivate us to do, or continue doing, certain activities.

Ventricles: Ventricles are gaps or cavities in the brain that contain cerebrospinal fluid.

Smooth Pursuit Eye Movement (SPEM) Dysfunction: This is a phenomenon where schizophrenic individuals have trouble tracking a moving target visually (such as a pendulum) while their head is held still.

Smooth pursuit eye movement dysfunction may instead indicate poor motor control, which is a symptom indicative of many other disorders, not necessarily psychiatric in nature. For example, Parkinson's Disease victims often have poor motor control in the disease's later stages. Would you expect their SPEM to be dysfunctional before they contract this disease? People with SPEM dysfunctions who do not have a diagnosable mental illness have been found to have interpersonal difficulties and some type of neurological impairment. Thus, SPEM dysfunctions might serve as a marker for an individual's vulnerability to developing Schizophrenia.

We will conclude this section with a simple statement. As fascinating as all of these hypotheses are, they in turn present more questions than provide solid answers. We can say with certainty that the Schizophrenic Disorders do not have a single causal factor, but we can also say that somewhere in the etiological mix we will find some biological, biochemical, or neurological abnormalities. For definitions of key terms, see Rapid Reference 7.5.

Sociocultural Factors

It is a simple fact that prevalence rates of the Schizophrenic Disorders vary throughout the world. At the least this can be attributed to cross-cultural variances in defining mental illness and, more to the point, defining what qualifies as symptoms of a mental illness. For example, is paranoia abnormal in Pyongyang, North Korea? How about demonstrating an abnormal and exaggerated startle response in Tikrit, Iraq? What about the prevalence of apathy and unipolar depressive symptoms in cities such as Tromso, Norway, which lies way above the Arctic Circle and where it is completely dark during a portion of the winter months? These differences in the prevalence rates of Schizophrenia could also reflect religious differences and thus differences in religious values. Little research has occurred examining which cultural factors, if any, both increase and decrease the risk of developing Schizophrenia. It appears that the field just accepts the fact that differences exists and leaves it at that.

Schizophrenic disorders appear to occur less often in what we consider to be third-world, or less industrially developed, countries. More important for our present needs, evidence has been presented for many decades that the Schizophrenic Disorders are more prevalent among individuals with lower SES. The lower the SES, the more prevalent the Schizophrenic Disorders appear to be. A famous study by Faris and Dunham (1939) that is often presented in psychology and social work programs discovered that in Chicago the greatest prevalence of the Schizophrenic Disorders was in the neighborhoods with the lowest SES. Statistically speaking, this and many future studies point to an inverse correlation (or relationship) between SES and the prevalence of Schizophrenic Disorders. These data can be interpreted in a few ways.

First, being a member of a lower SES is itself highly stressful and this membership can harm an individual's ability to properly handle difficult situations. The *downward drift hypothesis* refers to individuals who are already in a low SES and who, when they begin developing prodromal symptoms of a Schizophrenic Disorder, drift even further downward on the SES scale because these symptoms prevent them from finding jobs or from forming interpersonal relationships that would offer support to help them handle the impending Schizophrenic Disorder (Gottesman, 1991). Support has been dis-

CAUTION

Once again we need to use care when we examine sociocultural factors. Coming from a low SES can be considered either a risk factor or an exacerbating factor for virtually all illnesses, mental and psychological. The ability to prevent or treat a disorder probably has a direct relationship with one's SES.

covered for this hypothesis, but the support is far from conclusive. We can, however, state that the Schizophrenic Disorders are partially influenced by the patient's sociocultural factors.

Psychological Factors

As you might have expected, much of the research focus into psychological factors has focused on behaviors and communications that occur within an individual's family. In essence, disrupted or unclear communication between parents (assuming an intact nuclear family) and dysfunctional family interactions were presumed to have led to the initial onset of schizophrenic symptoms. We will begin this section therefore with a conclusion: Research has not supported either of these hypotheses.

Bateson, Jackson, Haley, and Weakland (1956) proposed an interesting theory for the development of Schizophrenia that considers disruptive familial communication. Their double-bind communication theory of Schizophrenia posits that the individual develops Schizophrenia because she or he receives mixed messages at home. For example, Robert's father Henry tells him "Robert, I love you more than anything, and I am so proud of you" when Robert brings home a straight A report card. When Robert tries to approach him for a hug to give and receive affection, Henry freezes up and perhaps punishes him. Robert is thus constantly placed in situations where no matter what he does, he cannot win, and this increases any anxiety that is already present. Bateson posits that the individual has a psychotic break over a period of time because the mixed messages confuse him or her and because such disorganized and contradictory communication is eventually reflected in the child's own thinking and speech (1956). The individual does not know what the truth is or what reality is, and he or she has a break from reality. The parents of a schizophrenic individual are unable to clearly communicate with their child, and this leads to confusion on the child's part and to disrupted conversations within the family. This theory is no longer supported (Miklowitz, 1995) and, in fact, if used in family therapy, can be extremely damaging to the parents. If the parents or caregivers hear this theory, they may feel extreme guilt that the Schizophrenia developed in their child because of their mistakes in parenting (either what they said or did), causing them to feel very guilty and creating emotional duress for them. As many clinicians will state, any parent that has a child who has a serious mental illness, but especially one as devastating as Schizophrenia, does not need this additional burden.

A brief mention of Fromm-Reichmann's concept of the *schizophrenogenic mother* (Fromm-Reichmann, 1948) is warranted. You might expect at this point in your reading that based on the date this concept is archaic, and it is. For Fromm-Reichmann, the schizophrenogenic mother is typically a cold, dominant, rejecting mother, similar to a refrigerator mother, steely cold and frosty with no feelings. This type of mother was believed to cause the development of Schizophrenia in her child or children. Similar to the double-bind theory, this concept would most likely cause extreme guilt and has not been supported by research.

What we *do* appear to agree upon regarding a family's influence on the development of Schizophrenia is that the family's environment does indeed influence Schizophrenia. However, it has an impact on its course, not on its etiology. The when, where, and how regarding the onset of schizophrenic symptoms is not important, but instead these concepts examine how the individual adjusts once symptoms appear and the patient has already been treated for Schizophrenia. What has been discovered with discharged schizophrenic patients in remission is that relapse seems to be linked to a type of negative communication called *expressed emotion* (EE). Two factors appear to have been discovered that are critical in EE. First, the patient receives hostility or excessive criticism from his or her relatives. The second factor involves overinvolvement and overprotectiveness of family members. Research has supported overall results, especially among chronic schizophrenics and their families. Family members had a high EE when they accepted positive symptoms as the product of a mental illness, and, in addition, EE is high when the family members believe that Schizophrenia and its symptoms are under the patient's control (Hooley & Hiller, 1998). We can conclude that EE appears to be a critical component in the development of an active schizophrenic episode.

CAUTION

Butzlaff and Hooley (1998) note that high EE is a good predictor of a Schizophrenic Disorder before its onset, but it is an even better predictor of the outcome of a mood disorder and of an eating disorder. What this simply implies is that this etiological concept is shared with other mental illnesses and, perhaps more important, that there may be some common causal factors (or common links) among many mental illnesses.

Finally, we will again mention the diathesis stress model of mental illness, which is accepted by many psychologists today as a plausible explanation for the development of a Schizophrenic Disorder. To review, the individual is born with a diathesis to develop Schizophrenia, the diathesis being a genetic vulnerability. Recall that this does *not* mean that they will develop Schizophrenia. The stress portion explains the development of Schizophrenia thusly: The individual will develop Schizophrenia if they experience some type of stress so severe that they are unable to cope (Zubin & Spring, 1977). Such stressors may include extreme trauma, interpersonal conflicts, marital problems, the loss of a loved one, or a total loss of income and savings. If the individual can effectively handle the stress brought about by the trauma, the Schizophrenic Disorder *may* never develop.

Thus, what can we conclude about the etiology of Schizophrenic Disorders? The conclusion is a simple one, but it leads to many complications: There is no single causal factor, a certain causal sequence of events, or one entity (genetic or otherwise) in the etiology of the Schizophrenic Disorders. Clinicians seem to be dealing with a variety of disorders combined under one diagnostic criterion; this amalgam of disorders is probably caused by a combination of biological, neurological, psychological, and sociocultiural factors. Until we have isolated one specific factor (or factors), this viewpoint is truly the most responsible one. For definitions of key terms, see Rapid Reference 7.6.

☰ *Rapid Reference 7.6*

Key Terms to Know

Double-Bind Communication Theory: This is Bateson's and his colleagues' theory that Schizophrenia develops because an individual receives mixed messages at home; it is archaic and disproven.

Schizophrenogenic Mother: This is Fromm-Reichmann's concept that Schizophrenia develops because an individual has a cold, dominant, rejecting mother, similar to a refrigerator mother, steely cold and frosty with no feelings; it is archaic.

Expressed Emotion (EE): Expressed emotion may be involved with helping to develop active episodes of Schizophrenia; it involves two factors: The patient receives hostility or excessive criticism from his or her relatives, and family members are overinvolved and overprotective.

TREATMENT MODALITIES

The most effective approach toward treating Schizophrenia seems to be a combination of pharmaceutical, behavioral, cognitive, and family therapy, with the use of antipsychotic medications seen as the primary treatment modality for the Schizophrenic Disorders. Even though many psychologists and others agree that these approaches tend to be more effective, none of them, alone or in combination, can be said to cure or, in quite a few instances, improve the Schizophrenic Disorder. Effective treatments modalities will work on attempting to rid the individual of hallucinations, delusions, and disorganized aspects of behavior or, at the least, to attempt to lessen these symptoms. An additional concern for clinicians is that many schizophrenic individuals will relapse, even if their treatment is maintained.

Before the 1950s, the expected outcome for schizophrenic individuals was poor. Unless the schizophrenic patient's family was quite wealthy and could afford a private psychiatric hospital (this also presumes that the family was involved and supportive and did not wish to disown the patient), schizophrenic patients were usually transported to public institutions that served as warehouses for the mentally ill. Once the patients arrived, they rarely received treatment, and, if they did, the treatment at this time was often cruel as well as being ineffective. For example, schizophrenic patients often received ECT therapy, which was ineffective in treating hallucinations or delusions. The patients were often tied up in straitjackets and left alone in their beds or in the dayroom. Some may have received prefrontal lobotomies. The staff at these facilities was poorly trained, burned out, and overworked. The staff did not wish to deal with these patients, and neither did the general population. Therefore, many of the public psychiatric hospitals served a function similar to prisons: They removed sometimes dangerous and bothersome individuals from population and society. Many of these patients were never expected to leave the hospital.

Because of the chronic hospitalization, daily living and coping skills needed to survive outside of the hospital were forgotten. Thus, in a type of self-fulfilling prophecy (or perhaps learned helplessness), the individuals deteriorated to such a degree that they really never could survive on their own in the world outside of the hospital without significant assistance. Because there was no real need to use these skills in the hospital (such as trimming a Christmas tree, using a telephone, or making change from a dollar), they would deteriorate and perhaps vanish.

Antipsychotic Medications

One of the most important advances in psychology and psychiatry occurred in the mid-1950s when the first group of antipsychotic medications, the *phenothiazines*, was introduced. Known then as *major tranquilizers*, these medications calmed down some of the more violent inpatients, but they also worked on the schizophrenic patients' positive symptoms, specifically their hallucinations and delusions. Thorazine (chlorpromazine) was accidentally discovered by the French doctor Henri Laborit (1914–1955) in 1952 when he used Thorazine as a supplement to anesthesia. In 1953 Thorazine was first used to treat psychiatric patients. Thorazine went beyond simple sedation, with patients showing improvements in thinking and emotional behavior.

We must mention the terminology before we examine antipsychotic medications. In the past antipsychotics were divided into *typical* and *atypical* classes (Bezchlibnyk-Butler & Jeffries, 2005). Typical antipsychotics were dopamine antagonists and include medications such as Thorazine. Atypical antipsychotic medications are newer medications that are more effective at alleviating positive symptoms and also appear to work on serotonin levels. Drugs in this class include Clozaril. This distinction between typical and atypical antipsychotics sometimes is unclear; some authors now use the terms *second generation* to refer to the atypical antipsychotics and *Conventional* to refer to typical antipsychotics (Bezchlibnyk-Butler & Jeffries, 2005). Throughout the remainder of this chapter, we will use the more familiar terminology, typical and atypical.

The changes that these discoveries brought about were stunning in their suddenness. Many chronic inpatients previously seen as hopeless were now released because they could continue their treatment in an outpatient setting. The discovery and successful employment of these medications changed the field of psychology and psychiatry and made people realize that individuals with a mental illness could be treated effectively and should be afforded proper treatment.

The field of antipsychotic medications is rapidly changing, with newer and better (i.e., fewer side effects and more effective at reducing negative symp-

DON'T FORGET

Statistics vary, but anywhere from 10 percent to 25 percent of schizophrenic patients do not demonstrate improvement when using typical antipsychotic medications (Bezchlibnyk-Butler & Jeffries, 2005). Approximately 35 percent respond somewhat to these medications; they demonstrate improvement, but not full remission of the schizophrenic symptoms. Finally, some estimates list the percentage of schizophrenic individuals who do not respond to any type of treatment (including atypical antipsychotic medications) as approximately 10 percent.

DON'T FORGET

Recall that a side effect is temporary. That is, side effects will drop out for most people once they have physiologically adapted to the medication.

toms) appearing often. Statistics show that a schizophrenic individual has an excellent chance of being discharged from the hospital after a few weeks or perhaps months, and the concept of the eternal stay is considered to be an artifact. A small percentage of the discharged patients experience a full recovery from their Schizophrenic Disorder without residual aftereffects or relapses. However, many schizophrenic patients get involved in recidivism—or the revolving door of mental illness as some call it—because they are often readmitted due to relapses, then they are treated, discharged, readmitted, and so on as the cycle continues.

Typical Antipsychotic Medications
These medications include Thorazine (chlorpromazine), Mellaril (thioridazine), and Stelazine (trifluroperazine). These medications seem to be dopamine antagonists, and they have short half-lives, which denotes that they must be taken daily, sometimes several times a day. This medication class works much better on positive symptoms of Schizophrenic Disorders rather than the negative symptoms. Sometimes therapeutic efficacy is realized in about a week, but, generally speaking, noticeable improvements do not occur until several weeks after the medication regimen has begun. In general, no one typical antipsychotic medication is more effective than another. The choice of medication might be determined by the desire to minimize side effects and may also be based on the half-life of the medication (i.e., how long it takes for one-half of the medication to be metabolized by the body). A major advantage of the antipsychotic medications is that it is

virtually impossible to become physiologically dependent on any of them. As is true with any substance (or situation, for that matter), it is always possible to become psychologically dependent on them. Ironically, the medications that we will discuss (and have previously examined in other chapters) that have a very low physiological dependence potential also seem to have the most significant side effects.

The typical antipsychotic medications tend to produce some of the most severe side effects in some patients. Some of the most common side effects of the typical antipsychotics are drowsiness, dizziness, dry mouth, urinary hesitancy, and constipation. These side effects are known as *anticholinergic side effects,* and they are similar to the effects produced by antihistamines, medications that include the over-the-counter cold and allergy pills like Benadryl, Chlortrimetron, and Contac. Because of the nature of these side effects, some clinicians call them *drying side effects.* If nothing else, these side effects are bothersome and unpleasant, but for most people they are considered to be more an annoyance than a hazard. Recall that some of the antidepressants that we discussed in Chapter 3 also produce anticholinergic side effects.

Extrapyramidal side effects (EPS) include Parkinsonism, or Parkinson's Disease-like side effects, such as tremors, shaking, rigidity, and drooling. These effects tend to be more common in adults and in senior citizens and can be treated by adjusting or changing the medication, or by adding Symmetrel (amantadine) to the patient's list of required medications (Amantadine is an antiviral drug that has been used to treat influenza). Other effects can include akathisia (restless agitation) and unusual involuntary postures. Extrapyramidal side effects can diminish after 3 to 4 months of continuous typical antipsychotic treatment. Medications such as Cogentin (benztropine), Benadryl (diphenhydramine), and Artane (trihexyphenidyl) can also be administered during the first few months of treatment to help minimize the EPS severity, although akathisia may require beta blockers (medications designed to lower heartrate and blood pressure) or even benzodiazepines. Cogentin is most often administered; it is an anticholinergic drug used to treat muscle-rigidity, restlessness, and stiffness. It is believed that the risk of Tardive Dyskinesia, which is a serious side effect caused by the extended usage of various antipsychotic medications such as Thorazine, can be reduced with the use of Cogentin. Cogentin can also be used to treat Parkinson's disease (Bezchlibnyk-Butler & Jeffries, 2005). These medications have their own side effects, such as dry mouth, urinary hesitancy, nausea, and insomnia.

What occurs when a patient has Tardive Dyskinesia? The patient will demonstrate involuntary face, trunk, and limb movements, such as a protruding tongue, chewing, and lip puckering. They will also demonstrate spastic bodily limb and trunk movements. These involuntary bodily movements may include jiggling of the legs, writhing motions, and head and pelvic jerking. Individuals who have Tardive Dyskinesia may also have seizures. As you might expect, Tardive Dyskinesia is very upsetting to the patients who contract this side effect as well as to the patient's families. An additional concern is that Tardive Dyskinesia is irreversible in some patients. We know that Tardive Dyskinesia is caused by antipsychotic medications, but once the symptoms appear in some patients, even removal from the medication does not alleviate or eliminate the condition. In some patients the Tardive Dyskinesia becomes significantly worse once antipsychotic medications are discontinued.

Depot antipsychotics, a second type of typical antipsychotic medication, are medications that have a very long half-life, lasting about 2 to 4 weeks once administered. These medications are injected and are ideal for patients who have poor or inconsistence compliance with drug therapy. Medications in this category include Prolixin (fluphenazine) and Haldol (haloperidol). These medications produce a lower relapse rate if for no other reason that the schizophrenic patient does not need to remember to take his or her medication every day, and thus medication compliance is increased. The most critical concern remains side effects. If the individual has a bad side effect reaction, they will have to cope with the side effect as long as the medication is active. Haldol and Prolixin also take longer to reach maintenance levels.

DON'T FORGET

One reason why may schizophrenic individuals do not take their antipsychotic medications on an outpatient basis is specifically to avoid these side effects. What these individuals often do instead is turn to alcohol or illicit drugs when their hallucinations and delusions return (we call this *Self-medicating*).

CAUTION

The term *neuroleptic* refers to the side effects of the typical antipsychotic medications, specifically the Parkinsonian-like symptoms they can produce.

Atypical Antipsychotic Medications

Atypical antipsychotics appeared in the 1990s and again signaled some major advances in the treatment of the Schizophrenic Disorders. This group of medications is as effective as typical antipsychotics in reducing the positive symptoms of Schizophrenia, and they are more effective, in general, in reducing the negative symptoms of Schizophrenia. In general, they also have markedly fewer side effects than the typical antipsychotics (Bezchlibnyk-Butler & Jeffries, 2005). This newer type of antipsychotic includes Clozaril (clozapine) and Risperdal (risperidone). For example, Clozaril evidently does not cause Tardive Dyskinesia and other muscular problems, while Risperdal apparently does not cause EPS and has a much lower Tardive Dyskinesia risk (Bezchlibnyk-Butler & Jeffries, 2005; Maxmen & Ward, 1995). However, Clozaril may cause agranulocytosis in about one percent of the individuals who take it. *Agranulocytosis* is a drastic lowering of the individual's white blood cell count to the point where a minor cut or cold could potentially kill the individual. Knowing this, the FDA approved Clozaril in 1990 with the requirement that the individual taking the medication get weekly monitoring of their white blood cell counts. If this condition does occur, it is prudent for the psychiatrist to stop Clozaril treatment. Some of the other atypical antipsychotics that have appeared recently include Zyprexa (olanzapine) and Seroquel (quetiapine) (Bezchlibnyk-Butler & Jeffries, 2005).

Treatment compliance tends to be increased with the atypical antipsychotic medications because of their decreased EPS and other side effects. This does not by any means imply that the side effects produced by this medication class are harmless. One common side effect is significant weight gain leading to obesity. This can lead to hypertension, coronary disease, and Type II Diabetes, all of which can either maim or kill. Some research has demonstrated that at least 30 percent of schizophrenics who did not respond to typical antipsychotics or who were resistant to treatment in general responded well to atypical antipsychotics (Bezchlibnyk-Butler & Jeffries, 2005). Most professionals define treatment resistance of schizophrenic individuals as a failure to demonstrate significant improvement while taking a typical antipsychotic medication after at least 6 weeks of treatment time. The doses here are defined as having to be moderate to high levels. Note that much of the research examining atypical antipsychotics involved Clozaril as it has been on the market the longest (Bezchlibnyk-Butler & Jeffries, 2005).

Third Generation Antipsychotic Medications

We need to briefly mention Abilify (aripiprasole), which has been available since 2002 and is considered an atypical antipsychotic medication. Abilify falls into a new class of antipsychotics, the Third-Generation Antipsychotic medications. Abilify is somewhat unique in that it does not produce Parkinsonian-like side effects, tardive dyskinesia, agranulocytosis, weight gain, or diabetes. In addition, the patient discontinuation rate is approximately 9 percent, significantly lower than the other antipsychotic medications. This can be partially attributed to the absence of significant or debilitating side effects.

Abilify works by stabilizing dopamine receptors in the brain. In other words, Abilify will act as a dopamine agonist when the dopamine levels are too low, and will act as a dopamine antagonist when the levels are too high. This is in contrast to the typical and atypical antipsychotics which act as dopamine antagonists. Like some of the atypical antipsychotics such as Risperdal (risperidone), Abilify also blocks serotonin receptors.

As was previously mentioned, all of the antipsychotic medications block dopamine receptors in the cortical and limbic areas of the brain, while the atypical antipsychotics also block serotonin receptors. In general, the typical antipsychotics are better dopamine receptor blockers, while atypical antipsy-

DON'T FORGET
....

Just before this book's publication a major study involving 1493 schizophrenic patients appeared in the New England Journal of Medicine. Lieberman et al (2005) compared schizophrenic patients taking the conventional (first-generation or typical) antipsychotic medication Trilafon (perphenazine) with schizophrenic patients taking Risperdal (risperidone), Seroquel (quetiapine), and Zyprexa (olanzepine). Geodon (ziprasidone) was included in the study after FDA approval occurred. The results of their study are intriguing, to say the least: 1061 out of 1432 patients who received at least one dose of medication (74 percent) discontinued their medication use. Of all the medications studied, patients stayed on Zyprexa the longest. What is critical is that Lieberman et al (2005) discovered that Trilafon's efficacy appeared to be similar to that of Risperdal, Seroquel, and Geodon. The implication: Perhaps patients with Schizophrenia who do not have health insurance and must pay for their own medications may be served equally as well by typical (conventional) antipsychotics such as Trilafon, which cost about 10 times less than medications such as Geodon and Risperdal.

≡ *Rapid Reference 7.7*

Antipsychotic Medications and Side Effects

Typical (Conventional) Antipsychotic Medications: These include Thorazine (chlorpromazine), Mellaril (thioridazine), and Stelazine (trifluoperazine); they seem to be dopamine antagonists; they have short half-lives and work much better on positive symptoms of Schizophrenic Disorders.

Atypical (Second Generation) Antipsychotic Medications: As effective as typical antipsychotics in reducing the positive symptoms of Schizophrenia; more effective, in general, in reducing the negative symptoms of Schizophrenia and block serotonin receptors in the brain; these include medications such as Risperdal (risperidone) and Clozaril (clozapine).

Third-Generation Antipsychotic Medications: This includes medications such as Abilify (aripiprasole); Abilify does not produce significant or debilitating side effects; it acts as a serotonin receptor blocker and works to regulate dopamine levels in the brain rather than simply block dopamine receptors.

Depot Antipsychotics: This is a subclass of typical antipsychotic medications; these medications have a very long half-life, lasting about 2 to 4 weeks once administered; these medications are injected and include Prolixin (fluphenazine) and Haldol (haloperidol).

Anticholinergic Side Effects: These occur from using typical antipsychotics; some side effects are drowsiness, dizziness, dry mouth, urinary hesitancy, and constipation which are sometimes known as antihistamine effects or drying effects.

Extrapyramidal Side Effects (EPS): These includes Parkinsonism, or Parkinson's Disease-like side effects, such as tremors, shaking, rigidity, and drooling; they are produced by using typical antipsychotic medications.

Tardive Dyskinesia (TD): This is due to using typical antipsychotic medications; the patient demonstrates involuntary face, trunk, and limb movements and spastic bodily limb and trunk movements; the patient may also have seizures.

chotics are better serotonin blockers (Bezchlibnyk-Butler & Jeffries, 2005). See Rapid Reference 7.7 for a review of antipsychotic medications and side effects.

Psychotherapy

Psychotherapeutic approaches do not focus on the schizophrenic individual's active symptoms, that is, his or her psychotic episodes. Instead, psychotherapy focuses on making changes that will be effective for a much lengthier period of time. Of course, implementing these changes takes time, and it also takes time to make sure that these changes in behavior and so on remain.

Because of the significance of EE, family therapy and family-oriented treatment approaches have been demonstrated to have a somewhat positive impact on the schizophrenic individual. Family modalities help the family members handle the schizophrenic individual, especially during relapses and during times when she or he goes off of his or her medication. One presumption is that family members are under extreme duress because they need to care for an individual who has a chronic condition. A critical component is education. Family members are educated about the Schizophrenic Disorders—what it means to have one, the symptoms and their meanings—and are taught to accept the nature of the disorder and the fact that the patient may not be cured but might go into remission. The purpose of this is to eliminate the possibility that the family will develop unrealistic expectations for the schizophrenic patient that might lead to harsh criticism of him or her. Behavioral techniques, where family members are taught how to improve communication between themselves and the schizophrenic individual as well as how to improve communication among the family members themselves, are also taught. The obvious goal here is to try to get the family to work together to help the patient and to not be at odds with each other or allied against the patient. Hopefully, this will minimize the possibility of conflict.

There are some problems with this approach. Schizophrenic individuals may eventually relapse, and family treatment modalities may only serve to delay relapse, not prevent it. Finally, in the era of managed care, family treatment methods might not be permitted (Bellack, Haas, Schooler, & Flory, 2000).

Social skills training (SST) is also a widely used therapeutic modality. Even schizophrenics who successfully return to the community probably still have some residual symptoms that need to be addressed. Research has shown that social skill deficits remain and appear to act independently of positive and negative symptoms. These deficits may include being appropriately assertive, having a willingness to compromise, demonstrating socially appropriate behaviors, being able to regulate emotions, and recognizing appropriate boundaries (for example, recognizing that masturbation in public is not allowed and that if you are sexually attracted to a stranger, you do not run up and start fondling them). During SST the individual remains on his or her antipsychotic medication. Basic skills, as well as social problem solving skills and cognitive effectiveness, are taught to the individual. Skills are taught through the use of modeling, role playing, and verbal and social reinforcement. Management of medication and schizophrenic symptoms and basic conversation and self-care skills are also taught. When used in combination with antipsychotic medication, SST appears to lead to short-term improvements (e.g., Bustillo, Lauriella, Horan, & Keith, 2001). However, research remains unclear as to whether SST helps to prevent relapse and whether SST prevents symptoms from reappearing once the SST has concluded.

Another approach involves the community and is called *assertive community treatment* (ACT) This approach uses an interdisciplinary treatment team that provides education, rehabilitation, skills training, and overall support in addition to the antipsychotic medication. Usually the team provides services on a regular basis during the week and also provides services at any time, day or night, during crisis situations. The goals here are to help to maintain the schizophrenic individual (or other individuals with chronic, serious mental illnesses) in the community and to attempt to reduce the need for further hospitalization. What differs from traditional forms of treatment is that the team goes to the individual instead of expecting the patient to come to them. Research has offered support for ACT methods (e.g., Thornicroft & Susser, 2001); however, ACT is costly and is not easy to properly implement. It requires a well-organized and extensive treatment network. Because ACT appears to reduce the number of days spent in an inpatient psychiatric facility while at the same time improving the schizophrenic individual's level of functioning, in the long run ACT proves to be more beneficial and cost-effective than traditional serves provided by community mental health centers (CMHC).

Other treatment modalities use cognitive behavioral techniques to help schizophrenic individuals cope with stress and to help them handle some of their cognitive processing deficits, specifically to help them to attempt to reduce auditory hallucinations and thus to make them less upsetting. Skill training focuses on teaching the schizophrenic individual that these hallucinations are misattributed to an external source. By reattributing them to internal sources, they may be able to accept the hallucinations and realize that perhaps their thoughts about the voices, not the voices themselves, are what upsets them. They are also taught to recognize environmental situations and cues that may exacerbate the hallucinations.

Schizophrenic individuals are also taught to recognize cognitive, affective, and physiological and bodily indicators of stress and how to properly handle it, specifically progressive muscle relaxation techniques and cognitive restructuring (Hogarty et al., 1997). Hogarty et al. discovered that stress reduction was effective in reducing the relapse rate, but *only* for individuals who lived with their families (1997). Curiously, they also found that those who lived independently actually experienced an increased relapse rate when compared to controls, which the researchers suggested was caused by the schizophrenic individuals' experiencing more stress and more instability living away from their families. Thus, they became overwhelmed and decompensated (i.e., deteriorated and began to demonstrate active symptoms).

Finally, what about schizophrenic patients who require long-term inpatient hospitalization or, perhaps, are never at the point where they can safely leave sheltered care? *Token economies* have been beneficial for inpatients to get them to display desired behaviors and to decrease the display of undesirable behaviors. A list of desired positive behaviors is drawn up for each patient, such as shaving every day, proper toileting, and appropriate participation in social activities. For each instance in which the appropriate behavior is demonstrated, praise and a token are given to the patient. Both reinforce the desired behavior; praise and tokens are given out by the staff, who closely monitors the patients' behaviors. These tokens can be exchanged at the end of a period of time (a day or a week) for food or certain privileges, such as television time. Inappropriate behaviors are ignored with the idea that ignoring them will lead to a decrease and to extinction. If necessary, punishment, such as privilege removal, is administered, although this is not desired in this system. Research has shown that token economies are quite effective, even when examined over a lengthy period of time (Paul & Lentz, 1977). In fact, 11 percent of the patients in the treatment group were released to independent living situations and were not, at least during the study and its follow up, readmitted to the hospital. None of the patients in the control group was released to the community. Thus, behavioral modification programs can produce positive outcomes for chronic schizophrenic individuals who otherwise might never leave an inpatient setting.

Having said all of this, what can we conclude about effective treatment modalities for the Schizophrenic Disorders? It is clear to us that familial support as well as antipsychotic medications are two critical treatment modalities, and both should be included if we wish to successfully treat many schizophrenic individuals. Behavior modification techniques and stress reduction techniques (for the schizophrenic patient as well as for the family) have also proven to be effective. Finally, while combining many treatment modalities appears to be the most effective approach, one final modality is also critical: education. We cannot hope to make improvements in the treatment of schizophrenic individuals without proper education. While in this instance education may not necessarily lead to prevention, it may encourage family members to act more quickly if they recognize premorbid symptoms in the prodromal phase. Early intervention, as with all of the disorders discussed, is vitally important.

Putting It Into Practice

The Case of Jacob (Jack) Lunar

Jacob (Jack) is a 63-year-old White male who came to us because his daughter Rose was concerned about how Jack had arrived home 4 days prior. Rose told us that Jack was "picked up by the police because he was standing in the street, or sometimes against the building walls, beating the wall and the street with two large broom handles, all the while shouting at everyone around him. When the police arrived, he was lying down on the sidewalk, his pants were off, and he was wearing a hat that was made of shag carpet and a garbage bag. They saw his emergency ID bracelet and brought him back to us. My husband wants him back in the hospital, as he can't handle his craziness anymore."

We then asked Jack to tell us the reasons he was here. "Well, I think I'm getting the sickies again, like Dr. Jekyll there. You know, Frank was right all along, the pollen count is really high today ... [a very long silence] ... no, no, not to that. More of this, yes. I like pizza you know." Rose then interjected, "This has been happening a lot lately, it's impossible to converse with him. I think he's pouring his meds down the toilet. I love my father dearly, but please help him." Jack made poor eye contact throughout the initial intake session, as he frequently looked out the window, at his watch (which had stopped), often cleaned his glasses, and at times fixated on the stuffed animals in our office. He was sloppily dressed and looked like he needed a shower. He would giggle inappropriately at times during the interviews, but otherwise his affect remained flat.

(continued)

We then brought in our psychiatrist who evaluated Jack and determined that he was not a "threat to himself or to others as long as he is in his daughter's care. He should return tomorrow," which he did with Rose in tow. We had also obtained the hospital records that showed that Jack had spent a good part of the past 35 years in and out of state psychiatric hospitals. Jack had previously been diagnosed with Schizophrenia, Disorganized Type but had been discharged from the hospital because his schizophrenic symptoms had been in remission for a number of months. The hospital felt it more beneficial to release him into his daughter's care. The records also noted that he was on Thorazine (chlorpromazine) and responded very well, so the treatment team saw no reason to switch to another medication. The last note showed that Jack had made nice progress and showed few or no active schizophrenic symptoms (recall that active symptoms are Criterion A symptoms for Schizophrenia in the *DSM-IV-TR*).

We then asked Jack how he was feeling today. "Well, today ... today, today, today ... show ... I don't know ... should I blow, how am I? And how do you do Mr. Chips? I'm okay, cold but okay ... [long pause] ... yeah, well shut up, bitch...." We asked Jack to clarify what was occurring and he replied, "I'm listening to them say things, both of them, all day long, they don't shut up. They hate me I know, I'm too good for them, sexy guy like I am. Always smack talking about me ... [long pause] ... are too ... smells how? No, sunflowers in twiddly two." It appeared as though Jack was listening to voices carrying on a conversation about him or about some other topics, a common auditory hallucination in Schizophrenia. Rose also told us that "this listening to voices has occurred in the past and has been occurring the past three weeks, each day getting worse. I guess I trusted him too much to take his pills."

As you can readily see, it is impossible to carry on a conversation with Jack. Because Jack's auditory hallucinations consisted of two or more voices conversing with each other, Criterion A for Schizophrenia has been met. In addition, Jack also demonstrates disorganized speech, especially frequent derailment (sometimes called loose associations), tangentiality, and incoherence. Jack also meets Criterion B in that he has not been able to work or to be self-sufficient for many years. He always needs some form of total or partial care to make sure he survives each day. Finally, Jack's Schizophrenia has been present for decades, easily fulfilling the 6-month duration minimum. We thus arrived at the following diagnostic impressions; our Axis I diagnosis matched the psychiatric hospital's:

Axis I: Schizophrenia, Disorganized Type, Episodic with   295.10
          No Interposed Residual Symptoms
Axis II: No Diagnosis   V71.09
Axis III: Hypertension, Essential   401.9
Axis IV: Occupational Problems: Unemployment
Axis V: GAF = 20 (Current)

We diagnosed Jack with Disorganized subtype because all of the following symptoms were prominently displayed: disorganized speech, disorganized behavior, and flat or inappropriate affect. We used the episodic course specifier because his symptoms were not continuous when he was taking his antipsychotic medication. Jack did not display clinically significant residual symptoms between his active schizophrenic episodes, which led us to use the final course specifier with No Interposed Residual Symptoms. Jack received an Axis III diagnosis because he was also being treated for hypertension. Finally, his GAF is very low, which led us to formulate the treatment plan accordingly.

Treatment Plan

Once the initial intake was over, we asked Rose to bring Jack back the following day so the clinic team could meet. Because Jack was still actively hallucinating and because it appeared that he was not taking his medications, the clinic as a whole decided to rehospitalize him. The psychiatrist agreed as if left untreated, Jack could do something to hurt himself. Even though Rose loved him and was doing everything she could for him, she could not properly handle the situation.

When Jack arrived the next day, he was still incoherent, so we spent a lot of time talking with Rose and discussing the clinic's decision. "I was afraid you might come to that conclusion. I do believe that I can help Daddy, but he seems to be getting worse each day, and it's really draining me." We educated Rose on psychiatric hospitalization and told her there was no reason to be afraid. They treated Jack well before and they would do so again. We also explained to her that we would see Jack once he was released and work with him to get him more self-sufficient. The clinic also ran a support group for family members of schizophrenic patients, and we encouraged Rose to join. She agreed to take Jack back to the hospital and showed up later that day with his suitcase packed.

At last report Jack was still in the hospital and was responding well to his medication and to his treatment. Rose's husband did not want to take Jack back and would not move on this. Rose called us and told her that to preserve her marriage she was forced to agree. Because of this, Jack had nowhere to go if he was released. Thus, his chances of leaving the hospital are remote, and his prognosis is listed as Poor.

✍ TEST YOURSELF ✍

1. *Negative symptoms* refers to

   (a) responses, behaviors, or functions that are deficient or absent in an schizophrenic individual's behavior.

   (b) responses or behaviors that have been added to a schizophrenic's behavioral repertoire.

   (c) hallucinations and delusions.

   (d) the splitting of the schizophrenic's personality.

2. *Positive symptoms* refers to

   (a) responses, behaviors, or functions that are deficient or absent in an schizophrenic individual's behavior.

   (b) behaviors that have been added to a schizophrenic individual's normal behavioral repertoire.

   (c) anhedonia and flat affect.

   (d) alogia.

3. Hallucinations are

   (a) false beliefs that are held in spite of their impossibility of occurring or being so.

   (b) usually pleasant for a schizophrenic individual.

   (c) sensory experiences that are not caused by any external stimuli.

   (d) none of the above.

4. Delusions are

   (a) false beliefs that are held in spite of their impossibility of occurring or being so.

   (b) usually pleasant for a schizophrenic individual.

   (c) sensory experiences that are not caused by any external stimuli.

   (d) one example of loose associations.

5. Visual hallucinations are the most common type of hallucination with schizophrenic individuals. True or False?

6. The dopamine hypothesis states that Schizophrenia is caused by

   (a) a dopamine deficiency in their brains.

   (b) a dopamine excess in their brains.

   (c) dopamine reacting with serotonin.

   (d) a dopamine malfunction similar to that which occurs with Parkinson's Disease.

7. One critical treatment modality for schizophrenic individuals is

  (a) antipsychotic medications.

  (b) family therapy.

  (c) ECT.

  (d) both a and b.

8. Atypical antipsychotic medications such as Clozaril (clozapine) produce few serious side effects. True or False?

Answers: 1. a; 2. b; 3. c; 4. a; 5. False; 6. b; 7. d; 8. False

Eight

ESSENTIALS OF PERSONALITY DISORDERS

ersonality Disorders (sometimes called *character disorders*) affect about 15 million adults in the United States. Approximately 10 to 13 percent of the U.S. population meets the diagnostic criteria for a personality disorder at some point in his or her life. Personality Disorders are coded on Axis II of the *DSM-IV-TR* (APA, 2000). Generally speaking, Axis II diagnoses represent long-standing, deeply rooted problems (in this case personality traits) that are very difficult to treat successfully or modify. These disorders are also viewed as producing personality features that are maladaptive and inflexible and often cause adjustment problems or personal distress.

Personality Disorders are grouped into three clusters, based on the similarities among each disorder in the cluster. Cluster A includes disorders where the individual is viewed as being odd or eccentric. The individual may act socially detached, suspicious, and distrustful. Paranoid, Schizotypal, and Schizoid Personality Disorder fall into Cluster A. Cluster B includes disorders where the individual is viewed as being overly emotional or erratic in his or her behavior. The individual's behavior tends to be impulsive, may be dramatic, and may have antisocial features. Cluster B includes Histrionic, Narcissistic, Antisocial, and Borderline Personality Disorder. Individuals with Cluster B disorders are more likely to come in contact with mental health professionals, but not by choice. Cluster C includes disorders where the individual appears anxious or fearful. In this specific instance, these disorders, because they resemble Anxiety Disorders, are harder to differentially diagnose. Cluster C disorders include Avoidant, Dependent and Obsessive-Compulsive Personality Disorder. Because of the individual's anxieties, she or he is more likely to voluntarily seek help than an individual with a Cluster A or Cluster B disorder.

According to the *DSM-IV-TR* (APA, 2000), a personality disorder is ". . . an enduring pattern of inner experience and behavior that deviates markedly from the expectations of the individual's culture, is pervasive and inflexible, has an onset in adolescence or early adulthood, is stable over time, and leads to distress or impairment . . . The clinician should assess the stability of personality traits over time and across different situations" (pp. 685–686). One feature to look for when making a diagnosis is whether the patient displays extreme rigidity in relating to other people. Because of this rigidity, the patient cannot make adjustments to other people or to the environment. These individuals are caught up in a vicious cycle of self-defeating behaviors.

Generally, the Personality Disorders are not diagnosed in individuals under 18 years old. However, the *DSM-IV-TR* notes two critical exceptions. First, if the behaviors or symptoms (the authors call this *features*) have been present for at least *1 year*, then the individual can be diagnosed with a personality disorder even if she or he is under age 18. Second, Antisocial Personality Disorder (ASPD) *cannot* be diagnosed at all in an individual if she or he is less than 18 years old. This last condition is part of the formal diagnostic criteria for diagnosing ASPD. See Rapid Reference 8.1 for definitions of APA's personality disorder clusters.

≡ *Rapid Reference 8.1*

Personality Disorder Clusters

Cluster A: This cluster includes disorders where the individual is viewed as being odd or eccentric; the individual may act socially detached, suspicious, and distrustful; it includes Paranoid, Schizotypal, and Schizoid Personality Disorder.

Cluster B: This cluster includes disorders where the individual is viewed as being overly emotional or erratic in his or her behavior; behavior tends to be impulsive, may have antisocial features, and tends to be someone dramatic; it includes Histrionic, Narcissistic, Antisocial, and Borderline Personality Disorder.

Cluster C: This cluster includes disorders where the individual appears anxious or fearful; it includes Avoidant, Dependent, and Obsessive-Compulsive Personality Disorder.

HISTORY AND CHARACTERISTICS OF PERSONALITY DISORDERS

The history of Personality Disorders as such really began with the publication of the original *DSM,* or the *DSM-I* (1952). However, long before this publication, Hippocrates (460–377 B.C.) recognized that an individual's personality can be disordered or very unusual. His theory of normal brain functioning relied upon four bodily humors being balanced (a humor is a bodily fluid). These four humors are blood, phlegm, black bile, and yellow bile. Any imbalance of these humors produced a disorder. His theory does not hold up today against scientific scrutiny. However, his premise that a chemical imbalance produces abnormal behavior and that one's personality can be disordered were important harbingers of future thought.

The *DSM-III* (APA, 1980) and subsequent volumes and revisions placed Personality Disorders on Axis II. In the previous versions, personality disorder criteria were unreliable. Today our ability to accurately diagnose Personality Disorders has significantly improved because we have more specific diagnostic criteria and because we have a better idea of what to look for in patients. We also have better interview techniques that are designed to pick up more of these disorders.

Even though some clinicians will state that they are seeing more individuals with Personality Disorders, we need to exercise some degree of caution. More so than any other diagnostic category we have discussed, Personality Disorders tend to have a greater degree of misdiagnosis than any of the other categories. There are several agreed-upon reasons for this:

First, the diagnostic categories are not as clear as they are for many of the Axis I disorders. Let us quickly look at a diagnostic criterion for Paranoid Personality Disorder: ". . . is reluctant to confide in others because of unwarranted fear that the information will be used maliciously against him or her. . . ." (APA, 2000, p. 694). This criterion is based on the clinician's judgment and not on behavioral standards or operational definitions, which eliminate a lot of bias and subjectivity. What exactly does "reluctant to confide" mean? Because the *DSM-IV-TR* defines Personality Disorders by inferred traits or consistent patterns of abnormal behavior, clinicians run into difficulties making a reliable diagnosis.

A second problem is that until recently Personality Disorders have not received much research. Because of the lack of data-based research (with the exception of ASPD and Borderline Personality Disorder), we cannot make major improvements in their diagnostic criteria at present. In addition, people may have tendencies to demonstrate characteristics of more than one disorder. Widiger and Rogers (1989) found that

> **DON'T FORGET**
>
> Many individuals will be dually diagnosed or multiply diagnosed. This means that they can have an Axis II diagnosis as well as an Axis I diagnosis. Many individuals who have a personality disorder also have a comorbid Axis I disorder.

this occurred in 85 percent of the patients they researched! One of the most common diagnoses is Personality Disorder Not Otherwise Specified (NOS), which is really a catch-all category; if the individual cannot be diagnosed with something else, then they receive this diagnosis.

A final problem is that we cannot clearly distinguish between the presence and absence of a personality disorder. That is, normal expressions to pathological ones (some quite severe) can be found in many normal individuals, but with less intensity and on a smaller scale. Does being conscientious about minute details in your job mean that you have Obsessive-Compulsive Personality Disorder? Not necessarily if you are a neurosurgeon!

Because of these issues many clinicians are not terribly satisfied with Axis II diagnoses, particularly because the symptoms are more dependent on the clinician's judgment than we would like. Thus, we can view Personality Disorders as extreme expressions of normal behaviors we all have.

GENERAL SYMPTOMS OF PERSONALITY DISORDERS

One common feature of Personality Disorders is that they are deeply rooted in the individual, and their presence is also firmly established. Individuals who have these disorders are also not adaptable to changing situations. For example, these individuals may be unable to change the way they think about situations, interpersonal and otherwise. They are also unable to change the way in which they respond to the same situations. This usually does not create problems for the individual but almost always causes distress and problems for others involved with this individual. A more critical concern is that the individual with a personality disorder does not see his or her behavior as maladaptive, problematic, or undesirable, even if the consequences of these behaviors are evident to other people involved with this individual. Thus, you can see why these individuals rarely present themselves voluntarily for treatment. In their eyes, there is nothing wrong with their behaviors, even though the behaviors and their consequences are clearly problematic for other people!

Personality Disorders also have an early onset, with the symptoms generally present since at least late adolescence. Personality Disorders are also pervasive. In other words, they are evident across all situations in the individual's life (social, occupational, and personal). Personality Disorders are also quite stable during their course. This means that their behaviors and features are present on a consistent basis. This creates problems because this means that these disorders are more resistant to treatment and thus it is very difficult to establish treatment efficacy.

CLUSTER A DISORDERS

Cluster A disorders sometimes are confused with Schizophrenic Disorders or other psychoses. Indeed, some of the defining symptomatology is similar to Psychotic Disorders, so the confusion is understandable. Two critical differences are that individuals with a Cluster A disorder do not have hallucinations, and they maintain contact with reality. As you will soon see, some of these disorders are extremely difficult to differentiate from one another.

Paranoid Personality Disorder affects about 0.5 percent to 2.5 percent of individuals in the general population and affects anywhere from 10 percent to 30 percent of individuals in inpatient psychiatric hospitals, a somewhat large percentage. Anywhere from 2 percent to 10 percent of patients in an outpatient treatment facility are also affected. The disorder affects more males than females and typically is most often comorbid with Schizotypal, Borderline, and Avoidant Personality Disorders (APA, 2000).

DON'T FORGET

We would expect the percentages to resemble those given in the preceding because individuals with Personality Disorders generally do not voluntarily enter outpatient treatment facilities. Thus, we can presume that the percentages listed here, and those that follow, reflect mandated inpatients.

The *DSM-IV-TR* states that individuals who have Paranoid Personality Disorder have a pervasive suspiciousness and distrust of other people, to the degree that they see themselves as blameless for their faults and mistakes. Instead, they will blame others and may presume that others' motives are evil and malevolent. They suspect that others are exploiting or harming them even though no basis exists for such suspicions. They tend not to confide in others because they distrust others and fear that this information will be used against them. They tend to be extremely sensitive, so much so that they may read hidden threatening or demeaning meanings into benign remarks (e.g., "Oh, you look nice in that outfit! Is it new?" might be misinterpreted as "Huh? Did she think I was ugly before I wore this?" or something similar). They tend to bear grudges, have a quick temper, and react quickly with anger to perceived attacks that, in fact, are not apparent to other people. Finally, they will often believe that their spouse or partner is having an affair, even though these suspicions are unjustified (APA, 2000).

Individuals who have Paranoid Personality Disorder typically do not have psychotic features, that is, they are clearly in contact with reality, and they usually do not have hallucinations. What is important to remember is that these individuals do not have Schizophrenia, Paranoid Type because they do not have hallucinations, and their cognitive disorganization, typical of the Schizophrenias, is not present. In addition, they are able to function socially and in the workplace, although their functioning is affected by this disorder. These individuals are always guarded and alert for attacks from other people in their social, work, and home spheres.

Schizoid Personality Disorder affects less than 2 percent of the general population and is considered to be uncommon in clinical settings. It affects more males than females. Individuals with Schizoid Personality Disorder have no desire to form social relationships, and, if they do have them, these individuals do not enjoy them. Therefore, they have few close friends and rarely are close to anyone except to some first-degree relatives. They appear to be cold and distant when seen by other people, and they are unable to express their feelings. In fact, they generally do not have warm feelings for anyone. They have little or no interest in sexual activity, have few pleasures in their lives, and they are not emotionally reactive. That is, they rarely express any emotions at all, either positive or negative. These individuals tend to be loners who pursue solitary interests and occupations. This disorder's comorbidity is highest for Schizotypal, Avoidant, and Paranoid Personality Disorder. Thus, is it most likely that another Cluster A disorder will occur with Schizoid Personality Disorder.

Early research established a link between the presence of Schizoid Personality Disorder and the prodromal phase of Schizophrenia. This was not supported by later research, which did not establish a link between these disorders. Recent research also did not establish a genetic component for Schizoid Personality Disorder (Kalus, Bernstein, & Siever, 1995). There may, however, be a commonality with Schizophrenia in that schizophrenic individuals display anhedonia (an inability to experience pleasure and joy in activities and in life) and social withdrawal.

What we can confidently state is that these individuals do not desire or enjoy close relationships with other people, with the exception of their closest relatives. Perhaps the basic needs for love and approval (as outlined by Horney and others) never developed, disappeared, or somehow became dysfunctional during their lives. Thus, these individuals might lead emotionally empty lives. See Rapid Reference 8.2 for a classification activity.

Schizotypal Personality Disorder occurs in about 1 percent to 3 percent of the population and affects more males than females. Patients who have Schizotypal Personality Disorder will have the social and interpersonal shortcomings similar to those expressed by individuals with Schizoid Person-

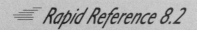

Rapid Reference 8.2

Classify These Individuals

Howard Hughes was a notorious loner who may have had OCD in addition to Schizoid Personality Disorder. Oscar the Grouch from *Sesame Street* really does not have any friends and tends to be a loner. When Satoshi Tajiri, the Pokemon creator, was profiled by *Time* a few years ago, he was made out to be a loner who had few friends and actually got attached to some of the creatures he created. When he was creating a new game, he would shut himself off from the outside world. Do any of these individuals fit the criteria for Schizoid Personality Disorder, or are they just loners?

DON'T FORGET

Prodromal means before the illness appears; *residual* means following the illness or after the illness has been cured or gone into remission. These two terms are usually used when describing Schizophrenia.

ality Disorder. This includes extreme social anxiety. A critical difference between schizotypal and schizoid is that schizotypal individuals demonstrate cognitive and perceptual distortions and eccentricities in their communication patterns. That is, their thoughts, speech, and perceptions are odd or magical. They may have beliefs that they are telepathic or clairvoyant. They may have illusions; for example, they may sense the presence of a person who is not actually there. Their speech is distinguished by unusual and unclear usages ("Only for a few whiles."). Their appearance and behavior may make them resemble someone who has Schizophrenia. Their clothing may be disheveled, they may be filthy, and they may talk to themselves (APA, 2000).

Ideas of reference are also common. The individual gets a sense that events and incidents occurring to him or her and in his or her environment have a meaning that is special to the individual. These are delusional thoughts where the individual reads personal significance into seemingly trivial remarks and activities of others and into completely unrelated events. These individuals will also be suspicious and have paranoid ideation. Their affect tends to be either constricted or flat (emotionless). Widiger, Frances, and Trull (1987) found that paranoid ideation, ideas of reference, and illusions were the most critical and telling diagnostic criteria.

Some other aspects of Schizotypal Personality Disorder are worth examining. A genetic and biological relationship has been demonstrated between this disorder and Schizophrenia (e.g., Kendler & Gardner, 1997). An intriguing side note is that some studies have demonstrated that individuals who have Schizotypal Personality Disorder have a visual deficit in that their ability to track a moving target is diminished (e.g., Siever, Bernstein, & Silverman, 1995). This is intriguing because the same deficit is present in schizophrenic individuals. Additional research demonstrates that schizotypal individuals have deficits in attention and in working memory, deficits also present in schizophrenic individuals (Squires-Wheeler et al., 1997). Kendler and Gardner (1997) consider Schizotypal Personality Disorder part of the schizophrenic spectrum, that is, it is a milder form of Schizophrenia where the individual is functioning at a somewhat higher level. The authors see Schizotypal Personality Disorder as occurring most often in the first degree biological relatives of schizophrenics. Finally, Siever et al. (1995) note that teenagers who have Schizotypal Personality Disorder are at an increased risk for developing Schizophrenia and Schizophrenia-like disorders (that is, disorders in the Schizophrenia spectrum) as adults.

One critical problem with accurately diagnosing Schizotypal Personality Disorder is that it is highly comorbid with several other personality disorders: Borderline, Narcissistic, Avoidant, Paranoid, and Schizoid Personality Disorder. Morey (1988) discovered that Schizotypal Personality Disorder has a 59 percent comorbidity rate with Paranoid and Avoidant Personality Disorder; the other comorbidity percentages range from 44 percent for Schizoid and 33 percent for Borderline and Narcissistic Personality Disorder. This is disturbing if we continue to view Schizotypal Personality Disorder as being its own diagnostic category.

Thus, the schizotypal individual has unusual thought patterns that end up disrupting their ability to communicate clearly with others. In addition, his or her ties to reality are impacted but not totally severed as in Schizophrenia. Because of this, many of these individuals are not able to realize their potential and are unable to lead truly productive lives.

CLUSTER B DISORDERS

Cluster B disorders tend to be those disorders that are better known to the layperson because of their hallmark criteria: Dramatic, emotional, or erratic behavior is displayed by the individual. In Histrionic Personality Disorder, the individual's behavior is characterized by excessive attention seeking and by extreme emotionality. They are uncomfortable if they are not the center of attention in most situations; however, their behaviors actually attract and seduce others into paying attention to them and being with them. These individuals tend to be emotional and appear as though they are on a Broadway stage. In addition, they tend to be sexually seductive and provocative, often in an inappropriate fashion. Their speech is dramatic but is also impressionistic and lacks detail. They are suggestible and thus easily influenced by other people and by circumstances they encounter. Finally, they often consider interpersonal relationships to be more intimate than they actually are (APA, 2000). They might attempt to control their partner through seduction and through emotional control and manipulation, which they are quite good at. Others view these individuals as self-centered, vain, and overly concerned about seeking and getting others' approval. However, many outsiders who interact with this individual see him or her as shallow and insincere.

Most statistics place the prevalence of Histrionic Personality Disorder at 2 to 3 percent. The APA (2000) also notes that the prevalence ratio between males and females is not statistically significant, so we can presume that the difference is negligible. The disorder may be overdiagnosed in females in Western cultures such as the United States because of sex role stereotypes. For example, a male who brags about his female conquests, his athletic skills, or his perceived prominence for a specific talent that is not a talent at all might be perceived as demonstrating a macho attitude. A female who talks about how much her professor desires her and who tells everyone that he always winks at her in class would be more likely to be diagnosed with Histrionic Personality Disorder (APA, 2000). When the individual does not get the attention she or he seeks and believes that she or he deserves, irritability and tantrums may result.

Individuals who have Narcissistic Personality Disorder demonstrate an exaggerated sense of self-importance and patterns of grandiosity in their fantasies or in their present-day behaviors. They have an extreme need to be admired and demonstrate a lack of empathy for others. Grandiosity is the most often used criterion to diagnose Narcissistic Personality Disorder and is also the most generalizeable criterion. These individuals exaggerate and overestimate their accomplishments and abilities, and they expect you to recognize them as being superior even though they have made no outstanding accomplishments. They, in turn, tend to underestimate the accomplishments and abilities of others. They have a tremendous sense of entitlement, which means that they have unrealistic expectations that they deserve special treatment ("Do you know who I *am*?") or that one should automatically comply with their expectations, even though others see this in a bemused, often astonished way. They believe that they deserve, and thus they require, excessive admiration. Their fantasies revolve around unlimited success, power, brilliance, beauty, or ideal love. Their behavior, which tends to be stereotypical (they are always discussing themselves and constantly bragging), attempts to get them the acclaim and recognition they think they deserve. Because of these haughty attitudes, they believe that they can only be understood by others who have a similar high status or that they should only associate with these types of individuals. Outsiders see this as a thinly veiled attempt to make themselves look good, worthy, and accomplished (APA, 2000).

Narcissistic individuals cannot (or are unwilling to) recognize or identify with others' feelings and needs, but in turn they are also envious of other people. They also believe that others are envious of them! The lack of empathy and the unwillingness or inability to take others' perspectives needs further examination. All children, according to Piaget (1896–1980) and others, start out as narcissists, but the reasons for this are clear: They cannot take the viewpoint of other people because cognitively they are incapable of doing so. Eventually most children acquire the ability (through maturation and experience) to be able to take others' perspectives and thus become less narcissistic. For reasons that researchers have yet to discern, some children do not grow out of this period and show either abnormal progress, little, or no progress. The children that demonstrate little progress in acquiring perspective may grow up to have Narcissistic Personality Disorder or perhaps one of the other Personality Disorders.

The prevalence of Narcissistic Personality Disorder within the general population ranges from 2 to 16 percent in the general population, but is less than 1 percent in the clinical population. Anywhere from 50 to 75 percent of the individuals diagnosed with Narcissistic Personality Disorder are male (APA, 2000). The fact that these individuals represent less than 1 percent of the clinical population is not surprising because these individuals rarely, if ever, seek out treatment. The reason is quite clear: These individuals see themselves (and their lives) as nearly perfect and do not see any need for change.

Widiger and Frances (1994) report, as do other researchers and clinicians, that people who have this disorder have very poor and fragile self-esteem underneath all of the bluster and grandiosity. In other words, they really do not like themselves very much, and their grandiosity is used as a cover for this. Clinicians agree that this low self-esteem might be the underlying reason why these individuals are so preoccupied with fantasies of outstanding achievement, why they demonstrate such an extreme need for admiration, and why they are so preoccupied with what others think of them and their supposed accomplishments. As a result, they tend to be extremely sensitive to criticism, which may lead to them feeling humiliated, empty inside, or full of extreme rage (e.g., throwing a fit if someone tells them their accomplishments are nothing special).

It can be difficult to separate out Narcissistic Personality Disorder from Histrionic Personality Disorder, but there are some critical yet subtle differences. Histrionic individuals tend to be more emotional and dramatic, while narcissists tend to be more exploitative of other people. Histrionics also tend to be overtly needy and much more so than narcissists. Both tend to be exhibitionists; however, the histrionic individual seeks constant attention, while the narcissist seeks constant praise and admiration (Widiger & Trull, 1993).

Individuals with Antisocial Personality Disorder (ASPD) violate the rights of others through deceit or aggression. They will lie repeatedly or will con other people for profit or pleasure. They are impulsive and lack the ability to plan ahead. Their behavior will generally be irresponsible, they will often be irritable, and they will often get into physical fights. An important criterion is that they will generally demonstrate a lack of remorse toward other people. For example, they will be indifferent to having hurt or mistreated another person, or they will rationalize this behavior. They are also unable to hold down a steady job and will often renege on financial commitments (APA, 2000).

The definition of ASPD includes two critical components, according to the *DSM-IV-TR*. First, Conduct Disorder must have been present before the age of 15. Some symptoms of Conduct Disorder are frequent lying, truancy, running away from home, theft, arson, aggression toward animals and other people, and destruction of property (graffiti for example). Second, this pattern of behavior (i.e., the ASPD behaviors) must have been occurring since the age of 15. Therefore, the ASPD diagnosis states that the initial ASPD signs and symptoms begin in childhood but continue on into adulthood. The individual must also be at least 18 before an ASPD diagnosis can be made.

What is intriguing is that close to 60 percent of children who have Conduct Disorder later develop ASPD (Myers, Stewart, & Brown, 1998). This means that left untreated or undiagnosed, it is likely that Conduct Disorder will later lead into the individual having ASPD. Men are more likely to receive the diagnosis of ASPD than are women; about 3 percent of males and about 1 percent of females receive an ASPD diagnosis. In clinical settings, the prevalence rate of ASPD ranges anywhere from 3 percent to 30 percent of the total clinical population. This prevalence rate increased substantially in substance abuse treatment facilities and in prison or other forensic settings (APA, 2000). The rates of ASPD are much higher for younger adults than they are for older adults; ASPD is also more common among individuals in lower SES strata. Antisocial Personality Disorder is most often comorbid with Substance Abuse or Substance Dependence, typically alcohol or illicit psychoactive substances.

In the past, individuals with ASPD were called *psychopaths* and *sociopaths*. Antisocial Personality Disorder individuals and sociopaths are usually involved with breaking laws, but there are some significant differences between the two concepts. The term *psychopath* implies that something is pathological with the individual's mind or with his or her psychological makeup. Hervey Cleckley (1982) spent a lot of time researching psychopaths and came up with 16 key characteristics for these individuals. According to Cleckley (1982), *psychopathy* includes criteria such as a lack of empathy, inflated and arrogant self-appraisal, and glib and superficial charm. These individuals have no sense of shame, and even when they demonstrate positive feelings for others, it is all an act. The superficial charm they demonstrate allows them to manipulate others for financial gain. These individuals do not experience anxiety about their behaviors, and thus they cannot learn from their mistakes and therefore hurt or harm others. Their behaviors are performed impulsively, for seeking and getting thrills as much as for seeking financial rewards.

Today most clinicians diagnose psychopathy using a checklist developed by Hare, Hart, and Harpur (1991) and refined by Hart and Hare (1997). The Revised Psychopathology Checklist is a 20-item checklist based on Cleckley's criteria. Research has demonstrated that there are two dimensions (clusters or factors) of psychopathic behaviors. The first refers to emotional detachment, is similar to Narcissistic Personality Disorder, includes traits such as a lack of remorse and callousness, and basically describes an individual who has inflated self-esteem and who exploits other people. The second factor characterizes an antisocial lifestyle and reflects the individual's behaviors: antisocial, socially deviant, irresponsible,

DON'T FORGET

Lynam (1997) created a children's version of Hare's checklist to be used by the child's mother to make diagnoses. In examining the results, it was discovered that children with psychopathy are similar to adults with the same disorder. They are impulsive and delinquent and show little remorse for some very cruel acts and behaviors.

and impulsive. Hart and Hare (1997) note that this second dimension is more closely related to the *DSM-IV-TR*'s diagnosis of ASPD than is the first dimension. Psychopathy is often comorbid with Substance Use Disorders. Finally, psychopathy occurs more often among men than among women.

Antisocial Personality Disorder and psychopathy are related, but both disorders are far from being identical. Hare and his colleagues dispute the *DSM-IV-TR* diagnostic criteria for ASPD. They state that it is inaccurate because it requires the individual to accurately recall events in his or her life that occurred many years ago. Why is this a problem? Antisocial Personality Disorder individuals are often habitual (or pathological) liars, yet we need to trust their recall of earlier events in their lives (Hare et al., 1991). Blurring the distinction between mental illness and criminality is an additional concern. Hart and Hare (1989) found that anywhere from 15 to 25 percent of convicted felons met the criteria for psychopathy, yet 75 to 80 percent of the same group of convicted felons studied met the criteria for ASPD! A concomitant problem is the criterion of having a lack of remorse. This is a key criterion of psychopathy, yet it is only one of seven criteria for the *DSM-IV-TR* definition of ASPD. Furthermore, the individual only needs to have three of the seven criteria to be diagnosed with ASPD. Thus, it is possible to receive an ASPD diagnosis while not having the lack of remorse critical to a psychopathy diagnosis. Obviously, further research is needed into these concepts.

Finally, we will examine Borderline Personality Disorder. This diagnosis has been in the *DSM* series since the *DSM-III* in 1980 and is characterized by impulsivity and instability in the individual's moods and relationships. The individual may have fears of abandonment that are real, or they can be imaginary. Their unstable interpersonal relationships tend to be intense and are characterized by alternating between extremes of idealization and devaluation. They suffer from identity disturbance; that is, their self-image is unstable. They are impulsive in the areas of spending, sexual behavior, gambling, substance use or abuse, reckless driving, and binge eating. Typically they will demonstrate repeated suicidal behaviors or threats, or they may be self-mutilators. Their affect is unstable because their moods tend to be erratic. They may show tremendous passion, and they abruptly demonstrate extreme anger, irritability, and are quick to take offense at something. Their anger will often be inappropriate and quite intense, and they will have difficulty controlling this anger. They cannot stand to be alone, demand constant at-

DON'T FORGET

The term *borderline personality* initially implied that the individual was on the border between what used to be called *neurosis* (or as is known today anxiety) and *psychosis* (or Schizophrenia). The implication was that the individual walked this tightrope between neurosis and psychosis, and no one knew (including the individual) what would cause him or her to tumble to either side. This definition is no longer current.

tention, and are very difficult to live with. They have chronic feelings of emptiness and depression. Finally, they will demonstrate transient psychotic and dissociative symptoms that will occur during extremely stressful periods (APA, 2000).

Borderline Personality Disorder affects about 1 to 2 percent of the population, but, again, it is much more highly represented in the clinical population: About 10 percent of outpatients and about 20 percent of inpatients in psychiatric settings are diagnosed with this disorder (APA, 2000). About 75 percent of those diagnosed are female. Borderline Personality Disorder is most likely to be comorbid with a mood disorder; the individual's parents are also more likely to have a mood disorder as well. Posttraumatic Stress Disorder, Panic Disorder, Substance Use Disorders, and Eating Disorders are also likely to be comorbid. Widiger and Trull (1993) discovered that the relationship between Mood Disorders and Borderline Personality Disorder is quite strong; about 50 percent of those who have Borderline Personality Disorder also qualified for a mood disorder at some point.

What is more intriguing is that depression for a borderline individual appears to have different symptoms than unipolar depressions for other individuals. The borderline's depression tends to be characterized by chronic lonely feelings; in addition, his or her familial and social relationships are typically seen as being hostile and the relationships as being quite fragile. Most intriguing is that, in general, borderline individuals who have unipolar depression do *not* respond as well to many types of antidepressant medications as do depressed individuals who do not have Borderline Personality Disorder (Gitlin, 1996). Finally, we often see Borderline Personality Disorder as being comorbid with ASPD, Histrionic, Dependent, and Schizotypal Personality Disorders. See Rapid Reference 8.3 for definitions of key terms.

≡ *Rapid Reference 8.3*

Key Terms to Know

Ideas of Reference: These occur in Schizotypal Personality Disorder; it includes delusional thoughts where the individual reads personal significance into seemingly trivial remarks and activities of others and into completely unrelated events.

Psychopathy: This is often confused with ASPD; it includes criteria such as a lack of empathy, inflated and arrogant self-appraisal, and glib and superficial charm; when individuals demonstrate positive feelings for others it is all an act.

Identity Disturbance: This is a criterion of Borderline Personality Disorder; the individual's self-image is unstable.

CLUSTER C DISORDERS

The disorders that appear in this cluster include anxiety and fearfulness as part of their hallmark features. This can create problems in that it might be difficult to separate these disorders from Anxiety Disorders. However, because the disorders in Cluster C include anxiety and fearfulness, these individuals are more likely to seek treatment.

Individuals with Avoidant Personality Disorder are fearful of the *possibility* of criticism, rejection, or disapproval and, therefore, will usually not engage in social relationships unless they are assured of being liked. However, these individuals desire affection and thus are often lonely and bored. It is possible that they may even avoid work situations that involve a lot of interpersonal situations and contacts. (Thus, becoming a psychologist who performs therapy would not be a wise career choice!) The interesting facet is that they do not enjoy their aloneness. In fact, their aloneness, caused by their inability to relate to others, causes extreme anxiety and often leads to low self-esteem and being excessively self-conscious. Because of this, they may see ridicule or rejection when in fact none exists. They also tend to say or do little when they have to be involved in social situations. They are fearful that they will say something silly or foolish or that they will be embarrassed and will blush. They see themselves as being incompetent, inferior to

CAUTION

It is difficult to distinguish Avoidant Personality Disorder from generalized Social Phobia because research seems to demonstrate that there is a significant overlap between the two. It is possible that they may be different ways of viewing the same condition or that Avoidant Personality Disorder is a more severe manifestation of generalized social phobia.

other people, and are thus not risk takers; they will generally not get involved with new activities.

Approximately 0.5 to 1.0 percent of individuals have Avoidant Personality Disorder, and its presence in mental health clinic outpatients is reported at 10 percent. This disorder is often comorbid with Dependent Personality Disorder. This occurs because the individual, when they do make a friend (or friends), they become extremely attached to and dependent on that individual. Avoidant Personality Disorder is also comorbid with Borderline Personality Disorder and the Cluster A disorders (Paranoid, Schizoid, and Schizotypal), and is often diagnosed with Mood and Anxiety Disorders, especially generalized Social Phobia and unipolar depression (APA, 2000).

Individuals who have Dependent Personality Disorder demonstrate a lack of self-confidence and lack a sense of autonomy. They see themselves as very weak and others as extremely powerful. They are extremely dependent on others and have a great need to be taken care of, which makes these individuals cling to others and to be submissive to others' wishes and demands. When a relationship ends, they become desperate and have to form another relationship to replace the broken one. If they have to be alone or be separated from these depended-upon people, they may panic and may end up in the hospital. These individuals often do not demonstrate appropriate anger with other people because they are terrified of losing their support. Thus, they may remain in psychologically and physically damaging and abusive relationships. In effect, these individuals lose their individuality because they let others make the decisions—both large and small—in their lives.

Although APA (2000) mentions that Dependent Personality Disorder is among the most frequently reported in mental health clinics, they do not give a percentage of prevalence. However, a reasonable estimate in the general population is about 1.5 percent (Torgersen, Kringlen, & Cramer, 2001). It is rather interesting that the percentage is significantly higher in Japan and in India, perhaps because dependent behavior may be encouraged here, especially for women. It does in fact occur more frequently among women. Dependent Personality Disorder is comorbid with Borderline, Schizoid, Histrionic,

> **DON'T FORGET**
>
> Bulimic women often have interpersonal problems and tend to alienate individuals when they get too close. What might the link be between Dependent Personality Disorder and Bulimia Nervosa?

Schizotypal, and Avoidant Personality Disorders. It is also comorbid with the Axis I disorders of Bipolar Disorder, unipolar depression (or Major Depressive Disorder), Anxiety Disorders, and Bulimia Nervosa.

Individuals with *Obsessive-Compulsive Personality Disorder* are perfectionists who are preoccupied with maintaining control mentally and in their interpersonal relationships. They make sure they do not make mistakes, and they will often check for the presence of mistakes. They pay so much attention to detail and are so afraid of making mistakes that their projects or schoolwork never get finished. Oddly, the details that consume them are often trivial, and so their work or school time is not put to good use. In addition, they tend to be workaholics and are not involved with leisure activities; they may have problems just relaxing or having any type of fun. In their relationships they demand that everything be done their way; they also tend to be quite stubborn. They are usually serious, rigid, formal, inflexible, and tend to be extremely moral. They may be hoarders, even if the objects have no sentimental or practical value, and they tend to be stingy. Others may view these individuals as being cold, rigid, and quite stiff, basically straitlaced individuals who cannot let loose. Freud would say that they have anal tendencies, most likely anal-retentive.

Obsessive-Compulsive Personality Disorder is very different from the anxiety disorder Obsessive-Compulsive Disorder (OCD) in that the personality disorder does not, contrary to popular belief, include the obsessions and compulsions that define OCD. People with Obsessive-Compulsive Personality Disorder are defined by their perfectionistic ways, their inflexibility, and their being too conscientious. Popular belief posits that the two disorders are related and are on the same spectrum, but, in fact, this is not the case. Obses-

DON'T FORGET

Recall that *obsessions* are persistent undesired thoughts or images that constantly intrude into the individual's head. The anxiety or distress realized by the individual because of these intrusive thoughts or images can only be alleviated by *compulsions*, rituals such as checking or cleaning endlessly.

sive-Compulsive Personality Disorder is often comorbid with Avoidant Personality Disorder, and is seen with Dependent Personality Disorder as well. This disorder is twice as common among men, and is seen in about 1 percent of the general population. Anywhere from 3 to 10 percent of individuals in mental health clinics have Obsessive-Compulsive Personality Disorder (APA, 2000).

ETIOLOGIES OF PERSONALITY DISORDERS

Perhaps because they were only really identified and noticed since 1980 (when the *DSM-III* was published), little is known about Personality Disorders' etiologies; they have also attracted sparse research attention as well. Another problem is that these individuals do not generally present themselves voluntarily to treatment settings, thus making these disorders more difficult to properly research. Those that do come in for treatment are usually in a severely debilitated state, and it becomes difficult to specify the causal factors because we have to go back and piece together the etiological pieces of the puzzle. Finally, the most critical problem is that many of the Personality Disorders are comorbid with each other, thus making it very difficult to separate out which factors are unique to each disorder.

We will begin by examining possible biological etiologies. Some research points to the heritability of certain Personality Disorders. For example, an infant's temperament may be a predisposing factor. In other words, is the infant a true people person, does the infant shy away from interpersonal contact, does the infant have a lot of energy and anger or not too much, and so on. Research has indicated that there may be some genetic etiological factors for the development of Paranoid, Schizotypal, Borderline, and Antisocial Personality Disorder (e.g., Nigg & Goldsmith, 1994). It also appears that a serotonin deficiency may be involved in the development of Borderline Personality Disorder. This may explain why these individuals engage in self-mutilation and why these individuals are impulsive, especially when it comes to aggressive behavior. Other research has implicated an irregularity of noradrenaline; in this case, the noradrenaline system is hyperresponsive in that it activates at inappropriate times and thus leads to chronic stress, similar to that seen in Anxiety Disorders, especially PTSD. Finally, dopamine, a neurotransmitter that has been implicated in the etiology of Schizophrenia (see Chapter 7), has also been posited to be involved in the etiology of Borderline Personality Disorder by Otto Kernberg (1928–). He states that dopamine deficiencies may be related to the fact that some borderline individuals demonstrate psychotic symptoms that are temporary (Kernberg, 1996).

When we examine psychosocial causal factors, two categories stand out: early childhood experiences and psychodynamic viewpoints. Some researchers believe that early learning experiences predispose a child to later developing a personality disorder. What is most interesting is that not much research has supported this belief, even though it remains popular. Perhaps not surprisingly, many studies have concluded that early childhood abuse and neglect may lead to the development of some of the Personality Disorders. In perhaps the most well-known study (Zanarini et al., 1997), over 350 Borderline Personality Disorder patients and over 100 individuals with other Personality Disorders were interviewed. The borderline individuals reported significantly higher rates of abuse when contrasted with the other individuals who had other Personality Disorders. Emotional and verbal abuse were the most common forms, and the least common forms of abuse were sexual and physical, respectively. The researchers concluded that over 90 percent of the borderline individuals suffered from some form of childhood abuse or neglect (Zanarini et al., 1997).

Two cautions need to be mentioned here. First, this study relied on self-reports from individuals whose diagnosis leads them to exaggerate and to distort their information and especially their views of other people. It is quite difficult to put much credence in what they say, especially when it involves self-reports of past situations. Second, as we have mentioned previously, there are many children outside of this study who experience abuse and neglect but do not grow up manifesting Personality Disorders or Axis I diagnoses. This is analogous to stating that because the Columbine killers played *Doom,* any adolescent who plays violent videogames will go and shoot up his or her school.

Heinz Kohut (1913–1981) wrote a lot about Narcissistic Personality Dis-

228 ESSENTIALS OF ABNORMAL PSYCHOLOGY

order (as well as other Personality Disorders), specifically examining possible etiological factors. Kohut believed that all children go through a stage where their behavior and beliefs are egocentric, to borrow a term from Piaget. That is, he believed that all events and needs revolve around them, and, additionally, they are unable to take another's perspective in all matters. Kohut argues that in order for the child to develop normally, his or her parents must mirror the child's grandiosity, which leads to the child developing a normal level of self-confidence and self-esteem.

Thus, how does Narcissistic Personality Disorder develop? If the parents are neglectful, if they show no empathy toward the child, or if they devalue the child, then the child will always be seeking out this ideal sense of self. While this perspective remains intriguing and is still espoused by some today, it has little research support. The opposite perspective has also received some support. This perspective states that Narcissistic Personality Disorder arises from parental overindulgence and pampering of the child; the child gets every wish and demand met, and the child learns that she or he is put on a pedestal and worshipped even if little or no effort is expended or no accomplishments have occurred. Thus, spoiling a child leads to the development of this disorder (Millon & Davis, 1996).

Finally, sociocultural factors merit a brief mention. Some researchers believe that the incidence of Personality Disorders has increased over the past few years in the United States. Reasons for this purported increase include the emphasis on instant gratification, quick fixes and instant solutions to all problems, and benefits of overindulgence that are relatively painless. Research on this concept is quite scarce, and thus more information is needed.

What can we conclude? Simply, that because research is so scarce on the etiologies of most of the Personality Disorders, we cannot arrive at any firm conclusions yet. More research is required, and perhaps a reformulation of the *DSM-IV-TR*'s diagnostic criteria for Personality Disorders is also warranted.

Etiologies of Antisocial Personality Disorder and Psychopathic Individuals

More research has been conducted on ASPD than on any of the other Personality Disorders. Because of this, we are somewhat better able to see what the etiological factors might be. We will examine biological factors first, then we will examine developmental factors, and we will conclude our brief discussion with an examination of sociocultural factors.

We will first focus on genetic factors that may lead to the development of ASPD. There seems to be a strong genetic link to the development of ASPD and criminality. (DiLalla & Gottesman, 1991). In addition, there seems to be a modest heritability factor for antisocial or criminal tendencies (Carey & Goldman, 1997). Researchers conclude that genetic factors may contribute to ASPD and to the development of psychopathy and to criminal behavior, but environmental factors help to influence the development of these (and other) conditions.

Biological factors have also been extensively researched. The underarousal hypothesis (Quay, 1965) states that psychopaths have low levels of arousal in their brain's cortex. This is the main reason for their antisocial behaviors. They will specifically seek out thrill-seeking behaviors and other unusual types of stimulation in order to boost the brain's arousal levels. These levels are presumed to be constantly low.

The fearlessness hypothesis states that psychopaths have a higher fear threshold, that is, frightening things for most people (a burning building, gunshots, auto accident) have little, if any, effect on these individuals (Lykken, 1982). We can conclude that because of this fearlessness, punishment will have little or no effect on these individuals. It is also possible that these individuals do not associate certain stimuli or cues with punishment or danger, such as an alarm going off. Lykken (1957) found that psychopaths did not show normal anxiety reactions when anticipating a punishment response and, more to the point, they were slow at learning how to stop responding when punishment was inevitable. They were unable to avoid punishment.

Fowles and Missel (1994) supported this hypothesis: Because psychopaths have problems learning how to properly respond to anxiety-producing situations, they are deficient in normal avoidance responses. Therefore, they do not successfully avoid punishment, and thus their impulsive behaviors remain unrestrained. Fowles and Missel attribute this to a deficient behavioral inhibition system, which is simply the neurological system that allows an individual to learn to inhibit certain responses so that she or he can avoid punishment. Inhibiting the responses must be learned in the face of cues that signal upcoming punishment. This is called *passive avoidance learning* and appears to be deficient in psychopaths and in individuals with ASPD.

The *behavioral activation system* is also an interesting concept. Briefly, this system activates a behavioral response to cues for an upcoming reward, and it also activates a behavioral response to cues for an upcoming punishment by avoidance of the upcoming punishment. This system may at the least be normal and at the most be overactive in psychopaths. This may help to explain why these individuals are so focused on obtaining rewards. In addition, if they are caught demonstrating a deviant or unwarranted (or illegal) behavior, they will be quite focused on avoiding punishment through lying, running away, or through deceit. Thus, when these individuals are being threatened with punishment, they will be overactive in avoiding the punishment by any means necessary.

Research into psychological factors has discovered an interesting concept. Psychopaths appear to persist in situations where failure is guaranteed. Even when they were informed about this, they continued to engage in the situation (Newman, Patterson, & Kosson, 1987)! Newman et al. concluded that once a psychopath sets his eyes on a goal, very little if anything will stop him from attaining that goal. Let us use an example to clarify this interesting hypothesis.

Imagine that you are hired to move a very large refrigerator out of a tight kitchen in New York City. You take the measurements and realize that it will not fit through the front door no matter what you do. Your supervisor shows up and tells you the same and tells you to give up because a wall will need to come down before the refrigerator can be removed. Most people, upon hearing this news, will listen to the supervisor and give up. The psychopath, goal-fixated, will continue at this task, refusing to believe this information.

One aspect of ASPD and psychopathy that has been well known for a while is the notion that these disorders begin early on in a child's life. According to Robins (1978), the greater the number of antisocial behaviors the child demonstrates in his or her childhood, the more likely that child will develop ASPD later on. In fact, Robins states that this criterion is the single best predictor of developing ASPD or psychopathy. Many of these behaviors are also criteria for Conduct Disorder: theft, truancy, and school discipline problems. Robins also noted that the earlier these symptoms are demonstrated, the greater the likelihood of developing ASPD (1978; 1991).

Some research has demonstrated that children who have Oppositional Defiant Disorder (ODD), especially at an early age, are more likely to develop ASPD, psychopathy, or other serious mental illnesses when they reach adulthood. Oppositional Defiant Disorder is characterized by hostile and defiant behaviors that begin by age 6 and is followed by Conduct Disorder that has an early onset around age 9. Research has also demonstrated that those who develop Conduct Disorder in adolescence usually do not develop psychopathy or ASPD, but instead they have problems that remain during adolescence but are not seen in adulthood (Hinshaw, 1994).

Children that have ADHD, which includes symptoms of restlessness, an extremely limited attention span, impulsive behavior, and extreme distractibility, are more likely to manifest psychopathy or ASPD. When ASPD occurs with Conduct Disorder, Lyman (1996) notes that there is a good possibility that the individual will later develop psychopathy. Attention Deficit/Hyperactivity Disorder occurs about 30 to 50 percent of the time with Conduct Disorder.

Some of Hare's early work discovered that parental rejection of the child, child abuse (not necessarily sexual), and being inconsistent parents might be important premorbid indicators of psychopathy developing later on in the individual's life. Dishion and Patterson (1997) later modified these indicators, and they included a parent's (or parents') own antisocial behaviors, divorce, low SES, parental stress and parental unipolar depression, and living in an impoverished neighborhood as being potential premorbid indicators of ASPD and psychopathy.

Another perspective sees parents as perhaps contributing to the development of ASPD (Patterson, 1982). The issue here is parents who give in to their children too much and do not discipline their children. What can occur is the following: Parents, losing their patience with a child who does not listen, may walk away or just give in, basically saying "fine, go ahead and do it, see if we care." What occurs next is that the child ends up learning not to give up. The parent's behavior is also reinforced because the arguing with the child has decreased or stopped. If this is combined with other factors involved in a dysfunctional household, such as parental pathology, the antisocial behaviors will continue and thus be strengthened.

We finally need to briefly examine sociocultural factors. Psychopathy and

ASPD both occur in many cultures, including nonindustrialized ones. What is worth noting is that the etiologies and prevalence of these disorders is related to whether a culture either encourages or discourages these disorders' development and manifestations. For example, how often are aggressive and violent behaviors expressed in the culture being examined? Are these behaviors expected or reinforced, making it more likely that they will continue to be expressed? Whether the society is individualistic or collectivist is also important.

The United States is an individualist society. By that we mean that independence, self-confidence, and competitiveness are all emphasized in the United States and are seen as the means to get ahead financially as well as professionally (promotions and such). In a collectivist society, the individual is expected to contribute to the group, accept authority usually without question, and usually has stable relationships. When one interprets these statements, one can see that societies like the United States may promote milder forms of antisocial behaviors in order to get ahead. In other words, demonstrating grandiosity and superficiality, perhaps with promiscuity, are psychopathic features. When these traits are minimized, the individual might be seen as having a lot of self-confidence, being a lady's man, and being dedicated to work because he really does not socialize with his co-workers. This concept is certainly intriguing and warrants further research.

In sum, as with many of the disorders, an integrative model best explains the etiology of ASPD and psychopathy. Perhaps the individual is fearless and is also chronically underaroused. Perhaps the individual comes from a dysfunctional household where Mom is working the streets and Dad has been in prison for many years. Because the child is underaroused, he seeks great thrills, and nothing is more thrilling than breaking the law and getting away with it. Once the young man enters treatment (against his will of course), it is discovered that he actively avoided punishment by lying and running away from home because his Mom would beat him if she found him. Therefore, his avoidance was reinforcing, as were the antisocial and psychopathic behaviors, and thus the antisocial behaviors continued. See Rapid Reference 8.4 for a review of some etiological theories for psychopathic individuals.

≣ *Rapid Reference 8.4*

Some Etiological Theories for Psychopathic Individuals

Underarousal Hypothesis: This states that psychopaths have low levels of arousal in their brain's cortex, the main reason for their antisocial behaviors; individuals will specifically seek out thrill-seeking behaviors and other unusual types of stimulation in order to boost the brain's arousal levels. These levels are presumed to be constantly low.

Fearlessness Hypothesis: This states that psychopaths have a higher fear threshold, that is, frightening things for most people (a burning building, gunshots, auto accident) have little, if any, effect on these individuals.

Behavioral Activation System: This system activates a behavioral response to cues for an upcoming reward, and it also activates a behavioral response to cues for an upcoming punishment by avoidance of the upcoming punishment; it may be overactive in psychopaths.

TREATMENT MODALITIES

Treatment for any of the Personality Disorders is problematic for a variety of reasons. First, as was previously mentioned, individuals who have either a Cluster A or a Cluster B disorder (or both) are unlikely to seek treatment voluntarily as they see nothing wrong with them or with their behavior and, more important, their behavior is not causing them enough stress to drive them to seek treatment. Research has also demonstrated (and you could also conclude, logically) that individuals who have a personality disorder as well as an Axis I diagnosis are less likely to succeed in treatment (Crits-Christoph & Barber, 2002). These patients will require longer-term treatment because of their personality disorder (which, by definition, includes long-standing traits and chronicity) and more extensive treatment (i.e., broader spectrum) as opposed to being able to focus on only one disorder. An additional concern is that individuals who have Personality Disorders also tend to be charming and fascinating and highly manipulative, thus making treatment efficacy more difficult. Because of these features, it is prudent for the psychologist to be on guard and not to get drawn in to the pathology, to lose objectivity, and perhaps display countertransference.

Psychodynamic techniques will attempt to alter the patient's present-day views of his or her problems that occurred in childhood that are presumed to underlie Personality Disorders. For example, the analyst would work with a Narcissistic Personality Disorder individual and attempt to get him or her to realize that it is okay not to be the center of attention all of the time, and that it is possible to be in the background and still maintain one's self-esteem. In other words, it is not essential to win all of the time or always be in the spotlight. An Obsessive-Compulsive Personality Disorder individual would be asked to understand that perfection as an adult is not necessary and that other adults will not reject him or her because he or she is not always perfect. The perfection might be seen as being tied to the patient's childhood desires to be perfect to win the love of his or her parents who were rejecting to the patient.

The behaviorists and the cognitive behaviorists pay attention to cognitions and situations and not to underlying traits of the individual. The situations, and the faulty cognitions, are the causal factors, not traits. These therapists would look at various smaller problems that when combined resemble the Personality Disorders. They would then use behavioristic techniques to treat the disorder. For example, individuals with Avoidant Personality Disorder would be taught assertiveness training and would be taught to be more assertive in social and in other situations, a rather successful modality (Alden, 1989). The behaviorists might also help a Paranoid Personality Disorder patient to not be so antagonistic and argumentative with others. They might be taught how to argue in a fair way.

Rational emotive behavioral therapy would also be a usable approach. The therapist would point out how the patient's irrational beliefs were causing blocks and problems in his or her life. For example, the therapist would point out that the Dependent Personality Disorder patient does not need to always be involved with someone in order to succeed and to survive. The Obsessive-Compulsive Personality Disorder patient does not need to be a control or a neat freak, and he or she would be taught that it is okay to fail. If they do fail (which is inevitable) the world does not come to an end, and they are not a bad person because of these failures.

Beck would treat Personality Disorders in a fashion similar to how he would treat unipolar depression. Beck and his colleagues would examine each personality disorder on the basis of faulty logic errors and faulty and dysfunctional schemata. Beck might, for example, work with an Obsessive-Compulsive Personality Disorder patient and help him or her to realize that they are using faulty logic when he or she believes that he or she is unable to do anything right because of failing in one activity. This is, of course, an example of overgeneralization that leads to aberrant behavior and perhaps to mental illness.

Treatment for Borderline Personality Disorder

Borderline individuals remain some of the most difficult to treat effectively in therapeutic situations, whether they are outpatient or inpatient. Borderline individuals do not leave their personality traits at the entrance, so their traits are quite visible during treatment.

Trust is a critical concern for borderline patients; it is difficult to create and, if created, difficult to maintain. Typical in this therapeutic relationship is alternation between putting the therapist on a pedestal ("Oh, thank you *so* much for listening to my silly problems today; I'm *so* grateful,") and then disparaging the therapist in the next moment ("You're telling *me* that there's something wrong with *me*? Look at yourself, I'm fine! You're a *&^%"). The borderline individual might make constant phone calls to the therapist at all hours when he or she is in a crisis (which is often), and the individual will demand special treatment, for example, coming in for Saturday sessions if this is not the norm. After insisting on having extra appointments or special times for them, they will not keep their next appointment and will blame this on the therapist. They will ask for understanding and empathy but will also tell you that certain topics are taboo, not to be touched.

The risk of suicide with borderline individuals cannot be overemphasized. However, it can be difficult to separate out a true cry for help when a gesture or a serious attempt is made from a manipulative gesture designed to see, for example, how the therapist will react to the patient at that specific moment. In general, borderline individuals do not intend to take their own lives, but they do intend, at the least, to make realistic attempts to hurt themselves. Of course, if any patient's behavior becomes too unstable or too unmanageable for the therapist, in-

CAUTION

Many therapists do *not* give out personal contact information to patients, no matter how critical the patient might be. The therapist's phone numbers should, as a rule, not be divulged; in today's world, no one remains totally unreachable.

patient hospitalization becomes necessary. This is also the case when suicidal gestures or attempts are too frequent or too close to being lethal.

It is also not unusual for the therapist treating borderline individuals to seek consultation and perhaps even therapy on his or her own. Usually this occurs because the therapist cannot manage his or her own emotions and ends up having countertransference toward the patient, thus harming the therapist's objectivity. It is also, as a rule, difficult to handle manipulative, emotionally erratic, and perhaps suicidal, individuals.

Linehan, Tutek, Heard, and Armstrong (1994) describe a technique called *dialectical behavior therapy* (DBT). This technique combines cognitive behavioral techniques with Rogerian techniques, specifically providing much empathy to the patient, as well as social skills training. The three goals of DBT all encompass working with the borderline patient to get him or her to control his or her behaviors. The first goal is to teach the individual to moderate and to control extreme emotions and erratic behaviors. The second goal is to teach the patient to learn how to tolerate the feelings that occur when he or she is distressed. The final goal is to work with the patient to help them to trust his or her own thoughts and emotions. The therapist takes an unusual position in therapy with borderline patients: The therapist accepts the patient as she or he is, yet at the same time works with the patient to get him or her to change his or her behaviors. The borderline patient also is taught that she or he need *not* see the world only in absolutes, that is, that situations are either all good or all bad, and so on. They are also taught to realize that life is always changing.

Initial studies of DBT demonstrated that borderline individuals decreased their suicidal behaviors, reduced their time in inpatient psychiatric facilities, were consistent in showing up for their therapy, and did not leave treatment early. However, a 1-year follow up found that many of the patients studied were really not much better off than when they began therapy (Linehan, Heard, & Armstrong, 1993). Dialectical behavior therapy continues to garner research, but this study (and others) again demonstrates how difficult it is to treat borderline patients.

Treatment of Antisocial Personality Disorder (ASPD)

As with Borderline Personality Disorder, treatment of patients with ASPD is very difficult due to their lack of remorse and insight (Andreasen & Black, 1995). Treatment is also problematic because ASPD individuals rarely come into treatment voluntarily because they do not see anything wrong with their behavior. In addition, these individuals often present with much charm, making it easier for them to be extremely manipulative with their therapists. Because of these reasons, it is not surprising that many clinicians do not predict successful treatment for an individual with ASPD. Some well-known researchers have stated that it is a fruitless endeavor to make any attempt to either treat, or to try to alter the behavior of, a patient with ASPD (see, for example, Cleckley, 1982). Antisocial Personality Disorder patients also tend to be recidivists, that is, they are well known to jails, prisons, and to mental health clinics and hospitals. For them, all of these institutions have revolving doors, and they are always going in, staying for a short period of time while experiencing no changes, and then leaving, usually to go to jail or prison. These patients also have a tremendous tendency to relapse shortly after treatment has concluded.

The reasons for this are quite simple. It is hypothesized that the ASPD patient (or the psychopath) manipulates his or her way through therapy, pretending to work hard and trying to gain insight, while all she or he wants is to feign success so treatment will end. She or he could also be manipulating the therapist in order to regain something that was lost due to the behavior, such as an early jail or prison release or a driver's license. One perspective sees psychopaths or ASPD patients as being unable to benefit from therapy because of their symptoms, such as being unable to form a trusting relationship with the therapist (or anyone for that matter), lying without really knowing they are lying, only living in the present and not planning or foreseeing the future, and seeing nothing wrong with their behaviors even though they are crimes.

Some recent research has provided a more optimistic viewpoint (Salekin, 2002). Treatment was found to be effective when cognitive behavioral techniques were used and in some instances when psychoanalysis was used to work on building the patient's remorseful and empathic feelings and to reduce lying. The younger the patient, the more likely therapy would be effective. Finally, if treatment were to be successful, it needed to be extremely intensive, with sessions occurring at least four times a week for at least a year. Salekin found in his metanalysis that many studies examined had methodological flaws, harming their results. Finally, Salekin wondered if the patients who showed treatment success were in fact "faking good," that is, they wanted to look good for research and for the therapist. In other words, were they manipulating treatment (2002)?

Is incarceration an acceptable option? Prisons are certainly, in many peoples' views, not places for rehabilitation but instead places where criminals become more hardened and learn more about how not to get caught. Prisons do function as facilities where dangerous individuals are removed from society, but do psychopaths belong there? One way to view this is that, for whatever reason, ASPD patients and psychopaths seem to quiet down once they reach age 40 (Craft, 1969). Perhaps this is because their ways have finally exhausted them, or because of some biological changes we have yet to identify, or because they finally gain enough insight to make some changes.

Medications to Treat Personality Disorders

For most of the Personality Disorders, psychotropic medications are sometimes used in treatment. The determination as to which drug to prescribe is based on the Axis I disorder the personality disorder resembles. When unipolar depression occurs in a Personality Disorder, SSRIs such as Prozac (fluoxetine) can be prescribed. Avoidant Personality Disorder patients can be prescribed anxiolytics such as Xanax (alprazolam) to help alleviate their phobias and social anxieties. Of course, antipsychotic medications such as Risperdal (risperidone) can be prescribed to Schizotypal Personality Disorder patients.

No one medication stands out as the ideal treatment option for Borderline Personality Disorder. Antidepressants and anxiolytics may help calm some of the emotions of a borderline patient, but they will not alter the long-term maladaptive behavioral patterns. Prozac (fluoxetine) seems to be helpful in reducing aggression, depression, and impulsivity in individuals with Borderline Personality Disorder. Lithium appears to reduce anger and suicidal behaviors and gestures, while antipsychotics appear to reduce anxiety, suicidal behaviors and gestures, and their psychotic symptoms. As you might have guessed, due to the manipulative nature of borderline patients, their increased potential for abusing drugs, and their being a greater risk for a successful suicide attempt, these drugs must be prescribed with extreme caution (Bezchlibnyk-Butler & Jeffries, 2005).

Sometimes medications such as Lithium and Tegretol (carbamazepine, an anticonvulsant) have been prescribed for the anger or rage that ASPD patients may have, but the data substantiating their usage are scarce. Anxiolytics may be used, but because impulse control for ASPD is poor, using highly addictive medicines is not wise. Antisocial Personality Disorder remains poorly understood in many ways, so at the present time medication usage is not recommended. For definitions of key terms, see Rapid Reference 8.5.

≡ Rapid Reference 8.5

Key Terms to Know

Dialectical Behavior Therapy (DBT): This is a technique used to treat Borderline Personality Disorder; it combines cognitive behavioral techniques with Rogerian techniques, specifically providing much empathy to the patient as well as social skills training.

Tegretol (carbamazepine): This is an anticonvulsant, sometimes prescribed to treat the anger or rage that may occur with ASPD.

Xanax (alprazolam): This is an anxiolytic sometimes prescribed to Avoidant Personality Disorder patients to help alleviate their phobias and social anxieties.

Risperdal (risperidone): This is an atypical antipsychotic medication sometimes prescribed to Schizotypal Personality Disorder patients.

Putting It Into Practice

The Case of Emily Borderbender

Emily is a 31-year-old African American female who was referred to us by her probation officer, Molly. Emily works for a major utility and has been there for 9 years. She is single and has no children. Molly told us that Emily had a rather lengthy rap sheet that stretched back over 5 years and not to be deceived by her demeanor and appearance. Most of Emily's offenses involved assault as she was involved in many fights. Emily has spent some time in jail, but never more than 9 months and has never been to prison. Emily came in to our office and immediately took charge. "I was arrested again, because of the fights and the cuts. I beat the s*** out of my last boyfriend because he was looking at other women, not paying attention to me. He thought he'd dump me. Well, screw him. I dumped him before he could get to it. I always dump them. I've laid the past three out, knocked out some of my last ex's teeth. My ex and I had sex at a concert recently. Later on that night I cut myself. See [shows us her belly]? It felt pretty good actually, the pain and the warm blood. I do that sometimes, like on my stomach and on my legs."

We asked Emily about her past boyfriends, "Well, I've had many, a lot, yeah. I go through guys. Use them for a few weeks and then go to the next. See, I like sex, and I like variety, but nothing too kinky, no bondage and stuff. I get bored easily. Right now I hooked up with this major hottie. We're hooking

(continued)

up tonight after I'm done here." We also asked Emily about her alcohol usage. "Well, I drink some. Sometimes I get really hammered. Coke? I use the stuff whenever I can. It really gives me energy and makes me feel sexy. Lots of times when I'm high I'll buy stuff, shoes and things. I've got lots of shoes and lots of debt [laughs]. You know, sometimes I get into fights as well when I'm high." We asked Emily how she feels when she's having sexual relations or when she's spending a lot of money. "Well, to be honest, I don't really feel much. I love my sex, but it's lost something, you know? Buying things is dope, but what's the point? I feel blank all the time. What's missing in my life? I don't know. I wonder if I'm Emily or a prostitute. Did I tell you that I once turned tricks as well? Great money but too risky. A john tried to cut me once, so I messed him up bad."

So far we have seen Emily demonstrate feelings of emptiness, impulsive sexual behaviors, substance abuse, impulsive spending behaviors, unstable and intense short-term interpersonal relationships that vary between idealization and devaluation, unrealistic feelings of abandonment, self-mutilating behavior, and anger-control problems. Her self-image also appears to be unstable. We wanted more information for further clarification.

We asked Emily to tell us more about her substance usage, and she promptly blew up, "Who the hell are you to ask me about this? Ask G-ddamned Molly if you want to know. She tests me all the time. Geez, I should lay you out. Typical jerk-off guy with the questions. Are we done here, because I've got a hookup to go to. . . ." At that point Emily refused to answer any more questions. We ended the session and contacted Molly to inform her about what occurred. Molly called us back quickly and told us to expect Emily again in 2 days. Later that day Emily called back, telling us, "I really need to see you now, or perhaps tonight, so I can get going on some stuff that's been bothering me. You're free later this evening, aren't you? If not we can get a few drinks and talk some more." Of course we informed Emily that she needed to be seen in our office, but this characteristic is typical of someone with Borderline Personality Disorder. Molly also told us that Emily had a huge amount of credit card debt and that part of her salary was garnished to help pay off the debts. In addition, Emily told Molly that she never used protection during sex because the thrill of perhaps getting pregnant helped arouse her. Therefore, Emily has a history of evidencing feelings of emptiness, impulsive behaviors, unstable and intense interpersonal relationships that vary between idealization and devaluation, unrealistic feelings of abandonment, self-mutilating behaviors, and anger-control problems. She needs to have at least five of nine *DSM-IV-TR* diagnostic criteria to be diagnosed with Borderline Personality Disorder. Therefore, the following were our initial diagnostic impressions:

Axis I: Cocaine Abuse   305.60
Axis II: Borderline Personality Disorder   301.83
Axis III: No Diagnosis
Axis IV: Arrest and Incarceration
Axis V: GAF = 55 (Current)

We gave Emily a diagnosis of Cocaine Abuse because the abuse causes problems in her life, specifically in her interpersonal relationships. She gets into fights while high, goes on spending sprees, and believes that cocaine use makes her sexier. Finally, cocaine is an illicit substance that she continues to use whenever she can. In this situation, our primary concern is treating the symptoms of her Borderline Personality Disorder.

Treatment Plan

The key treatment goals for Emily are to manage her symptoms and try and change her behaviors. Because Emily tends to be manipulative, we made it very clear who is in charge during the sessions. It is extremely difficult to effectively treat borderline individuals, but with Emily we used DBT techniques. By combining Rogerian techniques with cognitive behavioral techniques, we were able to initially make some progress with Emily. Once Emily was admitted to the clinic and began individual treatment, we worked on the following goals to get her to control her behaviors: to teach Emily to moderate and to control her extreme emotions and erratic behaviors, to teach Emily to learn how to tolerate the feelings that occur when she is distressed, and to work with Emily to help her to trust her own thoughts and emotions. We followed DBTs protocol and accepted Emily for who she was, but we also worked with her to change her aberrant behaviors. Finally, Emily began to see things differently and not view the world in absolutes, and she saw that her life is constantly changing and, in many instances, for the better.

Emily made decent progress in therapy during the 10 months she was involved, especially because she got into no physical fights during this time. She managed to reduce her promiscuity somewhat, and her outbursts were contained in the clinic, but not outside of it. She now used protection when she had sexual relations, and she reported that she was now able to feel pleasure and that it was okay if things went wrong at times. "I'm basically a bit happier now than I was, but I'm not there yet."

Once the eleventh month came around, Emily began to miss her appointments. At first she would call and cancel; eventually, she did not call and did not show up. We contacted Molly, who was also having problems with Emily remaining consistent with her appointments. Molly felt sorry for Emily and so let her slide somewhat, but she had enough. When Emily appeared for her next appointment with Molly, Molly had Emily escorted back to jail. That was the last time we saw Emily; her prognosis is Guarded.

☙ TEST YOURSELF ❧

1. **A characteristic of a Cluster A disorder is**
   - (a) overly emotional or erratic behavior.
   - (b) anxious or fearful behavior.
   - (c) odd or eccentric behavior.
   - (d) bizarre hallucinations.

2. **A characteristic of a Cluster B disorder is**
   - (a) overly emotional or erratic behavior.
   - (b) anxious or fearful behavior.
   - (c) odd or eccentric behavior.
   - (d} bizarre hallucinations.

3. **A characteristic of a Cluster C disorder is**
   - (a) overly emotional or erratic behavior.
   - (b) anxious or fearful behavior.
   - (c) odd or eccentric behavior.
   - (d) bizarre hallucinations.

4. **All Personality Disorders are coded on Axis II.** True or False?

5. **Which is the only personality disorder that *cannot* be diagnosed at all in an individual if she or he is less than 18 years old?**
   - (a) Borderline Personality Disorder
   - (b) Schizotypal Personality Disorder
   - (c) Obsessive-Compulsive Personality Disorder
   - (d) Antisocial Personality Disorder (ASPD)

6. **Which personality disorder is seen by some researchers as being a milder form of Schizophrenia?**
   - (a) Schizotypal Personality Disorder
   - (b) Schizoid Personality Disorder
   - (c) Borderline Personality Disorder
   - (d) Antisocial Personality Disorder (ASPD)

7. **Which personality disorder is closely related to psychopathy?**
   - (a) Schizotypal Personality Disorder
   - (b) Schizoid Personality Disorder
   - (c) Borderline Personality Disorder
   - (d) Antisocial Personality Disorder (ASPD)

8. **The Personality Disorders respond well to treatment interventions.** True or False?

Answers: 1. c; 2. a; 3. b; 4. True; 5. d; 6. a; 7. d; 8. False

Appendix A

Glossary of *DSM-IV-TR* Terms

Course: This section describes the typical lifetime patterns of the presentation and the evolution of the disorder. Age of onset and mode of onset, episodic or continuous course, and whether single or recurrent episodes have occurred are listed.

Differential Diagnosis: This section describes how the clinician should differentiate the presenting disorder from other disorders that have some similar features.

Dual Diagnosis: This is when an individual has more than one diagnosis. Sometimes it is difficult to ascertain which diagnosis is the principal diagnosis, especially when each diagnosis contributed to the individual's admission and to the services rendered.

Duration: This characterizes the typical length of the mental illness and its episodes.

Familial Pattern: This refers to the frequency of the disorder among the patient's first-degree biological relatives as contrasted with the frequency in the general population. This section also lists disorders that may occur more frequently in family members of the patient. If information on heritability is known, that also appears in this section.

Prevalence: This section, present in many of the diagnostic categories, provides data on lifetime prevalence of the disorder, incidence within the general population, and lifetime risk. If information is known for different settings (community, outpatient mental health clinics, inpatient psychiatric hospitals), this is also provided.

Principal Diagnosis: Sometimes called the *Primary Presenting Problem,*

> **DON'T FORGET**
> ....
> In most cases of multiple diagnoses, the principal diagnosis is an Axis I disorder, and this disorder is listed first. The remaining disorders are listed in order of the focus of clinical attention and the focus of treatment.

this is the presenting condition that is primarily responsible for the individual being admitted to an outpatient clinic.

Prior History: This specifier tells us that the individual has met the criteria for a certain disorder in the past even if they appear to be recovered, such as Separation Anxiety Disorder, Prior History. While the individual may have no disorder at the present time, she or he has a history of Separation Anxiety Disorder (APA, 2000).

Progression: This characterizes the general trend of the disorder over time, that is, is the disorder stable, worsening, or improving?

Provisional: This specifier is used when not enough information is available to make a firm diagnostic decision, but it is presumed that the full diagnostic criteria will ultimately be met.

Reason for Visit: This term is used when there is more than one diagnosis for an individual in an outpatient setting. This refers to the condition that is primarily responsible for the services received during the patient's visit.

Recurrence: In some instances, individuals who are in partial or in full remission or are recovered may develop symptoms that suggest that the disorder may be recurring; however, they may not at that time satisfy the diagnostic criteria for the particular disorder. There are three possible options:

- If the symptoms are judged to be a new episode of a recurrent condition, the clinician may diagnose the condition as *current* or *provisional,* even before the full diagnostic criteria have been met.
- If the symptoms are clinically significant but it is unclear to the clinician if the symptoms denote a recurrence of the original diagnosis, the category "Not Otherwise Specified (NOS)" is given.
- If the displayed symptoms are not clinically significant, no additional or provisional diagnosis is given, but the clinician may use "Prior History" (APA, 2000, p. 3).

Severity Specifiers: The *DSM-IV-TR,* in some diagnostic categories, asks the diagnostician to indicate the severity of the disorder *at the present time.* There are six severity specifiers:

- *Mild.* Few if any symptoms outside of the minimum number required to arrive at the diagnosis are present during the initial intake assessment. The present symptoms result in little more than mild social or occupational impairment.

- *Moderate.* This specifier is used when the patient's symptoms are between Mild and Severe.
- *Severe.* Many symptoms outside of the minimum required to make the diagnosis are present during the initial intake interview, or, in some cases, several symptoms that are so severe are also present. Finally, this specifier is used if the symptoms result in significant social and occupational impairment.
- *In Partial Remission.* This is used when only some of the signs or symptoms of the disorder are present. The full diagnostic criteria for the disorder must have previously been met.
- *In Full Remission.* This is used when there are no longer any symptoms of the disorder present, but it is still prudent and clinically sound to note the disorder. For example, if an individual with Bipolar I Disorder has been asymptomatic while on Lithium for 3 years, clinicians might opt to deem this individual as being fully recovered. If this is the case, they would no longer receive the Bipolar I Disorder diagnosis. For disorders not believed to have cures at present, this specifier will not be present in those diagnostic categories (e.g., Borderline Personality Disorder). The *DSM-IV-TR* is vague when describing the difference between "In Full Remission" and "Recovered" (which does not appear anywhere as a severity specifier). Many factors need to be taken into account, including the typical course of the disorder (i.e., is it chronic?), the time since the last disturbance (e.g., when did the last hallucination occur?), the total length of time of the active disturbance (For how many months did the hallucinations last?), and the need for additional evaluation or continued treatment, either medication or otherwise.

Specifiers: A specifier is not intended to be mutually exclusive or jointly exhaustive. When a

DON'T FORGET

Specific criteria are listed for defining Mild, Moderate, and Severe for the following disorders: Mental Retardation, Conduct Disorder, Manic Episode, and Major Depressive Episode. Additionally, specific criteria for defining In Partial Remission and In Full Remission are listed for the following disorders: Manic Episode, Major Depressive Episode, and Substance Dependence (APA, 2000, p. 2).

specifier is required, the *DSM-IV-TR* will state "specify" or "specify if" in the diagnostic criteria. Specifiers allow the diagnostician to group similar individuals within the general disorder who share certain features. For example, with Pedophilia, the diagnostician is required to specify whether the individual is sexually attracted to males, to females, or to both, and they must also specify if the pedophilia is "limited to incest."

Subtypes: This term refers to mutually exclusive and jointly exhaustive subgroupings within a specific diagnosis. When a subtype is required, the *DSM-IV-TR* tells the clinician to "specify type." For example, Anorexia Nervosa has two subtypes, based on how the anorectic individual attempts to control or lose weight: Restricting Type, or Binge-Eating/Purging Type.

Appendix B

Essentials of the Multiaxial System and How to Code an Individual Using the *DSM-IV-TR*

The *DSM-IV-TR* (APA, 2000) uses a multiaxial system to make diagnoses for individuals with mental illnesses. Each axis refers to different information that can help clinicians plan treatment and perhaps make prognoses about the patient in question. The multiaxial system facilitates communication for both organizing and communicating the information about the patient in question to other people and to other entities (e.g., probation officers, psychiatrists, and so on). The multiaxial system also allows clinicians to get a complete picture of the individual and not just see them as a set of symptoms or mental illnesses. That is, psychosocial and environmental problems, general medical conditions, and an overall level of functioning are also examined, evaluated, and listed in their record. This ensures that no critical aspect is overlooked when making diagnoses. Finally, this system allows for the application of the biopsychosocial model of mental illness, where all factors are considered pertinent in the etiology and in the expression of each disorder.

THE FIVE AXES OF THE *DSM-IV-TR*

Axis I: Clinical Disorders; Other Conditions That May Be a Focus of Clinical Attention

All of the clinical syndromes except for the Personality Disorders and Mental Retardation (these are reported on Axis II) are reported on Axis I. If a patient has more than one Axis I disorder, all of the present disorders should be reported. If more than one Axis I disorder is evidenced, the principal diagnosis or the reason for the visit (discussed in Appendix A) should be listed first. If a patient has both an Axis I and an Axis II disorder, the principal diagnosis or the reason for visit is presumed to be the Axis I disorder unless the Axis II diagnosis is qualified by the terms *Principal Diagnosis* or *Reason for Visit*. Axis I disorders include the following:

- Disorders Usually First Diagnosed in Infancy, Childhood, or Adolescence (excluding Mental Retardation, coded on Axis II)
- Delirium, Dementia, and Amnestic and Other Cognitive Disorders
- Mental Disorders Due to a General Medical Condition
- Substance-Related Disorders
- Schizophrenia and Other Psychotic Disorders
- Mood Disorders
- Anxiety Disorders
- Somatoform Disorders
- Factitious Disorders
- Dissociative Disorders
- Sexual and Gender Identity Disorders
- Eating Disorders
- Sleep Disorders
- Impulse-Control Disorders Not Elsewhere Classified
- Adjustment Disorders
- Other Conditions that May Be a Focus of Clinical Attention

Axis II: Personality Disorders; Mental Retardation

The *DSM-IV-TR* codes these disorders on Axis II to ensure that they are not overlooked because more attention is typically paid to the more obvious and sometimes dramatic displays of the Axis I disorders. The APA also notes that by coding these disorders on Axis II, this does not imply that their treatment options or pathogeneses differ from the Axis I disorders. According to some clinicians and theorists, Axis II disorders generally do not respond well to treatment interventions, and to some researchers these disorders have no cure.

Axis III: General Medical Conditions

Axis III is used to report general medical conditions that may be relevant to the clinician's understanding, treatment, or management of their disor-

der. The APA states that by coding medical conditions on Axis
III, this does not imply that mental
disorders are unrelated to physical
or biological factors or, more important, that general medical conditions are unrelated to behavioral
or psychosocial factors (2000). In

CAUTION

Many psychologists and mental
health clinics only code on Axis I or
Axis II. Some clinics state that only
medical doctors should provide
Axis III diagnoses.

some instances the medical condition is directly related to the mental illness, particularly to its etiology or to the worsening of the symptoms. That
is, the medical condition may be directly responsible for causing a mental
illness or for exacerbating the symptoms; when this is clearly the situation, a
physiological cause (or mechanism) is presumed to be present (although not
necessarily apparent).

Axis IV: Psychosocial and Environmental Problems

Psychosocial and environmental problems that can affect the diagnosis, treatment, and prognosis of the mental illness are coded on Axis IV. The APA
states that a psychosocial or an environmental problem can be a negative life
event (such as a death in the family), an environmental stressor, familial or
interpersonal stress, a lack of a social support system, or a lack of personal or
interpersonal resources. Positive stressors, such as a promotion or the birth
of a child, should be listed only if the individual has difficulties adapting to
the new situation and only if they either constitute a problem or lead to the
development of a problem. Psychosocial problems can also develop as a result
of the individual's mental illness. Finally, they can also constitute problems
that need to be considered in the patient's overall treatment plan. Axis IV
psychosocial and environmental problems include the following:

- Problems with Primary Support Group
- Problems Related to the Social Environment
- Educational Problems
- Occupational Problems
- Housing Problems

> **DON'T FORGET**
> ....
> The APA states that only psycho-social and environmental problems that have been present for 1 year prior to the current evaluation be listed. The clinician can (and should) list problems prior to the past year if they clearly have contributed to the current mental illness, such as combat experience leading to PTSD, even though the experience occurred, for example, in Vietnam.

- Economic Problems
- Problems with Access to Health Care Services
- Problems related to Interaction with the Legal System or Crime
- Other Psychosocial and Environmental Problems

Axis V: Global Assessment of Functioning (GAF)

This Axis is often seen as the most controversial because it is the most subjective of the five axes. Here the clinician uses his or her judgment about the patient's overall level of functioning, based on a scale ranging from 1 to 100 (0 is used if the clinician does not have adequate information in order to reach a reasonable conclusion). On this scale, the higher the number, the more mentally healthy the individual is presumed to be. The clinician considers the individual's psychological, social, and occupational functioning when making a GAF assessment. The GAF rating should only represent the individual's current level of functioning at the time of the evaluation; however, at times clinicians will define the current period of time as being the past week when the individual's level of functioning was at its lowest.

The GAF is reported on Axis V as "GAF = 70 (Current)." The term in parentheses refers to the time period reflected by the rating. This example denotes that the individual, currently, is demonstrating some mild symptoms (such as depressed mood) or some social, occupational, or school difficulties (truancy). See Rapid Reference B.1 for an example of how to record an individual on all five *DSM-IV-TR* axes.

≝ *Rapid Reference B.1*

How to Record an Individual on All Five *DSM-IV-TR* Axes

Axis I: Schizophrenia, Disorganized Type, Continuous, With   295.10
          Prominent Negative Symptoms

          Alcohol Abuse   305.00

Axis II: Borderline Personality Disorder   301.83

Axis III: Palsy, Cerebral   343.9

Axis IV: Unemployment

Axis V: GAF = 35 (Current)

References

Abraham, S. (1996). Characteristics of Eating Disorders among young ballet dancers. *Psychopathology, 29,* 223–229.

Abramowitz, J. S. (1998). Does cognitive-behavioral therapy cure Obsessive-Compulsive Disorder? A meta-analytic evaluation of clinical significance. *Behavior Therapy, 29,* 339–355.

Agras, W. S., Walsh, B. T., Fairburn, C. G., Wilson, G. T., & Kraemer, H. C. (2000). A multicenter comparison of cognitive-behavioral therapy and interpersonal psychotherapy for Bulimia Nervosa. *Archives of General Psychiatry, 57,* 459–466.

Alden, L. E. (1989). Short-term structured treatment for Avoidant Personality Disorder. *Journal of Consulting and Clinical Psychology, 57,* 756–764.

American Psychiatric Association. (1980). *Diagnostic and statistical manual of mental disorders* (3rd ed). Washington, DC: Author.

American Psychiatric Association. (2000). *Diagnostic and statistical manual of mental disorders* (4th ed., text rev.). Washington, DC: Author.

Andreasen, N. C., & Black, D. W. (1995). *Introductory textbook of psychiatry* (2nd ed.) Washington, DC: American Psychiatric Press.

Apter, J. T., & Allen, L. A. (1999). Buspirone: Future directions. *Journal of Clinical Psychopharmacology, 19,* 86–93.

Avila, M. T., McMahon, R. P., Elliott, A. R., & Thaker, G. K. (2002). Neurophysiological markers of vulnerability to Schizophrenia: Sensitivity and specificity of specific quantitative eye movement measures. *Journal of Abnormal Psychology, 111,* 259–267.

Barbach, L. G. (2000). *For yourself: The fulfillment of female sexuality.* New York: Penguin Putnam.

Barlow, D. H. (Ed.). (2002). *Anxiety and its disorders: The nature and treatment of anxiety and panic.* New York: Guilford.

Barlow, D. H., Raffa, S. D., & Cohen, E. M. (2002). Psychosocial treatments for panic disorders, phobias, and generalized anxiety disorder. In P. E. Nathan & J. M. Gorman (Eds.). *A guide to treatments that work* (2nd ed., pp. 301–336). New York: Oxford University Press.

Bassett, A. S., Chow, E. W., Waterworth, D. M., & Brzustowicz, L. (2001). Genetic insights into Schizophrenia. *Canadian Journal of Psychiatry, 46,* 131–137.

Bateson, G. D., Jackson, D., Haley, J., & Weakland, J. (1956). Toward a theory of schizophrenia. *Behavioral Science, 1,* 251–264.

Beck, A. T. (1979). *Cognitive therapy and the emotional disorders.* New York: Penguin.

Beck, A. T., Rush, A. J., Shaw, B. F., & Emery, G. (1979). *Cognitive therapy of depression.* New York: Guilford.

Beck, A. T., Steer, R. A., Kovacs, M., & Garrison, B. (1985). Hopelessness and eventual suicide: A 10 year prospective study of patients hospitalized with suicidal ideation. *American Journal of Psychiatry, 142,* 559–563.

Begley, S. (1998, January 26). Is everyone crazy? *Newsweek*, 48–56.

Bellack, A. S., Haas, G. I., Schooler, N. R., & Flory, J. D. (2000). Effects of behavioural family management on family communication and patient outcomes in Schizophrenia. *British Journal of Psychiatry, 177*, 434–439.

Bertelsen, A., Harvald, B., & Hauge, M. (1997). A Danish twin study of manic depressive disorders. *British Journal of Psychiatry, 130*, 330–351.

Bezchlibnyk-Butler, K. Z., & Jeffries, J. J. (2005). *Clinical handbook of psychotropic drugs*. Ashland, OH: Hogrefe & Huber.

Bierut, L. M., Dinwiddle, S. H., Begleiter, H., Crowe, R. R., Hesselbrock, V., Nurnberger, J. I., et al. (1998). Familial transmission of substance dependence: Alcohol, marijuana, cocaine, and habitual smoking: A report from the collaborative study on the genetics of alcoholism. *Archives of General Psychiatry, 55*, 982–988.

Borkovec, T. D., Newman, M. G., Pincus, A. L., & Lytle, R. (2002). A component analysis of cognitive-behavioral therapy for Generalized Anxiety Disorder and the role of interpersonal problems. *Journal of Consulting and Clinical Psychology, 70*, 288–298.

Bowden, C. L., Calabrese, J. R., McElroy, S. L., Gyulai, L., Wassef, A., Petty, F., et al. (2000). A randomized, placebo-controlled 12-month trial of Divalproex and Lithium in treatment of outpatients with Bipolar I Disorder. *Archives of General Psychiatry, 57*, 481–489.

Bruch, H. (1982). Anorexia Nervosa: Therapy and theory. *American Journal of Psychiatry, 139*, 1531–1538.

Bruch, H. (2001). *The golden cage: The enigma of Anorexia Nervosa*. Cambridge, MA: Harvard University Press.

Bustillo, J. R., Lauriella, J., Horan, W. P., & Keith, S. J. (2001). The psychosocial treatment of Schizophrenia: An update. *American Journal of Psychiatry, 158*, 163–175.

Butzlaff, R. L., & Hooley, J. M. (1998). Expressed emotion and psychiatric relapse: A meta-analysis. *Archives of General Psychiatry, 55*, 547–552.

Cannon, M., Jones, P. B., & Murray, R. M. (2002). Obstetric complications and Schizophrenia: Historical and meta-analytic review. *American Journal of Psychiatry, 159*, 1080–1092.

Cannon, T. D. (1998). Neurodevelopmental influences in the genesis and epigenesis of Schizophrenia: An overview. *Applied and Preventive Psychology, 7*, 47–62.

Cannon, T. D., Kaprio, J., Loennqvist, J., Huttunen, M., & Koskenvuo, M. (1998). The genetic epidemiology of Schizophrenia in a Finnish twin cohort: A population-based modeling study. *Archives of General Psychiatry, 55*, 67–74.

Carey, G., & Goldman, D. (1997). The genetics of antisocial behavior. In D. M. Stoff, J. Breiling, & J. D. Maser (Eds.), *Handbook of antisocial behavior* (pp. 243–254). New York: Wiley.

Chorpita, B. F., Brown, T. A., & Barlow, D. H. (1998). Diagnostic reliability of the *DSM-III-R* Anxiety Disorders: Mediating effects of patient and diagnostician categories. *Behavior Modification, 22*, 307–320.

Clark, D. M. (1996). Panic Disorder: From theory to therapy. In P. Salkovskis (Ed.), *Frontiers of cognitive therapy* (pp. 318–344). New York: Guilford.

Clekley, H. M. (1982). *The mask of sanity* (6th ed.). St. Louis: Mosby.

Cohen, D. (1997). A critique of the use of neuroleptic drugs in psychiatry. In S. Fisher & R. P. Greenberg (Eds.), *From placebo to panacea: Putting psychiatric drugs to the test* (pp. 173–228). New York: Wiley.

Cornelius, R., Salloum, I. M., Ehler, J. G., Jarrett, P. J., Cornelius, M. D., Perel, J. M., et al. (1997). Fluoxetine in depressed alcoholics. A double-blind, placebo-controlled trial. *Archives of General Psychiatry, 54,* 700–705.

Craddock, N., & Jones, I. (1999). Genetics of bipolar disorder. *Journal of Medical Genetics, 36,* 585–594.

Craft, M. J. (1969). The natural history of psychopathic disorder. *British Journal of Psychiatry, 115,* 39–44.

Craske, M. G. (1999). *Anxiety Disorders: Psychological approaches to theory and treatment.* Boulder, CO: Westview Press.

Craske, M. G., & Rowe, M. K. (1997). *Nocturnal panic. Clinical psychology: Science and practice, 4,* 153–174.

Crits-Christoph, P., & Barber, J. P. (2002). Psychological treatments for Personality Disorders. In P. E. Nathan & J. M. Gorman (Eds.), *A guide to treatments that work* (2nd ed., pp. 611–624). New York: Oxford University Press.

Daley, D. C., & Marlatt, G. A. (1992). Relapse prevention: Cognitive and behavioral interventions. In J. H. Lowinson, P. Ruiz, & R. B. Millman (Eds.), *Substance abuse: A comprehensive textbook* (2nd ed., pp. 533–542). Baltimore, MD: Williams & Wilkins.

DePaulo, J. R., & Horvitz, L. A. (2002). *Understanding depression: What we know and what you can do about it.* New York: Wiley.

DiLalla, D. L., & Gottesman, I. I. (1991). Biological and genetic contributions to violence—Wisdom's untold tale. *Psychological Bulletin, 109,* 125–129.

Dishion, T. P., & Patterson, G. R. (1997). The timing and severity of antisocial behavior: Three hypotheses within an ecological framework. In D. M. Stoff, J. Breiling, & J. D. Maser (Eds.), *Handbook of antisocial behavior* (pp. 205–217). New York: Wiley.

Eisler, I., Dare, C., Russell, G. F. M., Szmukler, G., le Grange, D., & Dodge, E. (1997). Family and individual therapy in Anorexia Nervosa: A five year follow-up. *Archives of General Psychiatry, 54,* 1025–1030.

Fairburn, C. G. (1985). Cognitive-behavioral treatment for bulimia. In D. M. Garner & P. E. Garfinkel (Eds.), *Handbook of psychotherapy for Anorexia Nervosa and Bulimia* (pp. 160–192). New York: Guilford.

Fairburn, C. G., Jones, R., Peveler, R. C., Hope, R. A., & O'Connor, M. (1993). Psychotherapy and Bulimia Nervosa. Longer-term effects of interpersonal psychotherapy, behavior therapy, and cognitive behavior therapy. *Archives of General Psychiatry, 50,* 419–428.

Fairburn, C. G., Welch, S. I., Doll, H. A., Davies, B. A., & O'Connor, M. E. (1997). Risk factors for Bulimia Nervosa: A community-based case-control study. *Archives of General Psychiatry, 54,* 509–517.

Fallon, P., Katzman, M. A., & Wooley, S. C. (1994). *Feminist perspectives on Eating Disorders.* New York: Guilford.

Faris, R. E. L., & Dunham, H. W. (1939). *Mental disorders in urban areas: An ecological study of Schizophrenia and other psychoses.* Chicago: University of Chicago Press.

Fink, M. (2001). Convulsive Therapy: A review of the first 55 years. *Journal of Affective Disorders, 63,* 1–15.

Fowles, D. C., & Missel, K. A. (1994). Electrodermal hyporeactivity, motivation, and psychopathy: Theoretical issues. In D. C. Fowles, P. Sutker, & S. H. Goodman (Eds.), *Progress in experimental personality and psychopathology research* (pp. 263–283). New York: Springer.

Foy, D. W., Resnick, H. S., Sipprelle, R. C., & Carroll, E. M. (1987). Premilitary, military, and postmilitary factors in the development of combat related Posttraumatic Stress Disorder. *The Behavior Therapist, 10,* 3–9.

Frank, E., Swartz, H. A., & Kupfer, D. J. (2000). Interpersonal and social rhythm therapy: Managing the chaos of bipolar disorder. *Biological Psychiatry, 48,* 593–604.

Franklin, M. E., & Foa, E. B. (2002). Cognitive behavioral treatments for obsessive compulsive disorder. In P. E. Nathan & J. M. Gorman (Eds.). *A guide to treatments that work* (2nd ed., pp. 367–386). New York: Oxford University Press.

Friedman, S., Jones, J. C., Chernen, L., & Barlow, D. H. (1992). Suicidal ideation and suicide attempts among patients with Panic Disorder: A survey of two outpatient clinics. *American Journal of Psychiatry, 149,* 680–685.

Fromm-Reichmann, F. (1948). Notes on the development of treatment of schizophrenics by psychoanalytic psychotherapy. *Psychiatry, 11,* 263–273.

Fuller, M. A., & Sajatovic, M. (2000). *Drug information handbook for psychiatry* (2nd ed.). Cleveland, OH: American Pharmaceutical Association.

Gagne, F. F., Furman, M. J., Carpenter, L. I., & Price, L. H. (2000). Efficacy of continuation ECT and antidepressant drugs compared to long-term antidepressants alone in depressed patients. *American Journal of Psychiatry, 157,* 1960–1965.

Galea, S., Ahern, J., Resnick, H., Kilpatrick, D., Bucuvalas, M., Gold, J., et al. (2002). Psychological sequelae of the September 11th terrorist attacks. *New England Journal of Medicine, 346,* 982–987.

Garbutt, J. C., West, S. I., Carey, T. S., Lohr, K. N., & Crews, F. T. (1999). Pharmacological treatment of Alcohol Dependence: A review of the evidence. *Journal of the American Medical Association, 281,* 1318–1326.

Garfinkel, P. E., Kennedy, S. H., & Kaplan, A. S. (1995). Views on classification and diagnosis of Eating Disorders. *Canadian Journal of Psychiatry, 40,* 445–456.

Garfinkel, P. E., Lin, B., Goering, P., Spegg, C., Goldbloom, D. S., Kennedy, S., et al. (1996). Purging and nonpurging forms of Bulimia Nervosa in a community sample. *International Journal of Eating Disorders, 20,* 231–238.

Garner, D. M., Garfinkel, P. E., Rockert, W., & Olmsted, M. P. (1987). A prospective study of eating disturbances in the ballet. *Psychotherapy and Psychosomatics, 48,* 170–175.

Garner, D. M., Garner, M. V., & Rosen, L. W. (1993). Anorexia Nervosa "restrictors" who purge: Implications for subtyping Anorexia Nervosa. *International Journal of Eating Disorders, 13,* 171–185.

Getzfeld, A. R. (1993). Characteristics of female bulimics and the effectiveness of desipramine treatment. *Dissertation Abstracts International, 54* (6-B), 3378. (UMI No. AAT 9331697).

Getzfeld, A. R. (1999, April). *Bulimia Nervosa, Anorexia Nervosa, and Alcohol Abuse: Differential diagnoses using the* DSM-IV, *a case study, and some potential treatment methods.* Poster session presented at the meeting of the National Association of School Psychologists, Las Vegas, NV.

Getzfeld, A. R. (2004). *Abnormal psychology casebook: A new perspective.* Upper Saddle River, NJ: Pearson Prentice Hall.

Gitlin, M. J. (1996). *The psychotherapist's guide to psychopharmacology* (2nd ed.). New York: Free Press.

Goldstein, D. J. (Ed.). (1999). *The management of Eating Disorders and obesity.* Totowa, NJ: Humana Press.

Goodwin, D. W. (1979). Alcoholism and heredity: A review and hypothesis. *Archives of General Psychiatry, 36,* 57–61.

Gottesman, I. I. (1991). *Schizophrenia genesis: The origins of madness.* New York: W. H. Freeman.

Hammen, C., & Garber, J. (2001). Vulnerability to depression across the lifespan. In R. E. Ingram & J. M. Price (Eds.), *Vulnerability to psychopathology: Risk across the lifespan* (pp. 258–267). New York: Guilford.

Hare, R. D., Hart, S. D., & Harpur, T. J. (1991). Psychopathy and DSM-IV criteria for Antisocial Personality Disorder. *Journal of Abnormal Psychology, 100,* 391–398.

Hart, S. D., & Hare, R. D. (1989). Discriminant validity of the Psychopathy Checklist in a forensic psychiatric population. *Psychological Assessment, 1,* 211–218.

Hart, S. D., & Hare, R. D. (1997). Psychopathy: Assessment and association with criminal conduct. In D. M. Stoff, J. Breiling, & J. D. Maser (Eds.), *Handbook of antisocial behavior* (pp. 22–35). New York: Wiley.

Heiman, J. R. (2000). Orgasmic disorders in women. In S. R. Leiblum & R. C. Rosen (Eds.), *Principles and practice of sex therapy* (3rd ed., pp. 118–153). New York: Guilford.

Herbener, E. S., & Harrow, M. (2002). The course of anhedonia during 10 years of schizophrenic illness. *Journal of Abnormal Psychology, 111,* 237–248.

Hinshaw, S. P. (1994). Conduct disorder in childhood: Conceptualization, diagnosis, comorbidity, and risk status for antisocial functioning in adulthood. In D. C. Fowles, P. Sutker, & S. H. Goodman (Eds.), *Progress in Experimental Personality and Psychopathology Research* (pp. 3–44). New York: Springer.

Hoek, H. W. (2002). Distribution of eating disorders. In C. G. Fairburn & K. D. Brownell (Eds.), *Eating disorders and obesity: A comprehensive handbook* (2nd ed., pp. 233–237). New York: Guilford.

Hogarty, G. E., Greenwald, D., Ulrich, R. F., Kornblith, S. J., DiBarry, A. L., Cooley, S., et al. (1997). Three year trials of personal therapy among schizophrenic patients living with or independent of family, II: Effects on adjustment of patients. *American Journal of Psychiatry, 154,* 1504–1512.

Hollon, S. D., DeRubeis, R. J., & Seligman, M. E. P. (1992). Cognitive therapy and the prevention of depression. *Applied and Preventive Psychology, 1,* 89–95.

Holzman, P. S. (2000). Eye movements and the search for the essence of Schizophrenia. *Brain Research Reviews, 31,* 350–356.

Hooley, J. M., & Hiller, J. B. (1998). Expressed emotion and the pathogenesis of relapse in Schizophrenia. In M. F. Lezenweger & R. H. Dworkin (Eds.), *Origins and development of Schizophrenia* (pp. 447–468). Washington: American Psychological Association.

Hsu, L. K. G. (1990). *Eating Disorders.* New York: Guilford.

Hudson, J., Pope, H., Jonas, J. M., & Yurgelun-Todd, D. (1983). Family history study of Anorexia Nervosa and Bulimia. *British Journal of Psychiatry, 142,* 133–138.

Hunicutt, C. P., & Newman, I. A. (1983). Adolescent dieting practices and nutrition knowledge. *Health Values: The Journal of Health Behavior, Education, and Promotion, 17,* 35–40.

Huttunen, M. O., & Niskanen, P. (1978). Prenatal loss of father and psychiatric disorders. *Archives of General Psychiatry, 35,* 429–431.

Iacono, W. G., & Clementz, B. A., (1993). A strategy for elucidating genetic influences on complex psychopathological syndromes. In L. J. Chapman, J. P. Chapman, & D. Fowles (Eds.), *Progress in experimental personality and psychopathology research* (pp. 11–65). New York: Springer.

Johnson, W. G., Tsoh, J. Y., & Varnado, P. J. (1996). Eating Disorders: Efficacy of pharmacological and psychological interventions. *Clinical Psychology Review, 16,* 457–478.

Kaemingk, K., & Paquette, A. (1999). Effects of prenatal alcohol exposure on neuropsychological functioning. *Developmental Neuropsychology, 15,* 111–140.

Kallman, F. J. (1938). *The genetics of Schizophrenia.* New York: Augustin.

Kalus, O., Bernstein, D. P., & Siever, L. J. (1995). Schizoid Personality Disorder. In W. J. Livesey (Ed.), *The DSM-IV Personality Disorders* (pp. 58–70). New York: Guilford.

Kaplan, H. S. (1974). *The new sex therapy: Active treatment of sexual dysfunction.* New York: Brunner/Mazel.

Kaplan, H. S. (1979). *Disorders of sexual desire.* New York: Simon & Schuster.

Karel, M. J. (1997). Aging and depression: Vulnerability and stress across adulthood. *Clinical Psychology Review, 17,* 847–879.

Keel, P. K., & Mitchell, J. E. (1997). Outcome in Bulimia Nervosa. *American Journal of Psychiatry, 154,* 313–321.

Kelsoe, J. R. (1997). The genetics of bipolar disorder. *Psychiatric Annals, 27,* 285–292.

Kendler, K. S., & Diehl, S. R. (1993). The genetics of Schizophrenia: A current, genetic-epidemiologic perspective. *Schizophrenia Bulletin, 19,* 261–285.

Kendler, K. S., & Gardner, C. O. (1997). The risk of psychiatric disorders in relatives of schizophrenic and control probands: A comparison of three independent studies. *Psychological Medicine, 27,* 411–419.

Kendler, K. S., McGuire, M., Gruenberg, A. M., O'Hare, A., Spellman, M., & Walsh, D. (1993). The Roscommon family study: Methods, diagnosis of probands, and risk of Schizophrenia in relatives. *Archives of General Psychiatry, 50,* 527–540.

Kernberg, O. E. (1996). A psychoanalytic theory of Personality Disorders. In J. F. Clarkin & M. F. Lezenweger (Eds.), *Major theories of personality disorder* (pp. 106–140). New York: Guilford.

Kessler, R. C. (2000). Gender differences in major depression: Epidemiological findings. In E. Frank (Ed.), *Gender and its effects on psychopathology* (pp. 61–84). Washington, DC: American Psychiatric Press.

Kessler, R. C., Keller, M. B., & Wittchen, H. (2001). The epidemiology of Generalized Anxiety Disorder. *Psychiatric Clinics of North America, 24,* 19–39.

Kiefer, F., Jahn, H., Tarnaske, T., Helwig, H., Briken, P., Holzbach, R., et al. (2003). Comparing and combining Naltrexone and Acamprosate in relapse prevention of alcoholism: A double-blind, placebo-controlled study. *Archives of General Psychiatry, 60,* 92–99.

Kilpatrick, D. G., Saunders, B. E., Amick-McMullan, A., Best, C. I., Veronen, L. J., &

Resnick, H. S. (1989). Victim and crime factors associated with the development of crime-related Posttraumatic Stress Disorder. *Behavior Therapy, 20,* 199–214.

Klein, D. F. (1994). Klein's suffocation theory of panic [Reply]. *Archives of General Psychiatry, 51,* 506.

Klerman, G. L., Weissman, M. M., Rounsaville, B. J., & Chevron, E. S. (1984). *Interpersonal psychotherapy of depression.* New York: Basic Books.

Ladouceur, R., Dugas, M. J., Freeston, M. H., Leger, E., Gagnon, F., & Thibodeau, N. (2000). Efficacy of a cognitive-behavioral treatment for Generalized Anxiety Disorder: Evaluation in a controlled clinical trial. *Journal of Consulting and Clinical Psychology, 68,* 957–964.

LeDoux, J. E. (2000). Emotion circuits in the brain. *Annual Review of Neuroscience, 23,* 155–184.

Leon, G. R., Fulkerson, J. A., Perry, C. L., & Early-Zald, M. B. (1995). Prospective analysis of personality and behavioral vulnerabilities and gender influences in the later development of disordered eating. *Journal of Abnormal Psychology, 104,* 140–149.

Lewinsohn, P. M. (1974). A behavioral approach to depression. In R. J. Friedman & M. M. Katz (Eds.), *The psychology of depression: Contemporary theory and research* (pp. 157–185). Washington, DC: Winston-Wiley.

Lewis, G., Croft-Jeffreys, C., & Anthony, D. (1990). Are British psychiatrists racist? *British Journal of Psychiatry, 157,* 410–415.

Ley, R. (1999). The modification of breathing behavior: Pavlovian and operant control in emotion and cognition. *Behavior Modification, 23,* 441–479.

Li, F., Duncan, T. E., & Hops, H. (2001). Examining developmental trajectories in adolescent alcohol use using piecewise growth mixture modeling analysis. *Journal of Studies on Alcohol, 62,* 199–210.

Lieberman, J. A., Stroup, T. S., McEvoy, J. P., Swartz, M. S., Rosenheck, R. A., Perkins, D. O., et al. (2005). Effectiveness of antipsychotic drugs in patients with chronic schizophrenia. *The New England Journal of Medicine, 353,* 1209–1223.

Linehan, M. M., Heard, H. L., & Armstrong, H. E. (1993). Naturalistic follow-up of a behavioral treatment for chronically parasuicidal borderline patients. *Archives of General Psychiatry, 50,* 971–974.

Linehan, M. M., Tutek, D. A., Heard, H. L., & Armstrong, H. E. (1994). Interpersonal outcome of cognitive behavioral treatment for chronically suicidal borderline patients. *American Journal of Psychiatry, 151,* 1771–1776.

Lucas, A. R., Crowson, C. S., O'Fallon, W. M., & Melton, L. J. (1999). The ups and downs of Anorexia Nervosa. *International Journal of Eating Disorders, 26,* 397–405.

Lykken, D. T. (1957). A study of anxiety in the sociopathic personality. *Journal of Abnormal and Social Psychology, 55,* 6–10.

Lykken, D. T. (1982). Fearfulness: Its carefree charms and deadly risks. *Psychology Today, 16,* 20–28.

Lyman, D. R. (1996). Early identification of chronic offenders: Who is the fledging psychopath? *Psychological Bulletin, 120,* 209–234.

Lynam, D. R. (1997). Pursuing the psychopath: Capturing the fledging psychopath in a nomological net. *Journal of Abnormal Psychology, 106,* 425–438.

Lyon, H. M., Startup, M., & Bentall, R. P. (1999). Social cognition and the manic defense: Attribution, selective attention, and self-schema in bipolar affective disorder. *Journal of Abnormal Psychology, 108,* 273–282.

Manji, H. K., Chen, G., Shimon, H., Hsiao, J. K., Potter, W. Z., & Belmaker, R. H. (1995). Guanine nucleotide-binding proteins in bipolar affective disorder: Effects of long-term lithium treatment. *Archives of General Psychiatry, 52,* 135–144.

Marlatt, G. A., Blume, A. W., & Parks, G. A. (2001). Integrating harm reduction therapy and traditional substance abuse treatment. *Journal of Psychoactive Drugs, 33,* 13–21.

Marlatt, G. A., Demming, B., & Reid, J. B. (1973). Loss of control drinking in alcoholics: An experimental analogue. *Journal of Abnormal Psychology, 81,* 233–241.

Masters, W. H., & Johnson, V. E. (1966). *Human sexual response.* Boston: Little, Brown, and Company.

Masters, W. H., & Johnson, V. E. (1970). *Human sexual inadequacy.* Boston: Little, Brown, and Company.

Mathews, A., & MacKintosh, B. (2000). Induced emotional interpretation bias and anxiety. *Journal of Abnormal Psychology, 109,* 602–615.

Maxmen, J. S., & Ward, N. G. (1995). *Psychotropic drugs: Fast facts* (2nd ed.). New York: W. W. Norton.

McBride, W. J., Murphy, J. M., Yoshimoto, K., Lumeng, L., & Li, T. K. (1993). Serotonin mechanisms in alcohol-drinking behavior. *Drug Development Research, 30,* 170–177.

McGrath, J. J., & Welham, J. L. (1999). Season of birth and Schizophrenia: A systematic review and meta-analysis of data from the Southern Hemisphere. *Schizophrenia Research, 35,* 237–242.

McGue, M. (1999). The behavioral genetics of alcoholism. *Current Directions in Psychological Science, 8,* 109–115.

McKim, W. A. (2003). *Drugs and behavior: An introduction to behavioral pharmacology* (5th ed.). Upper Saddle River, NJ: Prentice Hall.

Merckelbach, H., Muris, P. & Schouten, E. (1996). Pathways to fear in spider-phobic children. *Behaviour Research and Therapy, 34,* 935–938.

Michelini, S., Cassano, G. B., Frare, F., & Perugi, G. (1996). Long-term use of benzodiazepines: Tolerance, dependence and clinical problems in Anxiety and Mood Disorders. *Pharmacopsychiatry, 29,* 127–134.

Miklowitz, D. J. (1995). The evolution of family-based psychopathology. In R. H. Mikesell & S. H. McDaniel (Eds.), *Integrating family therapy: Handbook of family psychology and systems theory* (pp. 183–197). Washington, DC: American Psychological Association.

Millon, T., & Davis, R. D. (1996). An evolutionary theory of Personality Disorders. In J. F. Clarkin & M. F. Lezenweger (Eds.), *Major theories of personality disorder* (pp. 221–346). New York: Guilford.

Mineka, S., & Ohman, A. (2002). Born to fear: Non-associative vs. associative factors in the etiology of phobias. *Behaviour Research and Therapy, 40,* 173–184.

Mineka, S., & Thomas, C. (1999). Mechanisms of change in exposure therapy for Anxiety Disorders. In T. Dalgleish & M. J. Power (Eds.), *Handbook of cognition and emotion* (pp. 747–764). Chichester, England: Wiley.

Mitchell, J. E., Laine, D. E., Morley, J. E., & Levine, A. S. (1986). Naloxone but not CCK-8 may attenuate binge-eating behavior in patients with the bulimia syndrome. *Biological Psychiatry, 21,* 1399–1406.

Morey, L. C. (1988). Personality disorders in DSM-III and DSM-III-R: Convergence, coverage, and internal consistency. *American Journal of Psychiatry, 145,* 573–577.

Morrison, J. (1995). DSM-IV *made easy: The clinician's guide to diagnosis.* New York: Guilford.

Myers, M. G., Stewart, D. G., & Brown, S. A. (1998). Progression from Conduct Disorder to Antisocial Personality Disorder. *American Journal of Psychiatry, 155,* 479–485.

National Institute of Mental Health. (1999). *Facts about Anxiety Disorders* (Publication No. OM-99 4152). Rockville, MD: NIMH.

Newman, J. P., Patterson, C. M., & Kosson, D. S. (1987). Response perseveration in psychopaths. *Journal of Abnormal Psychology, 96,* 145–148.

Nietzel, M. T., & Harris, M. J. (1990). Relationship of dependency and achievement to depression. *Clinical Psychology Review, 10,* 279–297.

Nigg, J. T., & Goldsmith, H. H. (1994). Genetics of Personality Disorders: Perspectives from personality and psychopathology research. *Psychological Bulletin, 115,* 346–380.

O'Farrell, T. J. (1993). A behavioral marital therapy couples group program for alcoholics and their spouses. In T. J. O'Farrell (Ed.), *Treating alcohol problems: Marital and family interventions* (pp. 170–209). New York: Guilford.

Ohman, A., & Mineka, S. (2001). Fear, phobias, and preparedness: Toward an evolved module of fear and fear learning. *Psychological Review, 108,* 483–522.

Pallas, J., Levine, S. B., Althof, S. E., & Risen, C. B. (2000). A study using Viagra in a mental health practice. *Journal of Sex and Marital Therapy, 26,* 41–50.

Patterson, G. R. (1982). *Coercive family process.* Eugene, OR: Castalia.

Patton, G. C., Selzer, R., Coffey, C., Carlin, J. B., & Wolfe, R. (1999). Onset of adolescent Eating Disorders: Population based cohort study over 3 years. *British Medical Journal, 318,* 765–768.

Paul, G. I., & Lentz, R. J. (1977). *Psychosocial treatment of chronic mental patients: Milieu versus social-learning programs.* Cambridge, MA: Harvard University Press.

Paykel, E. S. (1982). Life events and social stress. In E. S. Paykel (Ed.), *Handbook of affective disorders* (pp. 149–170). New York: Guilford.

Prien, R. F., and Potter, W. Z. (1993). Maintenance treatment for mood disorders. In D. L. Dunner (Ed.), *Current psychiatric therapy* (pp. 255–260). Philadelphia: Saunders.

Prochaska, J. O., & Norcross, J. C. (2003). *Systems of psychotherapy: A transtheoretical analysis* (5th ed.). Pacific Grove, CA: Brooks/Cole.

Quay, H. C. (1965). Psychopathic personality as pathological stimulation seeking. *American Journal of Psychiatry, 122,* 180–183.

Read, J. P., Wood, M. D., Kahler, C. W., Maddock, J. E., & Palfai, T. P. (2003). Examining the role of drinking motives in college student alcohol use and problems. *Psychology of Addictive Behavior, 17,* 13–23.

Robins, L. N. (1978). Aetiological implications in studies of childhood histories relating to antisocial personality. In R. D. Hare & D. Schalling (Eds.), *Psychopathic behavior: Approaches to research* (pp. 255–271). Chichester, England: Wiley.

Robins, L. N. (1991). Conduct Disorder. *Journal of Child Psychology and Psychiatry, 32,* 193–212.

Robins, L. N., & Regier, D. A. (1991). *Psychiatric disorders in America: The Epidemiologic Catchment Area study.* New York: Free Press.

Rosenthal, D., Wender, P. H., Kety, S. S., Schulsinger, F., Welner, J., & Reider, R. (1975). Parent-child relationships and psychopathological disorder in the child. *Archives of General Psychiatry, 32,* 466–476.

Roy, A. (1992). Genetics, biology, and suicide in the family. In R. W. Maris, A. L. Berman, J. T. Maltsberger, & R. I. Yufit (Eds.), *Assessment and prediction of suicide.* New York: Guilford.

Roy-Byrne, P. P., & Cowley, D. S. (2002). Pharmacological treatments for Panic Disorder, Generalized Anxiety Disorder, Specific Phobia, and Social Anxiety Disorder. In P. E. Nathan & J. M. Gorman (Eds.), *A guide to treatments that work* (2nd ed., pp. 337–365). New York: Oxford University Press.

Russell, G. F. M. (1979). Bulimia Nervosa: An ominous variant of Anorexia Nervosa. *Psychological Medicine, 9,* 429–448.

Sadock, B. J., & Sadock, V. A. (2003). *Kaplan & Sadock's synopsis of psychiatry: Behavioral sciences/clinical psychiatry* (9th ed.). Philadelphia: Lippincott, Williams, and Wilkins.

Salekin, R. T. (2002). Psychopathy and therapeutic pessimism: Clinical love or clinical reality? *Clinical Psychology Review, 22,* 79–112.

Segal, Z. V., Williams, J. M., & Teasdale, J. D. (2001). *Mindfulness-based cognitive therapy for depression.* New York: Guilford.

Seligman, M. E. P. (1975). *Helplessness: On depression, development, and death.* San Francisco: Freeman.

Shenton, M. E. (1996). Temporal lobe structural abnormalities in Schizophrenia: A selective review and presentation of new magnetic resonance imaging findings. In S. Matthysse & D. L. Levy (Eds.), *Psychopathology: The evolving science of mental disorder* (pp. 51–99). New York: Cambridge University Press.

Siever, L. J., Bernstein, D. P., & Silverman, J. M. (1995). Schizotypal Personality Disorder. In W. J. Livesey (Ed.), *The DSM-IV Personality Disorders* (pp. 71–90). New York: Guilford.

Silberg, J., Pickles, A., Rutter, M., Hewitt, J., Simonoff, E., Maes, H., et al. (1999). The influence of genetic factors and life stress on depression among adolescent girls. *Archives of General Psychiatry, 56,* 225–232.

Sisson, R. W., & Azrin, N. H. (1989). The community-reinforcement approach. In R. K. Hester & R. W. Miller (Eds.), *Handbook of alcoholism treatment approaches: Effective alternatives* (pp. 242–258). New York: Pergamon.

Sobell, M. B., & Sobell, L. C. (1993). *Problem drinkers: Guided self-change treatment.* New York: Guilford.

Squires-Wheeler, E., Friedman, D., Amminger, G. P., Skodol, A., Looser-Ott, S., Roberts, S., et al. (1997). Negative and positive dimensions of Schizotypal Personality Disorder. *Journal of Personality Disorders, 11,* 285–300.

Steiner, H., & Lock, J. (1998). Anorexia Nervosa and Bulimia Nervosa in children and adolescents: A review of the past ten years. *Journal of the American Academy of Child and Adolescent Psychiatry, 37,* 352–359.

Steketee, G., & Barlow, D. H. (2002). Obsessive compulsive disorder. In D. H. Barlow (Ed.), *Anxiety and its disorders: The nature and treatment of anxiety and panic* (2nd ed., pp. 516–550). New York: Guilford.

Stice, E. (1994). Review of the evidence for a sociocultural model of Bulimia Nervosa and an exploration of the mechanisms of action. *Clinical Psychology Review, 14,* 633–661.

Strober, M., & Bulik, C. M. (2002). Genetic epidemiology of eating disorders. In C. G. Fairburn & K. D. Brownell (Eds.), *Eating disorders and obesity: A comprehensive handbook* (2nd ed., pp. 238–242). New York: Guilford.

Strober, M., Freeman, R., Lampert, C., Diamond, J., & Kaye, W. (2000). Controlled family study of Anorexia Nervosa and Bulimia Nervosa: Evidence of shared liability and transmission of partial syndromes. *American Journal of Psychiatry, 157,* 393–401.

Substance Abuse and Mental Health Services Administration. (2003). *2003 national survey on drug use and health.* Retrieved from http://oas.samhsa.gov/nhsda .htm#NHSDAinfo

Suppes, T., Baldessarini, R. J., Faedda, G. L., & Tohen, M. (1991). Risk of recurrence following discontinuation of lithium treatment in bipolar disorder. *Archives of General Psychiatry, 48,* 1082–1087.

Szasz, T. S. (1984). *The myth of mental illness.* New York: HarperCollins.

Thornicroft, G., & Susser, E. (2001). Evidence-based psychotherapeutic interventions in the community care of Schizophrenia. *British Journal of Psychiatry, 178,* 2–4.

Tienari, P., Wynne, L. C., Moring, J., Lahti, I., Naarala, M., Sorri, A., et al. (1994). The Finnish adoptive family study of Schizophrenia: Implications for family research. *British Journal of Psychiatry Supplement, 23,* 20–26.

Torgersen, S., Kringlen, E., & Cramer, V. (2001). The prevalence of Personality Disorders in a community sample. *Archives of General Psychiatry, 58,* 590–596.

Torrey, E. F., Bowler, A. E., Rawlings, R., and Terrazas, A. (1993). Seasonality of Schizophrenia and still-births. *Schizophrenia Bulletin, 19,* 557–562.

Tsuang, M. T., Lyons, M. J., Meyer, J. M., Doyle, T., Eisen, S. A., Goldberg, J., et al. (1998). Co-occurrence of abuse of different drugs in men: The role of drug-specific and shared vulnerabilities. *Archives of General Psychiatry, 55,* 967–972.

Vandereycken, W. (2002). History of anorexia nervosa and bulimia nervosa. In C. G. Fairburn & K. D. Brownell (Eds.), *Eating disorders and obesity: A comprehensive handbook* (2nd ed., pp. 151–154). New York: Guilford.

Vasey, M. W., & Borkovec, T. D. (1992). A catastrophizing assessment of worrisome thoughts. *Cognitive Therapy and Research, 16,* 505–520.

Vasterling, J. J., Brailey, K., Constans, J. I., & Sotker, P. B. (1998). Attention and memory dysfunction in Posttraumatic Stress Disorder. *Psychiatric Bulletin, 12,* 125–133.

Vitousek, K. B., (2002). Cognitive-behavioral therapy for anorexia nervosa. In C. G. Fairburn & K. D. Brownell (Eds.), *Eating disorders and obesity: A comprehensive handbook* (2nd ed., pp. 308–313). New York: Guilford.

Walsh, B. T., Wilson, G. T., Loeb, K. L., Devlin, M. J., Pike, K. M., Roose, S. P., et al. (1997). Medication and psychotherapy in the treatment of Bulimia Nervosa. *American Journal of Psychiatry, 154,* 523–531.

Wechsler, H., Lee, J. E., Kuo, M., & Lee, H. (2000). College binge drinking in the 1990's: A continuing problem. *Journal of the American College Health, 48,* 199–210.

Weeks, D., & James, J. (1995). *Eccentrics: A study of sanity and strangeness.* New York: Villard.

Weissman, M. M., Bruce, M. L., Leaf, P. J., Florio, L. P., & Holzer, C. (1990). Affective Disorders. In L. N. Robins & D. A. Regier (Eds.), *Psychiatric disorders in America: The Epidemiological Catchment Area study* (pp. 53–80). New York: Free Press.

Wickes-Nelson, R., & Israel, A. C. (2000). *Behavior disorders of children.* Upper Saddle River, NJ: Prentice Hall.

Widiger, T. A., & Frances, A. J. (1994). Toward a dimensional model for the Personality Disorders. In P. T. Costa, Jr., & T. A. Widiger (Eds.), *Personality Disorders and the five-favor model of personality* (pp. 19–39). Washington, DC: American Psychological Association.

Widiger, T. A., Frances, A., & Trull, T. J. (1987). A psychometric analysis of the social-interpersonal and cognitive-perceptual items for Schizotypal Personality Disorder. *Archives of General Psychiatry, 44,* 741–745.

Widiger, T., & Rogers, J. (1989). Prevalence and co-morbidity of Personality Disorders. *Psychiatric Annals, 19,* 132–136.

Widiger, T., & Trull, T. J. (1993). Borderline and narcissistic personality disorders. In P. B. Sutker & H. E. Adams (Eds.), *Comprehensive handbook of psychopathology* (2nd ed., pp. 371–394). New York: Plenum.

Wildes, J. E., Emery, R. E., & Simons, A. D. (2001). The roles of ethnicity and culture in the development of eating disturbance and body dissatisfaction: A meta-analytic review. *Clinical Psychology Review, 21,* 521–551.

Wilson, G. T., Loeb, K. I., Walsh, B. T., Labouvie, E., Petkova, E., Liu, X., et al. (1999). Psychological versus pharmacological treatments of Bulimia Nervosa: Predictors and processes of change. *Journal of Consulting and Clinical Psychology, 67,* 451–459.

Winters, K. C., & Neale, J. M. (1985). Mania and low self-esteem. *Journal of Abnormal Psychology, 94,* 282–290.

Zanarini, M. C., Williams, A. A., Lewis, R. E., Reich, R. B., Vera, S. C., Marino, M. F., et al. (1997). Reported pathological childhood experiences associated with the development of Borderline Personality Disorder. *American Journal of Psychiatry, 154,* 1101–1106.

Zilbergeld, B. (1999). *New male sexuality.* New York: Random House.

Zubin, J., & Spring, B. (1977). Vulnerability—New view of Schizophrenia. *Journal of Abnormal Psychology, 86,* 103–126.

Annotated Bibliography

American Medical Association. *Archives of General Psychiatry.*

Published continuously since 1954, this journal is one of the best sources for data-based research articles that examine the biological etiologies of mental illnesses and treatment of them with psychotropic medications. While somewhat difficult to comprehend at times, much critical research has been published here. It is a good place to start when seeking research on Eating Disorders, especially Bulimia Nervosa. Many past abstracts are available online. It is one of my favorite journals.

American Psychiatric Association. (2000). *Diagnostic and statistical manual of mental disorders* (4th ed., text rev.). Washington, DC: Author.

This is the definitive book for psychology and psychiatry, as well as for all other helping professions involving mental health assessment and treatment. It provides diagnostic criteria for all known mental disorders as well as etiological data (when available) and epidemiological data. It does not provide information on how to treat disorders and is a must for any student and professional; the hard- or softcover "big book" (not the desk reference) is strongly recommended. The revision is presently scheduled for 2011 at the earliest.

Bezchlibnyk-Butler, K. Z., & Jeffries, J. J. (2005). *Clinical handbook of psychotropic drugs.* Ashland, OH: Hogrefe & Huber.

This is an outstanding reference book that covers all psychotropic medications. It is updated yearly, usually just in time for APA's annual meeting. This book is written in a difficult manner, yet it provides important information about psychotropic medications (side effects, cautions for senior citizens, and so on). A great feature is the Patient Information Sheets in the back of the book. These sheets are written in everyday language and are designed to be given to patients who have just been prescribed a psychotropic medication. The sheets are ideal for students who have no background in psychotropic medications and for clinicians who are not comfortable with some of the highly technical terms in the text.

Gay, P. (1998). *Freud: A life for our time.* New York: W. W. Norton.

Not since Jones has such a comprehensive picture of Freud been presented until Gay's work was published. Many of Freud's letters, previously unpublished or not known, appear in this book. Well illustrated with many photographs, the book outlines the famous splits with Jung and Adler and chronicles his last days in Vienna before fleeing the Nazis. Gay's book became a New York Times bestseller, and once you read it, you will discover why.

Getzfeld, A. R. (2004). *Abnormal psychology casebook: A new perspective.* Upper Saddle River, NJ: Pearson Prentice Hall.

This casebook includes real-life individuals, unlike many casebooks that use sensational and famous individuals (Charles Manson, Jeffrey Dahmer, and so on). The book is designed to be used by undergraduate and graduate students, includes patients from a wide variety of racial, ethnic, and geographical backgrounds, and is written in an easily-accessible style. The book includes sections on appropriate medications for the treatment of each disorder discussed.

Livesley, W. J. (2001). *Handbook of personality disorders: Theory, research, and treatment.* New York: Guilford.

This edited volume is considered a classic in the field. It provides comprehensive information on the etiology, diagnosis, and treatment of Personality Disorders. The book also includes treatment modalities for special populations, such as groups and forensic patients. The writing is at times difficult to read; the book is aimed at professionals who have been practicing in the field, but it is usable as a doctoral-level text.

Maruish, M. E. (2002). *Essentials of treatment planning.* New York: Wiley.

A perfect accompaniment to the present book. This volume summarizes the entire treatment planning process, from the initial intake assessment of the patient to how to form a treatment plan, to how to monitor treatment progress. This information is especially important in today's era of managed care and treatment limitations. Written in the typical easy-to-approach Essentials style, I would recommend this book for masters- and doctoral-level graduate students and for clinicians as a handy reference.

Morrison, J. (1995). *DSM-IV made easy: The clinician's guide to diagnosis.* New York: Guilford.

This book is written in an easy-to-use style and tells the reader everything he or she needs to know regarding how to diagnose an individual using the DSM-IV-TR. It describes how to differentially diagnose someone and provides walkthroughs via case examples on how to diagnose someone. I like this book and recommend it to my students; it is especially helpful for upper-level undergraduates and for master's students who either have no background or whose program is not in the helping professions. The case examples are many and are enjoyable. In whole, it is a very approachable book.

Zilbergeld, B. (1999). *New male sexuality.* New York: Random House.

In my opinion, still the best book on male sexuality available. Many "how-to" sex books for men (and for women) are poorly written and only spread myths about sexual behavior. Zilbergeld debunks all of these myths in the first few chapters. Written in an easy to understand style that is highly approachable, this book is highly recommended for all clinicians. I would also recommend any books by Lonnie Garfield Barbach; she writes extensively on female sexuality.

Index

About the Author

Andrew R. Getzfeld received his BA in psychology from Vassar College, his MSSW from the University of Wisconsin-Madison, and his Ph.D. in school psychology from the University of Tennessee-Knoxville. He has frequently presented at APA and NASP, and has chaired poster sessions for Psi Chi at EPA. Andrew holds licenses in both New York and New Jersey- as a licensed master social worker in New York, and as a certified school psychologist, certified school social worker and a certified alcohol and drug counselor in New Jersey. Presently an Associate Professor in the psychology department at New Jersey City University, and an Adjunct Associate Professor teaching graduate courses in the psychology department at New York University, Andrew's areas of interest include eating disorders and the addictions, abnormal psychology, child development, and psychopharmacology. Andrew also serves as a Psi Chi Faculty Consultant and is the Psi Chi Faculty Advisor at New Jersey City University. His first book, *Abnormal Psychology Casebook: A New Perspective,* was published by Pearson Prentice Hall in 2004. In his limited leisure time he enjoys international and national travel, swimming, reading voraciously, writing books, watching movies, playing the occasional computer game, and spending as much time as possible with his family, especially his extremely precocious 4-year-old daughter Anya.